MIND

PSYCHOLOGY: The Untold Story of How Your Mind Works...

David Lloyd Shepard

Dedicated To all the Teachers
Who Were Afraid to tell their Students What they Know

Front cover: The Working Mind By agsandrew.

Disclaimer: Not for the Fainthearted. The purpose of this book is to provide knowledge. Combining Knowledge with Understanding, can make both of greater benefit.

TABLE OF CONTENTS

PROLOGUE

This is a book about the most important discoveries in psychology. Not just the bleached bones of the studies in a textbook, but what has been left out of our textbooks. From Genius to Suicide Bombers, from Science to Sex, we will cover the most censored facts in psychology.

Understanding how the mind works, gives us the potential to control our own mind. Only by coming to understand the forces that shape the human mind can we hope to change our psychology as effectively as science has changed our physical environment. We are way behind in that understanding.

How is it that the greatest minds in history were able to make some of the most astonishing discoveries of all time when others could not? How is it that others reacted with anger to the greatest discoveries of all time?

All of us want to read about the amazing, secret, hidden powers of the mind. This book is often about the opposite; not just the genius of the mind but the other 99.99% of reality, the part left out of our education.

For thousands of years, our doctors opened people's veins and bled them to make them well. No one could see that they were making patients worse. For decades doctors refused to believe the "germ" theory of disease, that tiny, microscopic organisms could kill a big adult. Only when they ran slam into reality were doctors forced to change. Psychology today is in a similar condition; caught between conflicting views of the mind, unwilling to accept the science in front of them. For fear of offending one point of view or another, we have censored our science, and made it into a bunch of conflicting ideas.

The problem we have in psychology is the same one described by the Nobel Prize physicist Richard Feynman who said of physics, *"We do not need more experiments. We need more imagination."* Yet in Psychology, we have tried to make psychology look more "scientific" by more experiments. And more. And more... Our textbooks are void of the connection with reality we need to understand what the experiments mean.

Einstein never did an experiment. He relied on imagination and math and the experiments of others. How did the greatest minds in history make their discoveries?

If we combine the two most successful scientific methods of all time; *Naturalistic Observation*, the area psychology ignores, the very methods that led to the success of

Copernicus, Galileo, Darwin, Einstein, Alexander Fleming, Margaret Mead, Jane Goodall, Watson and Crick, and many more, with the best of the *Experimental* methods, we will see something far more useful to understanding how our minds work.

Psychology has been presented as if it is only a series of conflicting ideas (behavioral, developmental, cognitive, perceptual, neuropsychology, etc. etc.). Yet all have found some important pieces. What we need is to put the known pieces together.

Yet psychology has gone more toward a philosophy of differing opinions, instead of a unity -of understanding. No other science does this. We cannot call ourselves a science if we are only a gaggle of conflicting opinions. We need a unified field theory.

MIND is about what has been left out, what others have not told us, in our high schools, our colleges, our psychology textbooks, and our daily news. Albert Einstein, in his autobiography, spoke of the realization of how much is censored from us. This led Einstein to "...*an orgy of freethinking*": About life, freedom, and the ideas they forced him to memorize in his physics textbooks.

One of the most dramatic examples of what has been censored from us came in news reports and a CNN special report in 2021 about the Tulsa Oklahoma race riots 100 years earlier. An unexamined report that a black teen had grabbed the arm of a white girl, triggered one of the worst riots in history. A mob of armed white men went on a rampage that killed an estimated 200 blacks and burned over 1,000 black homes and businesses. This, and four other white race riots were totally censored from our history books and our press for 100 years because it might offend the majority of Americans.

MIND is not for the fainthearted, it is for those who, like Einstein, have already run slam into a reality they never knew existed and who want to know what they were not told.

If you read each chapter to the end, I think you will see a unique insight from anything you have heard before, solely based on the evidence from psychology. Some of it may be liberating, some of it may painfully clash with what we have been told. Some of it may make you laugh at the extent of human stupidity. Let the chips fall...

1

OUTSIDE THE BOX
FROM THE MIND OF GENIUS

Out of tens of thousands of years of stumbling in the dark, banging rocks together to spark a fire, scraping in the dirt to plant enough grain to survive another hard winter, after endless wars and witch hunts, the human mind has produced works of genius so impossible to understand that we stand in awe of their ability.

The mind of Copernicus realized that the very earth under our feet is not in the center of the universe. Darwin discovered how the forces of nature have sculpted our body and mind. Einstein changed our illusions of gravity and forced us to reconsider the survival of our species with a simple equation; E=mc2. More recently, the discoveries in psychology of how the human mind works are equally striking but almost totally unknown.

How did such minds come to these discoveries when others could not see outside the box?

Our textbooks left us to marvel at their discoveries, but did not explain **how** their minds crossed this intellectual void. They left us to speculate: Superior DNA? Better Brains? Intense study? Secret Knowledge of the Illuminati? Ancient Aliens? NOVA talks about *Einstein's Brain.* Yet when we examine their own words of how they made their tremendous leap from the dirt to the universe, we see something dramatically different from what we expect.

The prestigious PEW research institute finds that America ranks 24th in the world in science. We are behind Canada, China, England, Germany, Japan, Russia, and South Korea. We are behind Czechoslovakia, India, Pakistan, Slovakia, Singapore, Lithuania, Latvia, Poland, and more. In a separate study, America is behind the nation of Lichtenstein. Can you say "Lichtenstein"?

Why?   What is it about science that Americans do not know?
And where do the ideas of "Genius" come from?

Stay with me for a journey into the intellectual understanding of *how* the great minds made their discoveries and I think you will see a rare flash of insight in your own mind, just as they had when they came to their insight, and some insight into why we are so far behind the world.

The Center of the Universe?

In the year of his death in 1543, Nicolaus Copernicus released his manuscript showing that the earth was only one planet going around the sun. He did not live to see its consequences. He probably could not have imagined that it would take nearly 400 years before the average person would know its truth.

Today, almost five hundred years after Copernicus, if you query the National Science Foundation about "*How many Americans believe the sun goes around the earth?",* you find that 25% of Americans still believe the sun goes around the earth, despite decades of astronauts in space. Yet nearly 90% of Americans know who the Kardashians are.

Challenge yourself to see if you can understand how the minds of genius came to understand something no one else in their time ever understood; and how others reacted to their heretical ideas.

We know how Galileo later came to understand this was an illusion. He looked through his new 20x telescope, saw four moons revolving around Jupiter, saw the phases of Venus-like the phases of our moon, and made the jump in part, by

Nikolaus Kopernikus.

analogy; our moon was going around us just like the moons around Jupiter, and we were all going around the sun.

But Copernicus had no telescope. How could he possibly have understood this with no telescope?

Few grasped the importance of Copernicus' manuscript. If you go outside and watch the Sun, you will see it move across the face of the Earth. Go outside at night and you will see the stars all move in unison across the face of the Earth. No one doubted we were in the center of all creation.

MARS MOVES BACKWARDS? Insight

Copernicus had no knowledge that was not readily available to every astronomer of his day. All knew that the planets, a Greek word that means 'wanderer', did not move in unison with the stars.

Over a period of months, Mars would move swiftly across the sky against the background of stars. Then Mars would start to slow down, hang suspended against the background of stars, then turn around and rush in the opposite direction. Astronomers called it the retrograde motion of the planets.

Mars would become brighter for months, and then become increasingly dim. This happened repeatedly, totally unpredictably. How could this be? It made no sense.

Copernicus compared two models of the universe, one with the Earth as the center, one with the Sun as the center. He realized that only the one with the Sun in the center, where the Earth and Mars were both planets going around the Sun, could explain what caused this mystery. What he saw in his model was this; because the Earth goes around the Sun almost twice, for every one-time Mars goes around the Sun, it follows that Earth will pass by Mars twice as Mars makes one orbit.

In the following example; when the Earth and Mars are going in opposite directions, as in Earth 1 and Mars 1, then Mars appears to be shooting across the sky against the static background of stars.

By the time the Earth 2 is going directly toward Mars 2, then Mars will appear to slow down and hang suspended in the sky.

When Earth 3 goes speeding past Mars 3 it will look as if Mars is rapidly moving backward against the background of stars

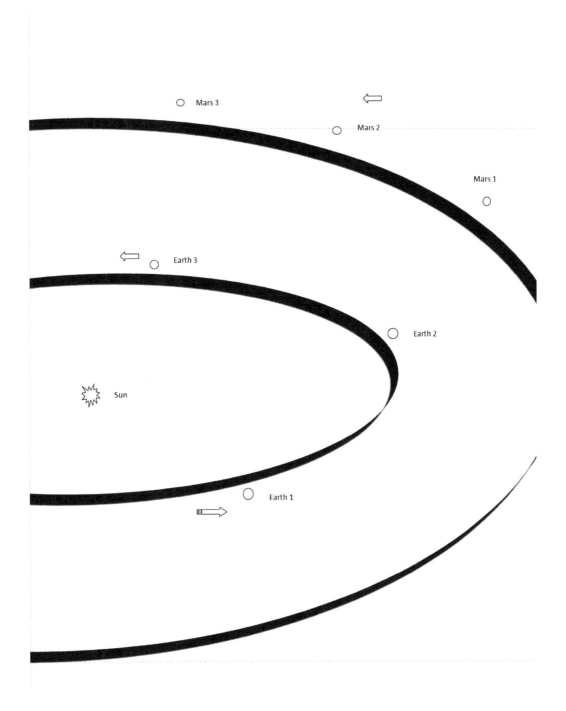

In Copernicus' own words, "*The apparent retrograde motion of the planets arises not from their motion but from the earth's. The motion of the earth alone, therefore, suffices to explain so many apparent inequalities in the heavens.*"

Suddenly, many more observations that astronomers had been making for centuries fell into place. Only the theory of Copernicus could explain so many disparate facts with elegant simplicity. When Mars and Earth are closest, Mars appears to be brighter. When they are farther away, Mars appears to dim. It was the simplest possible explanation.

The evidence had been there for centuries, hidden in plain sight. Now the pieces fit. Everything we thought we were seeing was only an illusion; an illusion created by the motion of the Earth around the sun.

If you now understand what Copernicus saw in these facts that told him we are not in the center of the universe, you can now understand the workings of a mind of genius. Does that make you a genius? At the very least you can explain how he understood something no one else on the face of the Earth understood. You now know something hardly one person in a million in the world can explain, even today, just because you now have learned something few people today ever learned. Learning is the key, not genius.

But this was only the beginning of the story. Many years later, his theory was adopted by the Monk Giordano Bruno. Bruno not only taught the heretical theory; he went far beyond his data. In an extrapolation more poetic than believable, he said that the stars in the sky were also planets, much like earth, and that they too could be inhabited. Bruno's teachings on the universe and of religion itself, he doubted the idea of hell, flailed in the face of what everybody else believed.

In the year 1594, over one hundred years after Columbus discovered America, they arrested Bruno for his heresies. They confined him to jail for six years while the inquisition debated his fate. Finally, in the year 1600, he was tried and convicted. Because he refused to repent for his sins and admit the error of his ways, they gave Giordano Bruno the maximum sentence. In the Square of Flowers in Rome, Bruno was burned alive.

In his ten-volume history, *The Story of Civilization*, Will and Ariel Durant, as part of their Nobel Prize for literature, vividly described the scene at Bruno's execution:

"On February 19, still impenitent, his body nude, his tongue tied, he was bound to an iron stake on a pyre in the plaza Campo de' Fiori and was burned alive, in the presence of an edified multitude."

Statue of Giordano Bruno, erected in his honor at the site of his execution in Campo de' Fiori. Nearly four hundred years too late.

Some thirty-two years after the burning of Bruno, Galileo Galilei, published his "*Dialogues on the Two Chief Systems of the World.*" Galileo also argued that the earth moves around the sun. With the publication of his "*Dialogues*" in l632, Galileo quickly became the subject of the Inquisition. Galileo was placed under house arrest and a special trial was convened to determine his fate.

Badgered by the questioning of the Inquisition, threatened with torture, Galileo, then in his seventies, got down on his knees before his tormentors and publicly read a confession, dictated by others, that he had been deluded, that he now saw the error of his ways, and that the earth was indeed the center of the universe.

The Confession of Galileo:

I, Galileo, son of the late Vincenzo Galilei, Florentine, aged seventy years, arraigned personally before this tribunal and kneeling before you Most Eminent and Reverend Lord Cardinals Inquisitors-General against heretical pravity throughout the entire Christian commonwealth, having before my eyes and touching with my hands the Holy Gospels, swear that I have always believed, do believe, and by God's help will in the future believe all that is held, preached, and taught by the Holy Catholic and Apostolic Church. ... I have been pronounced by the Holy Office to be vehemently suspected of heresy, that is to say, of having held and believed that the Sun is the center of the world and immovable and that the Earth is not the center and moves.

Galileo Galilei.

...with sincere heart and unfeigned faith I abjure, curse, and detest the aforesaid errors and heresies and generally every other error, heresy, and sect whatsoever contrary to the Holy Church, and I swear that in future... should I know any heretic or person suspected of heresy, I will denounce him to this Holy Office or the Inquisitor of Ordinary of the place where I may be... So help me God and these His Holy gospels, which I touch with my hands.
From G. De Santilana, *Crime of Galileo* University of Chicago Press.

"The good thing about science is that it's true whether or not you believe it."
Neil deGrasse Tyson

The anger felt toward Bruno and Galileo for their beliefs does not differ from the reaction we see in children, or politicians, who engage in bullying and name-calling, and put-downs, or racial prejudice and religious hatred. It is anger or disdain directed toward anyone who is different. We are kidding ourselves if we think this is different. Understanding prejudice is basic to understanding how the human mind works. Prejudice is learned. If we want to change society for the better, we must educate our children to understand reality.

Today, most of us know the Earth is only one of many planets going around the sun. But we only know it because we have taught this in our schools, we see it on TV shows, we watch it on *Cosmos*. Back then, no one knew this.

It took some 300 years before they ever taught this fact in the public schools; William and Mary's College taught the first known course in America in 1835. Even in the year 1900, the average American never went beyond the eighth grade. And all they learned in school was reading, writing, and arithmetic; back to basics, much like today.

Copernicus solved the mystery of the retrograde motion of the planets, but an equally important mystery may be to solve the mystery of how the mind of Copernicus came to solve that problem. Was it superior genes? A better brain? Secrets given him by the Illuminati? No. He used basic Trial and Error learning, contrasting one model against another, combined with putting two ideas together until the pieces fell into place, until he understood what could cause this mystery.

The brain of Copernicus needed no more special X-Men superpowers than yours needs to understand this idea. The evidence was there in plain sight, yet no one saw the connection.

Today, NASA has turned the Hubble Space Telescope toward a completely black part of the night sky, keeping it focused on the black for over a week. The time-lapse photo was described as "*like looking at the universe through a soda straw*". Through that "soda straw," they counted over 10,000 galaxies outside of our own Milky Way Galaxy.

NASA scientists estimate there are over 100 Billion galaxies outside our galaxy. Each of those, like our own galaxy, contains hundreds of billions of stars, like our sun.   That's billions with a "B". It makes our human problems seem tiny by comparison to the vastness of the universe.

> *"Looking at these stars suddenly dwarfed my own troubles and all the gravities of terrestrial life. I thought of their unfathomable distance, and the slow inevitable drift of their movements out of the unknown past into the unknown future."*

H. G. Wells

The idea of contrast and comparison used by Copernicus in comparing the two models of the cosmos is found throughout the entire of science today. Isaac Newton, the talented genius in physics, once said, "*I am unable to understand anything of which I cannot make a model.*" Mathematics itself is a model that allows for contrast and comparison.

DARWIN'S INSIGHT: In His Own Words

I once had a discussion with an editor over whether the great ideas of history were a product of hard work or of insight (putting two ideas together). His argument was based on Thomas Edison's comment that "*Genius is 1% inspiration and 99% perspiration*".   The idea is that only hard work leads to great ideas. Edison experimented with over 100 materials to use as filaments in light bulbs before coming up with a filament that worked. That is Trial and Error learning at its most basic. Yet the greatest ideas in history result from something quite different.   Consider the lifelong work of Charles Darwin.

In Darwin's *Voyage of the Beagle,* he recounts his long voyage around the world where he came into contact with enormous individual variations in the same species; "Darwin's Finches" and the sea turtles of the Galapagos Islands. Observing these variations gave him food for thought, but we have noted such variations throughout the history of biology, from Linnaeus to Huxley.

Darwin did not get his theory from the Galapagos, as is commonly believed. His first great insight came from accidentally reading an already famous work by

Thomas Malthus, *On Population*. What Malthus realized was human reproduction was so intense we would quickly overpopulate the earth, stripping it of all resources.

> *"In October 1838, that is, fifteen months after I had begun my systematic inquiry, I happened to read for amusement Malthus on Population, and being well prepared to appreciate the struggle for existence which everywhere goes on...* ***it at once struck me that under these circumstances favourable variations would tend to be preserved, and unfavourable ones to be destroyed.*** *The result of this would be the formation of new species. Here, then, I had at last got a theory by which to work..."*
> The *Autobiography of Charles Darwin* [italics and emphasis added]

Darwin is describing a sudden ***association*** *of ideas within his mind.* Some might call that association an insight. But what did Darwin see in the work of Malthus that so dramatically caught his attention?

For a more poignant example of what Darwin saw, if you start with two people or animals, they mate and reproduce, say two children (before birth control it was much higher). These two each go on to mate with two others and produce four (two children each), the four go on to produce 8, 16, 32, 64, 128, 256, 512, 1024, etc. In an incredibly short period of just 64 generations, you get:

GENERATION   **CHILDREN BORN**

1stgeneration...2
2ndgeneration...4
3rd...8
4...16
5...32
6...64
7..128
8..256
9..512
10..1,024
11..2,048

12..4,096
13..8,192
14...16,384
15...32,768
16...65,536
17..131,072
18..262,144
19..524,288
20..1,048,576
21..2,097,152
22..4,194,304
23..8,388,608
24...16,777,216
25...33,554,432
26...67,108,864
27..134,217,728
28..268,435,456
29..536,870,912
30..1,073,741,824
31..2,147,483,648
32..4,294,967,296
33..8,589,934,592
34...17,179,869,184
35...34,359,738,368
36...68,719,476,736
37..137,438,953,472
38..274,877,906,944
39..549,755,813,888
40......................................1,099,511,627,776
41......................................2,199,023,255,552
42......................................4,398,046,511,104
43......................................8,796,093,022,208

44	17,592,186,044,416
45	35,184,372,088,832
46	70,368,744,177,664
47	140,737,488,355,328
48	281,474,976,710,656
49	562,949,953,421,312
50	1,125,899,906,842,624
51	2,251,799,813,685,248
52	4,503,599,627,370,496
53	9,007,199,254,741,502
54	18,014,398,509,482,004
55	36,028,797,018,964,008
56	72,057,594,037,828,016
57	144,115,188,075,656,032
58	288,230,376,151,712,064
59	576,460,752,303,424,128
60	1,152,921,504,606,848,256
61	2,305,843,009,213,696,512
62	4,611,686,018,427,392,024
63	9,223,372,036,854,784,048
64	18,446,744,073,709,568,096

In just 64 generations, the mating of only two people could produce eighteen quintillion, four hundred forty-six quadrillion, seven hundred forty-four trillion, seventy-three billion, seven hundred nine million, five hundred and sixty-eight thousand, and 96 children.

Yes, really. If you doubt it, count them yourself.

That is not the total of all; it is just the number of children that would be born to the 63rd generation. And people were having more than two children generations ago. Benjamin Franklin was the 15th born child in a family of 17 children. And there were not just two people having children back then, there were hundreds of millions of people. Few of them were celibate.

Yet there are only about 7,600,000,000 people alive today, nothing like the 18,446,744,073,709,568,096 that would have been produced from only two people. To Malthus, only the endless wars, plagues, and famines prevented this.

Can you see what Darwin saw in this?

The number of individuals that would be born in the short space of sixty-four generations is staggering. But Darwin saw far more in the mathematics of life than overpopulation. He saw a law of nature that made all the unrelated, unexplainable observations that biologists had been making for over a century fall neatly into place.

Every animal reproduces far more of its own kind than could possibly be needed to replace its parents, including humans. If more than two of their children's children, on average, survived to reproduce their own kind, they would quickly overpopulate the earth.

To Darwin, it meant that any variation that would make it more likely to survive long enough to reproduce their own kind, even if that variation was small, could quickly become the majority. This is the basis of *natural selection.*

The reproducers inherit the earth.

Darwin's ideas met with anger and outrage when they appeared in the press. States passed laws forbidding the teaching of his ideas in schools. In the famous Scopes Monkey Trial, they put a teacher on trial, charged with the crime of teaching the forbidden theory. Today we forget, they found him guilty; he was fired and fined for his crime.

When Presidential candidate William Jennings Bryan denounced Darwin from the pulpit, audiences cheered in wild acclaim. Today, nearly one-third of Americans do not believe in evolution, it contradicts everything they were taught as children.

No one does the math.

Any eighth-grade child in Lichtenstein can do the math.

Yet if the public is not allowed to see the math, they cannot understand the science.

"There's an old saying among scientific guys: 'You can't make an omelet without breaking eggs, ideally by dropping a cement truck on them from a crane'." Dave Barry

Malthus' idea of dramatic overpopulation is not a "theory." It is a basic fact of nature. It is one of the two facts on which Darwin based evolution; it is **Natural Selection.**

Yet even today that is one of the most censored facts in the entire of America. You will not find it discussed in our textbooks; you will not find it in our mathematics texts, you did not hear it explained on the History Channel. Why? Perhaps because reality can be even more frightening than a Hollywood slasher movie.

It does not bother us one binary digit to see thousands of Zombies slaughtered on television or John Wick offing 36 men to get to kill the man who killed his puppy. At least he had a good reason. Hollywood, like politicians, is good at giving us good reasons. We are immersed in a sea of shiny objects.

But learning of nature's comment on the value of human life is uniquely disturbing. We are all rendered cowards in the face of reality.

"The great tragedy of science is the slaying of a beautiful hypothesis by an ugly fact."

Thomas Huxley

The overwhelming masses of all species, including humans, do not survive to reproduce.

In the last 100 years, we have made more progress than in the previous tens of thousands of years combined. Science, applied to medicine, has produced immunization and antibiotics to prevent the great plagues that killed off the vast majority of our young. The methods of science, applied to agriculture, reduced deaths from starvation. Thousands of years of bleeding people did not work. Thoughts and prayers did not work.

The overwhelming evidence suggests that we have only each other to cling to. We had better get good at understanding the importance of that.

Science has produced the plague that Malthus predicted, the

overpopulation of the earth; but it has also produced the cure, the Pill.

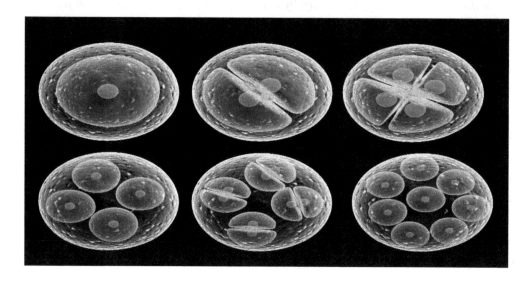

The mathematics of life is also what explains how a single fertilized egg cell, at conception, can double exponentially, at a similar exponential tempo as human life, until it becomes a living human with trillions upon trillions of cells. And it explains how the exponential increase in numbers of cars and factories have produced so much CO_2 in the atmosphere that it can cause major climate change in a very short time. Many people do not believe in Climate Change; they never did the math.

You see the same mathematics in the infection of Covid-19, although it only takes hours to double its number, not decades. If the body's immune system cannot catch up with it in a week, the outcome can be deadly.

In February 2020, President Trump repeatedly announced that there are only 15 Americans with the virus, and the numbers would soon be down to zero. In six months, there were six million infected Americans and 184,000 deaths. In just three more months there were over 12 million infected and a quarter of a million American's dead; more than died in all the wars we have fought since WWII. More than the Korean war (56,000), the eight years of the Vietnam war (58,000), and both of the Gulf wars all combined. One year after it first appeared, over 420,000 Americans had died from the virus, as many as died in four years of WWII.

"Human history becomes more and more a race between education and catastrophe." H. G. Wells

Not only the reproduction rate of the virus itself, but even the spread of the virus between people increases exponentially. Scientists guessed at its danger as soon as China announced in late January 2020 that their number of infections was doubling every week.

The hard evidence of math impacts every area of human life, from our understanding of the exponential growth of cells in the baby, to the exponential acceleration of global warming, to how viral epidemics spread, to the power of immunization to prevent our babies from dying early, to public opinions on the value of life and abortion, to why science is more important than personal opinion.

Yet every area of our educational system has been bankrupt, unable to deal with reality, crippled in the ability to educate our youth. In every conflict, from the Covid-19 crisis to the issue of abortion, scientists have had to fight each issue with their tongues tied, strapped to the iron stake of public opinion. All they could do is mumble incoherently: Their message coming out as if it were a foreign language. Society censored the math that showed the frailty of our species and the value of science. It is still censored.

All the while, cartoon characters repeatedly assured people that their personal opinions were worth more than reality. The pandemic is just fake news, they said. Just need a little hydroxychloroquine. Or maybe some injectable bleach. Or a strong UV light inserted in...

It is the math that rules; argue with that.

Why is it that even today the media coverage of Darwin's ideas continues to censor the hard evidence on which he based his theory? No one wants to be hated for telling you the truth. I certainly do not. The end result of that simple fact is that no one ever tells you the truth about anything when it conflicts with what people want to believe.

Philosopher Blaise Pascal put it well, *"It is dangerous to show man how nearly he is on a level with the brutes without also showing him his greatness..."*

Yet we spend all of our time glorifying our greatness.

DARWIN'S SECOND INSIGHT: Individual Variation

Darwin needed one more piece of the puzzle to solve the greatest mystery in history…

> *But at that time I overlooked one problem of great importance; and it is astonishing to me… how I could have overlooked it and its solution. This problem is the tendency in organic beings descended from the same stock to diverge in character* [Individual Variation] *as they become modified; and **I can remember the very spot in the road, whilst in my carriage, when to my joy the solution occurred to me…*** [Insight; the association of two ideas] *The solution, as I believe, is that the modified offspring of all dominant and increasing forms tend to become adapted to many and highly diversified places in the economy of nature* [italics and emphasis added].   Autobiography of Charles Darwin

The second fact on which Darwin's concept was based is that of **Individual Variation**. All species vary greatly in all physical traits. Some of us are very tall. Chinese basketball great Yao Ming was seven foot six inches tall; an advantage only in sports like basketball. Some are very short; General Tom Thumb of the Barnum and Bailey Circus was three-foot-tall, full-grown; an advantage if you are an Olympic gymnast or when food is scarce. Most of us fall in the masses in between the extremes.

If any variation increased the likelihood that the individual would survive to reproduce, then that trait would quickly overwhelm all others. Anything, even a tiny advantage, could, over time, result in that variation becoming the dominant species. Suddenly, the pieces fit.

The British writer-sociologist Herbert Spencer called it "*Survival of the Fittest*", a term Darwin liked. Yet a more accurate description would be; any variation that increases the chance that the individual would survive long enough to reproduce their own kind would eventually become the dominant species.

Most of those who do not survive were quite "fit" but the selection pressure was intense. Only within the last one hundred years has science, applied to medicine, brought about a great change in the death rate, due to immunization and antibiotics. These ideas began with Pasteur, Koch, and Jenner in the 1800s, but it took decades before they were accepted in medicine.

For decades, even medical doctors refused to believe the work of Pasteur, Koch and Jenner, that tiny, microscopic germs could kill an adult. They never did the math on the exponential growth of microorganisms.

DARWIN'S THIRD VARIABLE:
Human Selection--an Un-Natural Selection

More than this, Darwin knew we had long been breeding our horses for traits we wanted. We bred tall and swift horses to other tall and swift horses to become racehorses. We bred stout and strong horses to pull plows. Every egg you eat comes from chickens that have been bred for generations for their egg-laying ability. A single Leghorn can lay up to 200 eggs a year; that made eggs very cheap. Every chicken you eat comes from chickens that have been bred for generations for their meat quality.

Do you have a dog? What kind? A Chihuahua? A Great Dane? A Shiatsu? Few of the 198 AKC registered breeds of dogs even existed hundreds of years ago; all have been bred, by humans, from six original types of dogs, most within the last few hundred years. By selecting for whatever individual variation came along, and breeding like to like, we have produced dogs that do not even look like dogs.

Compare a Pekinese to a Great Dane or a Chihuahua to a Rottweiler. Darwin showed how nature, using natural selection, had been doing for hundreds of millions of years the same thing humans have been doing for a few hundreds of years by humans selecting for specific traits by breeding like to like for any new mutations.

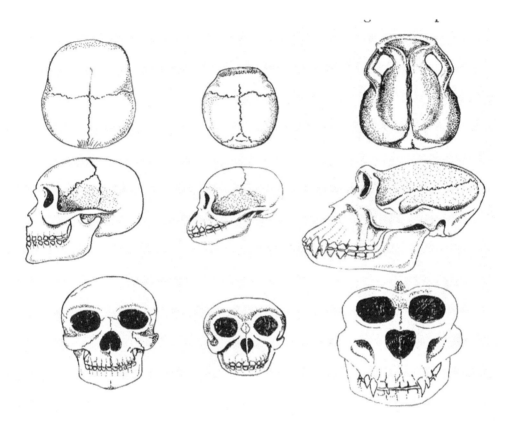

Based on Ernest Hooten, in *Up From the Ape.*

In the left column, you see an adult human. In the column on the far right, you see an adult gorilla. What is the animal in the middle? A missing link? A chimpanzee? No, the skull in the middle is from a newborn baby gorilla. It looks far more like a human than the adult it becomes. Massive jaw muscles pulling on the bone create the sagittal crest and deformation of the bone.

The adult skull looks nothing like the baby it started from.   Is the difference between a Chihuahua and a Great Dane any greater?

Above right, a baby orangutan, sucking his thumb, with a very modern-looking head. Its parent's skull will be less rounded than the baby's.

Top left, a baby gorilla with an almost modern skull. The parent's skulls will look nothing like this. Why?

Why is there such a dramatic difference in the skull of a baby gorilla compared to an adult? NASA noted that when rabbits were sent into space with the astronauts, that lack of gravity pulling on the muscles would cause the smaller bones in the foot of a rabbit to decalcify, to dissolve back into the bloodstream. The early astronauts suffered similar problems in the weightlessness of space. They needed daily exercise to force the muscles and bones to maintain their ability.

Compare the skull of a baby gorilla to that of an adult. If, at birth, we severed the jaw muscles attached to the bone of the sagittal crest on top of the skull, the skull of an adult would not develop nearly the same as when the massive jaw muscles are attached to the crest. It would be more rounded, like the baby.

AUSTRALOPITHECUS

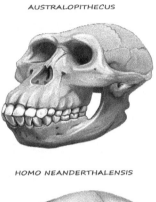

HOMO ERECTUS

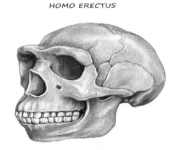

HOMO NEANDERTHALENSIS

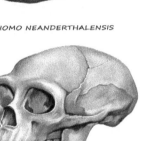

HOMO SAPIENS

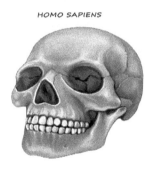

Genetics has changed so that it has reduced the heavy jaw and their muscles that an ape needs to chew tough vegetation. Today, apes spend about five hours a day just chewing. Becoming an omnivore and a meat eater made the heavy jaw and muscles unnecessary. Along with upright posture, which made the heavy neck muscle unnecessary, that allowed the braincase to grow much larger, making possible a larger brain. This took hundreds of thousands of years.

Biologist Thomas Huxley verbally kicked himself for *"...having seen the obvious for so long, but missed the conclusion"*. Darwin had no knowledge or ability that was not available to every other biologist of his day. But he could see outside the box.

Darwin saw in the mathematics of human reproduction a model for the driving force of evolution; Natural Selection. He saw in Individual Variation the raw material on which it acted. He saw in the artificial selection, the breeding of our horses, the hard evidence that it works. Darwin had put three ideas together as no one else ever had.

The evidence was all around us, known to every biologist, yet few could put these ideas together. It was hidden in plain sight.

There is one mistake in the above image. Neanderthal's, coming out of the north, would have had white skin. Our ancestors, coming out of Africa would all have had black skin. The darker the skin, the greater the protection from radiation from the sun that causes melanoma; skin cancer. The lighter the skin allows the skin to produce vitamin D, which prevents Rickets, a bone disorder. Small differences are the basis of this gradual evolution.

Since then, we have evolved into couch potatoes who only want to be entertained. That only needed the failure of our culture to value knowledge. We have made trivia entertaining and education boring. Sports, movies, video games rule. Science has yet to offer a cure for the entertainment that overwhelms our limbic system.

THE ORIGIN OF DARWIN'S GENIUS

Charles Darwin.

Darwin's insight was not the result of any new discovery but of sudden insight, the **association** of these ideas in his mind. In his own words, on reading the ideas of Malthus he made the association; **"…*it at once struck me that under these circumstances favourable variations would tend to be preserved and unfavourable ones to be destroyed*".** Further, he put two more ideas together in a moment of insight that was so profound that he even remembered the place on the road where it occurred, **"*I can remember the very spot in the road, whilst in my carriage, when to my joy the solution occurred to me…*"**

The media presents Darwin's ideas as if they were some mystical discoveries; again, he had acquired the knowledge, but putting the ideas together is what marks his insight as "genius". Most of us think of someone who is "smart" as someone who is quick-witted, constantly thinking about one idea or another, a fast talker, yet Darwin described himself as, **"*…a slow, plodding thinker.*"** Einstein himself said, **"*I am not smarter than most, I am just more persistent.*"** That is something that makes the rest of us feel better about ourselves. Yet we largely ignore it in a media obsessed with a magical-mystical view of genius and a nation wedded to superheroes.

In Darwin's words; *"At no time am I a quick thinker or writer: whatever I have done in science has solely been by long pondering, patience, and industry."*

"I have as much difficulty as ever in expressing myself clearly and concisely; and this difficulty has caused me a very great loss of time, but it has had the compensating advantage of forcing me to think long and intently about every sentence, and thus I have been led to see errors in reasoning and in my own observations or those of others."

Charles Darwin

It may well be that that *"slow, plodding"* thinking, that mulling over of ideas, is more important for the discoveries of genius than the quick-witted, fast-talking ability we often mistake for genius. Then, the sudden association of two ideas in the mind, led to a great realization. One reason I have put so many short paragraphs and even one-sentence paragraphs in this book, besides the fact that I have a simple mind, is the hope that it will slow the reader down to mull over each idea as had Darwin and Einstein. What does all of this say about how the mind works?

Edwin Boring, the historian of psychology, when he was asked to pick the greatest psychologists of all time, picked Darwin as number one. Darwin showed clearly that humans are subject to the same laws of nature as all other animals. So is our psychology.

Today, Darwin's concept of evolution is the cornerstone of biology. So much flows from that fact. The few biologists who doubt it are the ones who never did the math, the ones who never even heard about the math. The fact of evolution is evident in the overwhelming similarity found in the DNA of our species to so many others.

"The main idea in all of biology is evolution. To not teach it to our young people is wrong".

Bill Nye, "The Science Guy"

THE SPIRAL STAIRCASE: The Double Helix

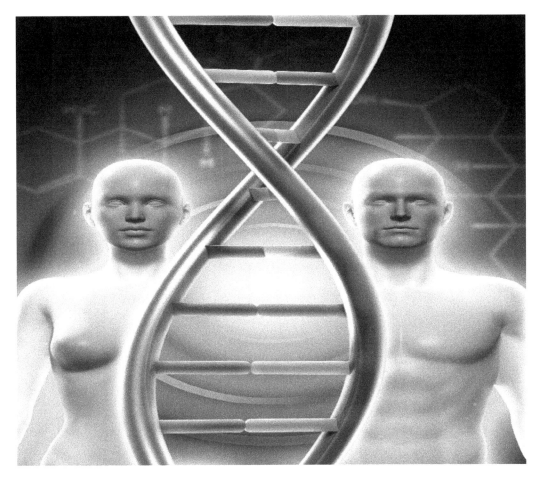

      The great Nobel Prize-winning discovery of the structure of DNA by Watson and Crick has a story behind it that is rarely told. Biologists had long been debating the structure of DNA. Some said it had a single strand, a single helix. The great genius of molecular chemistry, Linus Pauling, a two-time Nobel Prize winner, said it must have a three-helix construction.

      The story is told by Watson himself of how he was watching an old late-night TV movie, *The Spiral Staircase*, when the thought immediately hit his consciousness, after seeing the double banisters coming down the spiral staircase, that the shape that fits must be a double helix, with the four base pairs attached between the two banisters, like rungs on a ladder.

His discovery began with simply associating two ideas in the mind. Now they had a model. That model turned out to be the one that fit. Fitting the known chemicals, the four base pairs, into the rungs on the ladder, with each rung only able to support a large base and a small base, was the next step that made it possible to discover the DNA code. The pieces fit.

The structure of DNA

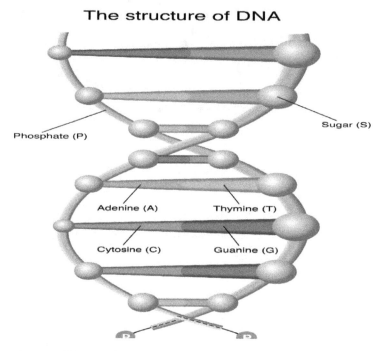

Throughout this series, from Copernicus to Darwin, we see an understanding of "genius" that differs greatly from the mysterious notion we have been given by the media of minds so brilliant that no one else could have done what they have done. The media looks to their "brain" as the cause of their brilliance, yet these new ideas did not come from any new knowledge, or from any mysterious mental ability, they came from **associating ideas** in the mind.

But this is not the entire story; consider the insight of Einstein that radically changed our view of physics.

EINSTEIN'S "GEDANKIN" EXPERIMENT:
The Thought Experiments of Einstein

Einstein used "thought experiments", what he called the "*gedankenexperiment*", such as his imagining gravity while being in an elevator that was dropping from a great height, as a form of modeling his ideas about gravity, just as Copernicus had contrasted two models to see the movement of the planets.

It may be that this was an insight Einstein gained from having been in an early elevator when they had no computer control over their descent. I remember from many years ago when they often dropped suddenly for a small distance, giving the passengers a brief feeling of weightlessness, floating in space. That was in the old days, when people were often the operators of the elevators and could not easily stop at the right point to balance the elevator with the floor. That brief period of weightlessness may have been when Einstein realized that the "pull" of gravity was no longer there. Today, computer control of decent has eliminated that fun experience.

NASA uses the same idea to simulate the weightlessness of space when training astronauts by dropping them in a plane for thousands of feet so they would experience what being without gravity is like; floating in the abyss of space for about twenty minutes. If the plane were to accelerate downward too fast, it would pin you against the ceiling, as if there were some mysterious force holding you to the ceiling. But there is no mysterious gravitational force holding you to the ceiling; that is an illusion.

The "force of gravity" Einstein thought, is also an illusion.

Einstein realized that, contrary to what everyone else believed, this gravity was not a force pulling you toward the Earth, but instead, the curvature of space causing us to accelerate toward the depression in space created by the mass of the earth. It was difficult for most to see, yet a profound insight.

As with Copernicus, Einstein's three great papers in his "miracle year" fell flat when first published. Few in physics understood them. Einstein was a Patent Clerk 3rd class, in a badly furnished government office, not even a respected professor. They ignored his publications for two years. Fortunately for Einstein, Max Plank, perhaps the most famous physicist of his day, could see something brilliant in Einstein's unique view of reality.

What we thought was reality, was only an illusion. It somewhat reminds one of the old joke about "He died because he fell off the roof." No, "It's not the fall that kills you; it is the sudden stop when you hit the ground." Two different ways of looking at the same thing.

The warping of space-time is vaguely similar to being sucked into the wake of a speedboat that is passing by. After the boat passes, all matter, the water, and fish get pushed toward the center of the vortex. There is no force in the center of the water pulling you toward the center. Einstein said that the mass of large planets and suns curves the fabric of space all around them, forcing everything nearby into that mass.

Yet we can see the wake of the speedboat, seeing that wake makes it easy to understand. No one can see the curvature of space-time. In science, as in everyday life, if you can't see it, it is hard to believe it. So, Einstein went out on a limb. He made a prediction so bold, so improbable, that few believed it was possible. He predicted that the light from stars many light-years away would be warped as it passed by the mass of our sun, distorted "like a lens" by the curvature of space. The force of the mass of the sun would enable us to see that a star's light, as it passed by the mass of the sun, would be displaced by the curvature of space. Yet no one had observed this.

Over a decade would pass before they put this to the test by observing the displacement of light from a star during a solar eclipse. Astronomer Author Eddington proved Einstein's prediction that the light of the star would, like a lens, would follow the curvature of space created by the sun as the light curved around the sun.

Not until 2014 did physicists announce they have discovered the "Gravitational waves" predicted by Einstein's theory, the wake of gravity traveling through the fabric of space from the big bang.

The pieces consistently fall into place.

In the year 2000, long after his death, Time magazine picked Einstein as the Man of the Century. It was a bit late to benefit Einstein, he had been dead for nearly fifty years. But it was not so much his prediction of the warping of space but the predictions of his theories of the atom that led to the atomic bomb that cemented his everlasting fame. Who cares about warping space? An atom bomb was something no one could ignore.

E=mc2. Argue with that.

Einstein continued to develop his grand Theory of General Relativity. He was about to present this in a symposium to the greatest minds in Europe when he realized that the math he depended on to support his theory was fatally flawed. He had done the math wrong. He went back to the drawing board, agonizing over what math he needed to support his theory. After trying many models (Trial and Error) he finally went back to an older model he had tried and rejected. This now worked. It fit the data.

Remarkably, Professor David Hilbert, one of the greatest mathematicians in Europe, had also taken up the challenge after hearing Einstein's talk. Both came to the same mathematical conclusion at the same time.

Again, the pieces fit.

The media portray Einstein's genius as if it were a magical property of his unique brain that we mortals cannot comprehend. Others have searched for some difference in the biology of the brain that might make this possible. Yet most ignore what Einstein himself said about his genius:

"I am not smarter than most, I am just more persistent."

Einstein first came up with a mental idea, his "thought experiments", to imagine alternative ways of looking at the question; a form of mental Trial and Error. Then he experimented with "mathematical models" until he found a model that would fit; again, Trial and Error. Next, we must compare it to reality, does it fit our observations? If the model did not fit the hard evidence, we must throw it out.

Einstein was aware of his fallibility. But what most of us never see in the way the media presents the work of genius, is the Trial-and-Error learning that is common to all scientific work. It is not magic; it is Fumble and Find until the moment of insight, when the pieces fit.

In Einstein's own words; "*But the years of anxious searching in the dark, with their intense longing, their alternations of confidence and exhaustion, and the final emergence into the light—only those who have experienced it can understand that."*
Emotion drives the effort. Trial and Error are basic to understanding.

Einstein recorded his moments of despair and ecstasy in his life. But this was a moment of pleasure at his success, very similar to Darwin's comment that he remembered exactly where he was when "*...to my joy*" he saw the solution.

Einstein's ideas were greeted with incredulity and even disdain, because few understood them. Yet no one hated Einstein, because there was no emotion associated with his ideas. Perhaps the comedian Charlie Chaplin said it best in a famous meeting with Einstein recorded by the press. Chaplin was known for his pratfall comedy; he would slip on a banana peel and everybody would laugh.

Chaplin told Einstein that, in effect; "people laugh because everybody understands what I do. People like you because no one understands what you do."

Einstein laughed.

Einstein had no knowledge that was not readily available to any physicist of his day. Others were equally motivated to succeed. What was unique to Einstein? Even though his theories of matter caused no anger from others, Einstein's controversial ideas, the ones that were critical to his ability to think outside the box, the ones noted below in his own words, are censored by the media to this day.

Something happened to Einstein early in his life that triggered a realization that much of the ideas embedded in our brain by society *"...could not possibly be true"*, that they were only ideas given us by the adults, that authorities rarely knew what they were talking about.

The part of the equation about Einstein's genius that is always left out of the stories about Einstein are his own thoughts, his distrust of authority. The effect of this early discovery was dramatic; in his own words, his realization that *"…youth is intentionally being deceived by the state through lies…"* led to:

> *"The consequence was a positively fanatic orgy of freethinking coupled with the impression that youth is intentionally being deceived by the state through lies; it was a crushing impression. Mistrust of every kind of authority grew out of this experience, a skeptical attitude toward the convictions that were alive in any specific social environment-an attitude that has never again left me, even though, later on, it has been tempered by a better insight into the causal connections.*

> He saw this as *"...a first attempt to free myself from the chains of the 'merely personal,' from an existence dominated by wishes, hopes, and primitive feelings. Out there was this huge world, which exists independently of us human beings... The contemplation of this world beckoned as a liberation...*

Einstein wrote of his distrust of authority, which began at the young age of 12, as an opinion, that *"...has never again left me...",* even at the age of 70 when he wrote those words. When everyone else was accepting the words of authority, he learned to distrust those words from a very early age. His *"supreme goal"* in life became to understand what no one else understood, to put the pieces together. He saw past the ideas of others, to see outside the box, into that "*great eternal riddle*". People who are certain they know everything are not the ones who question authority and change our knowledge.

"Only the guy who isn't rowing has time to rock the boat."

John Paul Sartre

This rejection of authority led him to question the ideas that were taught him in physics; you see this in all outstanding works from Copernicus to Darwin to Einstein. It is often essential to doubt authority, to doubt even the ideas embedded in our own mind, to see over the lid to peek at the reality outside the box.

"In the sciences, the authority of thousands of opinions is not worth as much as one tiny spark of reason in an individual ... "

Galileo

"I was an ordinary person who studied hard... There is no miracle person, it just happened they got interested in this and they learned all this stuff. They're just people, there's no talent, no special miracle ability to understand quantum mechanics or electromagnetic fields that comes without the need for reading and study and learning..."

Nobel Laureate in Physics Richard Feynman
Described in a book about him "*The Greatest Mind Since Einstein?*"

Einstein, Gandhi, and Martin Luther King. Three of the great minds of history, not because of their brains, but because of their ideas.

THE RUBIC'S CUBE OF GENIUS

From these studies and dozens of others, genius is not some new neurological phrenology where we diagnosis intelligence by reading the bumps in your brain. It is a combination of:

- 1. **Motivation**, Emotion motivates us to acquire the knowledge; Einstein was a genius in physics, he was thrilled by the idea of a "supreme goal" of understanding that "great eternal riddle." Einstein was an imbecile in geology. He said geology is boring. He wasn't motivated to study geology. If he had a better geology teacher, he might have come to love it. But he acquired no knowledge of geology.

"It will come to the question of the fire you have in your belly." Oliver Wendell Holmes. That "fire" motivates us to acquire knowledge.

- 2. **Knowledge**, if you were not motivated enough to acquire the knowledge, you have no information to work with and you cannot grasp the question.
  "All knowledge is through experience." Einstein.
  If you don't learn it, you don't know it.

- 3. **Organization** of that knowledge (putting ideas together). *"The true sign of intelligence is not knowledge but imagination."* Einstein said. That is; a new idea, a new imagination, a new organization of reality into which the pieces fit.

  In a prophetic statement that should apply to psychology, the Nobel Prize physicist Richard Feynman said, *"We don't need more experiments... we need more imagination."* Unfortunately, in its zeal to look more "scientific", psychology chose instead to go with more experiments. And more, and more, and...

- 4. **Critical Thinking: Being able to think outside the box,** a healthy distrust of the ideas that are alive in our *own* minds that led Einstein to *"...a positively fanatic orgy of freethinking,"* that combines both motivation and imagination.
  "If you find yourself agreeing with the majority, stop and reflect." Mark Twain

- 5. **A Strategy; the Scientific Methods** that allow one to understand how to put ideas to the test. In the entire of human history, no other idea has worked to lift the veil of ignorance, no other paradigm in human history has been as successful in every area of human knowledge as the Scientific Methods in physics, agriculture, medicine, psychology, and technology.

Systematic Observation and Experimentation are the two most powerful ideas that led to the success of science.

"Knowing how to think empowers you far beyond those who know only what to think." Neil deGrasse Tyson

Observation and Experimentation are the "how" in how to think.

- 6. The **Cumulative Effect** of **Knowledge**: Sir Isaac Newton said, "*If I have seen farther than most men it is because I have stood on the shoulders of giants*." Knowledge builds on knowledge.

- 7. Pure **Chance**: The chance of reading Malthus at a critical time or thinking of a new way to imagine the structure of the DNA molecule. Mark Twain said, "*Name the greatest of all inventors; accident.*"
Louis Pasteur said, "*Chance favors only the prepared mind.*"

- 8. **Selective Attention**: Ignore the trivia. Psychologist William James said, "*The art of being wise is the art of knowing what to overlook.*" Focus your attention on the important evidence.

Just as important, anyone can understand the greatest ideas in history. It does not take a genius with a better brain. The tendency of the media to present these ideas as a product of the mind of a unique *Jeopardy!* Champion who knows all the answers, ideas that only superior minds can read, detracts from our understanding of reality.

Of all the comments I have received by students over the years, one that I value highly is the student who wrote, "*He made me feel smart*". Just knowing that we can all understand the works of genius; that everyone on earth can be wrong; that others are not smarter than we are, can be a tremendous realization of what our mind can grasp.

Understanding that, is liberating.

THE DIRECTION OF HISTORY: THE BOX

Two thousand four hundred years ago Socrates went about Greece questioning the ideas of others. Is Zeus really the king of all the gods? How do we know this? Is a soldier who dies in battle a hero? How does that make him a hero? People did not like his questions.

In 399 B.C.E. They arrested Socrates for his questioning. They charged him with the crimes of not respecting the Gods of Greece and with corrupting the minds of students with his teachings; not unlike the charges in the Scopes Monkey Trial and the Inquisition of Galileo.

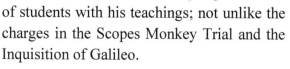

Socrates, 2,400 years ago, despised by so many, was sentenced to death by a vote of 500 and one of his fellow citizens in the Democracy of Athens. A statue to his courage was erected, 2,300 years too late.

They put Socrates on trial before a jury of five hundred and one of his fellow Athenian citizens in the Democracy of Athens. They found him guilty. They took a second vote, and they passed the sentence of death. Socrates drank the hemlock, becoming the first recorded martyr for free speech, but only one of many.

Many are destined to reason wrongly; others, not to reason at all, and others to persecute those who do reason. Voltaire

Just before the execution of Socrates 2,400 years ago, Plato recorded the comment of Socrates on the impossibility of going back to ignorance once we have been exposed to reality:

Most people, including ourselves, live in a world of relative ignorance. We are even comfortable with that ignorance, because it is all we know. When we first start facing truth, the process may be frightening, and many people run

back to their old lives. But if you continue to seek truth, you will eventually be able to handle it better. In fact, you want more. It's true that many people around you now may think you are strange or even a danger to society, but you don't care. Once you have tasted the truth, you won't ever want to go back to being ignorant." Socrates, via Plato.

The most profound discovery in human history may not be that made by Copernicus or Darwin or Einstein. The most profound discovery is one we do not want to know, that is, of how the human mind reacted to these new ideas and what this says about our mind. It was not just a difference of opinion, but often a dramatic hatred of those whose discoveries contradicted the ideas already in our minds.

You see this today in American politics, where the only thing that matters are personal opinions, the hard evidence is often ignored. The politics of hate have overwhelmed our limited ability to reason. And you see this prejudice in bullying in school, name-calling, the value judgments we dump on others, and in racial and religious prejudice. Of all these grand discoveries, none of them are as remarkable as what the human reaction to others says about the human mind.

Our mind is controlled by our emotions.

"Those who are able to see beyond the shadows and lies of their culture are unlikely to be understood, much less believed, by the masses."

Plato

We no longer put people to death to destroy an idea; as we did to Socrates and Bruno. Instead, we simply censor the ideas in our schools by labeling them "controversial". We reduce "controversial" ideas to nothing but a "matter of opinion" in our news. In politics, we destroy people by attacking their ideas with emotion. That has been effective in preventing reality from reaching the minds of the public, without the messy need to execute people.

We can see the overwhelming success of this censorship because few people can even imagine what we have censored from them.

"This institution will be based on the illimitable freedom of the human mind. For here we are not afraid to follow truth wherever it may lead, nor to tolerate any error so long as reason is left free to combat it."

Thomas Jefferson

In our schools, in debate classes, students are assigned an idea and forced to defend that position.   The very idea of debate is biased against the idea of seeking the truth.

In our law schools, they do not teach lawyers to seek the truth, but to argue to defend their client, regardless of their guilt. Lawyers, like politicians, often are judged on their ability to spin reality. Much of our politics is little more than an opinion that ignores the facts in favor of their party. The election of 2020 was a contest between facts and spinning reality. If politicians could agree on facts being more important than defending a point of view, we might accomplish far more in congress.

Lawyers represent only .08 % of the population yet over 40% of congressmen and senators are lawyers. Perhaps this is indicative of the fact that so many believe that their job is to spin reality in favor of their party, instead of doing what is best.

Prejudice is built into our educational system. Weekly pep rallies teach children to believe that *our* football team is better than *their* football team and that football is more important than education. The cheering and applause embed the emotion into the brains of our youth. We embrace Superheroes with the passion of religion; X-Men, Superman, Batman, Die Hard I, II, III, IV, John Wick, Harry Potter, etc., etc... All of whom possess magical powers never found in real live people. We have created a fantasy world devoid of any association with reality.

We live in a fairy tale of our own creation, unable to see the box into which we have stuffed reality, unable to see outside the box we have built around our mind.

Bullying, name-calling, racial prejudice, religious prejudice and anti-science bias are part of our society. Society's hatred of Bruno, Galileo, Darwin, Socrates and so many more is only one part of the overall prejudice against anything that differs from our emotionally held beliefs.

Scientists do disagree, but one great advantage of science over opinion is that, unlike politicians and the public, scientists agree that facts are far more important than opinions. Scientists do make mistakes. Unlike other ideas, science is self-correcting. When scientists make mistakes, many others are waiting to look critically at the evidence.

The very ideas we learn growing up in our culture, the ideas others embed in our minds, become the box that makes it difficult to see another reality. Understanding this is powerfully important to understanding human psychology.

The failure of our culture is a failure of our educational system.

For thousands of years, even before the time of Hippocrates, doctors opened a vein and bled people to make them well. How could we have failed to realize we were making them worse? Even when Pasteur, Koch, and Jenner showed that microorganisms could produce disease, doctors at first refused to believe the "germ" theory; that such tiny bacteria could kill a great adult. It took decades before the germ theory became accepted in medicine.

Why is it that the first ideas in our mind are so resistant to change?

The first ideas embedded in our minds become the criteria by which we judge reality. That is the *prime experience.* That is part of the prison of The Box. New ideas do not fit well into our mind.

Learning, imprinted in our brain by others, rule our thoughts. Emotions, imprinted in our brain by others, control our minds. Emotions are more powerful than thoughts or reason or reality. If we are to progress beyond this, we must first learn to understand how this happens. We must learn to get in control of our minds.

In the "real" world, shiny tin foil sells; reality you cannot give away.

Einstein on Human Nature: *"Only two things are infinite, the universe and human stupidity, and I'm not so sure about the first"*

Never forget, as you try to understand this life, that we are only a few hundred years away from a time when everyone on the face of the earth believed the earth was flat and in the center of the universe and that our grandmothers were witches who had to be tortured into confessing and burned alive to destroy the evil inside. The hangings at Salem were only a dot on the tail end of centuries of witch hunts. Based on news reports and court records well over 100,000 of our grandmothers were executed in Europe in the 16th century alone. It did not stop the plagues that ravaged our ancestors.

Never forget the thousands of years of endless wars, or how we believed for centuries that bleeding people made them well, and how we are only a few years away from invading Iraq for weapons of mass destruction that turned out not to exist.

Never forget we spent eight years at war in Vietnam. To what end? Or that we invaded Afghanistan and Iraq, spending over 15 years at war. To what end?

Never forget we are only a few hundred years away from a time when everybody in America believed that *"All Men are Created Equal"* (except for slaves, Indians, women, Gays, Irishmen, Slavs, immigrants, kids we bully, politicians we trash, religions that are not "ours", anyone we disagree with, etc., etc., etc...).

Only the discovery of a new, learned strategy, a method of studying reality, the Scientific Method -- Naturalistic Observation in Copernicus and Galileo, Fleming, Einstein, etc.; Experimental design, as in Placebo control and comparison in Medicine, have made it possible to go beyond the powerful trap of personal opinions and cultural bias.

> *"The only way to comprehend what mathematicians mean by Infinity is to contemplate the extent of human stupidity."* Voltaire

The human brain has not changed in tens of thousands of years; only the development of the scientific methods has changed the human condition.

The single most important lesson in the entire of human history, the one left out of our education, the one no textbook ever mentions, is that we are all reeeeealy stupid. No exceptions. No super brains. No heroes. *That,* is why we need the scientific methods.

We are stupid beyond the power of words to explain what stupid means.

Only the methods of systematic observation and experimentation, have improved our lives. Argue with that.

The mistakes of the past, in no way inhibit the people of the present from assuming that their current view of reality is somehow absolute truth.

It is not what we teach in schools that is important; it is what they have left out, what has been censored by society. The same is true of psychology.

Psychology too, has its controversial side, the untold story. You never hear about it because it is ignored by the press and reduced to stories of salivating dogs or lists of symptoms in our textbooks that never hint of what is important. Reality gets lost in textbooks that cover thousands of studies but ignore a more basic understanding.

The press ignores the serious issues in favor of sensationalism or credits the magical-mystical force of DNA and biochemicals in your brain with everything. The media studiously ignores the implications of psychology. So does psychology itself.

Psychology has failed in its efforts to look more "scientific" by pumping out textbooks that only include experiments. They have ignored the fact that the greatest discoveries of all time, of Copernicus, Darwin, Einstein, Alexander Fleming, Margaret Mead and many more, have been made using *Observation,* not Experimentation.

Einstein never did an experiment, he relied on imagination, math, and the experiments of others. The failure of psychology to understand that has left us without understanding of the most important issues of our time. But if we could combine Observation and Experimentation, we would have a far better science than what we have.

Our mind has its origins in our experiences, our potential is in our programming, but unless we come to understand the forces that shape our mind, we will continue to be a prisoner of our experiences.

Yet understanding what we know about the mind is critical in its implications, because it gives us the potential to gain control over our own mind, as Einstein's insights gave us the potential to control the atom.

What is it that the greatest minds in psychology have learned about how the mind works? Stay with me as we go further inside the Box, into what they left out of our textbooks, what the media never told us.

2

INSIDE THE BOX

QUEST FOR THE MIND CODE

"The obscure we see eventually, the completely obvious, it seems, takes longer." The Dean of news, Edward R. Murrow

KNOWLEDGE COMES ON LITTLE CAT FEET

The Amazing Subtlety of Learning

How is it possible that a 2-year-old American child grew up to speak only Chinese? DNA? The wiring in his brain? Free will?

Cultural anthropologist Clyde Kluckhohn tells of a two-year-old American boy who was the son of American missionary parents in China in his book, *"Mirror for Man"*. The two-year-old was orphaned when his parents were killed and he was taken in and raised by a Chinese family. All of his life he grew up in the outback of China, hearing only Chinese words, understanding only Chinese ideas.

Many years later, when westerners met him for the first time, they were astonished; not by his fair hair and western appearance, but by the fact that everything about him seemed Chinese, not American. He spoke only Chinese, English was lost to his mind; it had no meaning, it elicited no emotions. His personality, his deference, the way he held his hands, the ideas he believed were Chinese, not Western.

Not just language is determined by our experiences, but much of what we think of as embedded in our DNA is determined by experiences; Our mannerisms, our gestures, our deference, our temperament, our philosophy on life, our politics, our religion, our most basic beliefs.

When his American grandparents learned he had been found they brought him back to America. But he could not speak the language, he could not understand the customs, he did not understand our beliefs. He must have felt lost. Imagine us being lost in China, unable to read those strange Chinese symbols on their street signs and in their books; unable to understand their most basic words. Kluckhohn reports that after two years here, he went back to China.

吉 jí	好 hǎo	兴 xīng	富 fù
Fortune	good	Good luck fortune	lucrative
福 fú	宝 bǎo	顺 shùn	高 gāo
Happiness	Treasure	smooth	lofty

Experience is profound in determining what we know and what we become. *"All knowledge is from experience,"* said Einstein. Such a simple fact, yet no one notices? It is all relative to the environment we grow up in, and the unique experiences we have.

Everyone reading this book had ancestors that spoke not a word of English. They may have spoken Welch, or Gallic, or Deutsch, or Slavic or Latin or Hebrew. They may have spoken Toltec or Olmec, or Quechua, or Swahili, or any of a thousand different languages, but they did not speak a word of English.

THE BRAIN IS PROGRAMMED BY A PROCESS SO SUBTLE... IT SEEMS LIKE MAGIC.

We are not aware of learning the language we speak, yet it is clearly learned. It is learned by a process so subtle, so without our awareness, that we do not even notice it as it is happening.

Yet if we were not so certain that language is learned it is likely that we would be easily convinced that it was in our DNA. Biological researchers would compare the DNA of those who speak Chinese with those who speak Russian and those who speak English. They would look in DNA responsible for the motor cortex, in Brocca's area, in Wernike's area. They would quickly discover genes that differ between those who speak different languages.

Ah! It must be that genes determine their language! And the press might eagerly parrot this as if it were all we needed to know. Anytime there is no clear evidence of a cause for the behavior, the media automatically assumes it must be in our DNA, our biochemistry, or in the wiring of our brain.

Where does the intelligence in our brain come from? Is it already formed by a mysterious process, triggered by the question? Do the brains of "Genius" IQs work better than ours? Let's see how our mind works.

HOW DOES YOUR BRAIN COMPARE TO GENIUS?

Every year for fifteen years I have given college students in my classes, and some professors, the DETRN Test, with amazing results. Are you ready to see how your ability compares to the average college student or to college professors? Are you in the category of "Genius"?

All tests start with very simple questions, "*What is the shape of a box?*" (Answer: square or a cube) and progress to more difficult questions, the "genius" level such as "*What is an apocryphal story?*". This is a question that might be used because almost no one except the top 2% have ever heard of the Apocrypha.

In giving this test, I repeat the following questions twice, and they write their answers down on paper.

Starting with the very simple, challenge yourself to see how you do.

1. Take two apples from three apples. What do you have?

92% of college students say "one" apple. They know they are right. They are absolutely certain. Is that correct? Read the question again.

Even on the third reading of the question, few change their minds. It must be "one" apple. But the correct answer is "two" apples. Can you explain why that is the correct answer? Read it again.

I use this question to illustrate a profound principle of how the mind works, the **Primacy Effect**. What does the mind do to answer that question? We go back to what most of us learned in first grade: *"If you have three apples and you **take away** two apples, how many do you have **left**?"*

But the question does not say **"take away"** it says **"take"** and it does not ask how many do you have **"left"** it asks how many do you **"have"**. If you take two, you have two.

Many think this is a "trick" question. But no, it is a very straight forward question, and a terribly important rule of psychology. If you never went to first grade, you could easily answer that question.

What we have learned *first* takes precedence over any other possible answer to the question. We see this again and again in our reaction to the ideas of genius, or politics, religion, sports, and personal arguments. In the entire of human experience, the primacy effect rules.

Sometimes what we learn *first* makes it impossible to see any other way of understanding the question. In the same vein, everyone in Einstein's day believed gravity is a force that pulls you toward the earth, it was obvious to everyone. Einstein thought, in effect; what if that is the wrong way of looking at the question?

Over the years, as word has gotten out about this question, students are less likely to answer "one" and have learned from other students about the question. But, like Copernicus' insight, if you don't learn it, you don't know it.

2. *"What Four Words Appear Most Prominently on Every American Coin?"*

You are an eyewitness to thousands of American coins. You are now testifying in a court of law, under oath, as an expert witness. Remember, you are under oath. Answer one simple question: *What four words appear most prominently on every American coin?*

Nearly 100% of my college students know the correct answer. The four words are, "*In God We Trust*". So do all the professors who have been asked. They are certain of their answer. They have no doubt. Could everyone possibly be wrong? They are wrong. Try again.

How is it possible that after tens of thousands of experiences with American coins, almost no one can answer this simple question? Because no one really pays attention. The four words are, "*United States of America*".

Both statements are on the coins, but that one is several times larger than the first; "*most prominently*". Yet we all remember, *"In God We Trust"* because it has been a headline in the news, we have heard it mentioned, it was controversial, it is emotional, therefore, it is seared into our minds, we remember it because of what we have heard, not because of what we have seen. This illustrates a second major principle of psychology; ***Selective Attention.***

The forces of selective attention and the primacy effect bias every judgment we have in interpersonal relations, politics, religion, and personal choice.

If you still think these are "trick" questions, let's try one that is absolutely straight forward. Here is a question that might determine if you are ready for college.

3. *Divide 30 by one half. Then add 20. What is the answer?*

More than 90% of my college students know the correct answer is 35. They are "pretty sure" of their answer. Is that what you got? Wrong. Try again.

Even after trying again, only a few students in most college classes will say that the correct answer is 80. Usually, those are math or science majors. Why is the correct answer 80? Can you figure this out? Read it again.

Almost everyone's brain interprets this question as saying "Take half of 30" but it does not say that at all, it *clearly* says "***Divide*** 30 by one half". If you divide 30 by one half (.5) you get 60. Add 20 and you get 80. But if you don't learn it, you don't know it. Once you learn it, you get pretty good at it. But having to figure it out on our own is very hard because our minds have never been taught that exact kind of question.

Yet this is a profound question because of what it says about the human mind. All of us learned ***division*** in school. All of us learned *fractions* in school. But when it comes to putting two and two together to come up with an idea we have never learned, that is not easy. That is why the seemingly simple ideas of Copernicus, Darwin, and Einstein were so difficult for others to see.

We cannot easily answer this question because most of us have never had a question just like this one. In every case of "genius" from Copernicus to Darwin to Einstein, they could put ideas together that no one had ever taught them. That is very difficult to do, unless they have taught you to do so, then it seems easy.

Now let's go back to simpler questions. Here is a question that might determine whether or not you can get into medical school. And no, it is not a trick question.

4. *A doctor gives you three pills. He tells you to take one pill every half hour. How long before the pills are all gone?*

Almost every college student knows the correct answer is one and a half hours. Is that what you got? Wrong. Read the question again.

On the second try some guess wildly at ½ hour, some guess two hours. No. The answer is one hour. How could the answer be one hour?

Did you figure this out? Take one pill at 7:00 p.m. Take the second at 7:30 p.m. Take the third at 8:00 p.m. In one hour, they are all gone. We all learned math in school. Why is it so difficult to apply it to the real world?

5. Some months have 30 days, some months have 31 days. How many months have 28 days?

The majority of people will say "one", February, has 28 days. We generally go back to what we learned in first grade: "Thirty days has September, April, June, and November, all the rest have 31 except February which has 28." I could never make that rhyme. Some have heard the question before and get it right. Actually, they *all* have 28 days.

OK, this is a bit of a trick question because the way the question was asked leads you to think only in terms of which month has 28 days, yet that is still a problem with how we think about all questions. We *selectively attend* to the fact we learned that February is the only month with 28 days. Again, if you never went to first grade, you might easily answer this question. What we learn first interferes with our ability to answer the question.

6. *An airplane crashed on the border between Mexico and the United States. Almost everyone was killed. On which side of the border should the survivors be buried?*

Admittedly, this question has only one answer: You do not ever, ever, ever bury survivors. Yet the mind is often so consumed with what we *think* the question is (how we *perceive* the question) that we miss some of the subtlety of the question. Instead of reading the actual question, the mind guesses *(perceives)* what the question is and assumes the wrong question. Selective Attention makes the question confusing.

This is again an example of a major principle of psychology; **Selective Attention.** We see the same reaction in answering more serious questions dealing with politics, religion, interpersonal interactions, and public opinions.

7. **A man builds a cabin with four sides. Each side faces south. A bear comes by. What color is the bear?**

This is a question for Sherlock Holmes. Students guess black because that is the most common type of bear. Or brown. That is the second most common. The actual answer is white. Why? Can you figure out why white is the answer just from the words in the question?

The only place on earth where you can build a cabin where all four sides face south is the North Pole. It would have to be a Polar bear and Polar bears are white. This question requires you to put two ideas together. Not easy, is it?

My favorite question is the next one because it took me two years to figure out this one. I'm sure you will do better. I had been given the answer but the answer made no sense. Two years later this question popped into my mind again and I suddenly realized *why* this was the answer.

8. A rancher had 19 cows. The cows were struck by lightning. All but one of the cows died. How many were left?

92% of college students say "one". Even on re-reading the question, almost everyone says "one". After telling them that is wrong, students still say "one". Some wildly guess 18 or even 20. Wrong again. Read it again.

Can you figure it out? The correct answer is 19. Why is 19 the correct answer? Can you explain this?

This is like the first question about "*take two apples*". The mind automatically assumes that the question asks something it does not ask. We *perceive* the question based on past experiences. The question we hear is "how many were left *alive*" but that is not what the question asks, it asks "how many were **left**". There were 19 left; 18 dead ones and 1 live one. But we have difficulty in trying to think in any way except what the mind believes (perceives) the question to be. Einstein saw a whole new way of looking at the *question* of gravity.

9. How many animals of each species did Moses take aboard the Ark with him?

Most college students know the correct answer is "Two". Is that what you got? No. The answer is not "two". You never went to Sunday School? Read the question again.

The answer is "none". Can you explain why? Again, this illustrates the principle of **Selective Attention.** At first, the mind concentrates solely on how it *perceives* the question and ignores the details. Eventually, most everyone gets it after re-reading it. Moses didn't have an ark, that was Russell Crowe.

This may be the advantage given to Darwin by being "...*a slow, plodding thinker*" or to Einstein who said, "*I am not smarter than most people, just more persistent.*" If we spend more time mulling over the evidence, instead of quickly jumping to an assumption that we already know what the question is, then it might be easier to see what the answer is. Mulling things over may be an advantage by itself.

Speed reading is not the mark of genius.

Again, we see the same reaction in answering more serious questions dealing with politics, religion, and interpersonal relationships. We simply ignore the evidence and go back to what our brain perceives the question to be or to previous answers embedded in our brains by others.

This is **not** a *real* Intelligence Test. In a real I.Q. test, they would ask questions everyone would interpret the same way. You never find questions like this on a test designed to compare individuals with each other. I put this "test" together from questions that have been around for a while but are usually called "trick" questions.

They are not "trick" questions. They are questions that show the limits of our knowledge, how dependent we are on what we have already learned, how difficult it is to put two ideas together, how hard it is to think outside the box.

Even students and professors with "genius" level IQs do not do any better than average on this test, unless they have already learned the answers to these questions elsewhere.

"*All knowledge is from experience*", as Einstein noted.

Our failure to understand is also from experience.

COGITO, ERGO, COGITO COGITO:

I Think, Therefore, I Think I Think.

The fact that we can think has created the illusion that we do think.

In part, the question of what makes for "genius" is the wrong question. The question should be, "why are the rest of us unable to see outside the box?" These questions get at a problem different from what an I.Q. test does; they show major principles of psychology that make it difficult for any of us to think outside the box.

These are some of the Forces of Mind that shape and determine how we think, the emotions we feel, and what we believe in; the forces that control our mind.

The Basic Principles are first, **Perception:** We tend to answer the question as the brain *perceives* it rather than attending to the details of the question. As in; "*How many animals of each species...*"

Second, The **Primacy Effect**: The brain goes back to whatever we learned first, even in first grade, to answer the question; "*Take two apples from three apples...*"

Third, **Associating Two Ideas** that we have learned before: Such as *division* (Divide 30) and *fractions* (...by one half) is terribly difficult, even though we all learned division and fractions in school. This is the genius of Copernicus, Darwin, and Einstein that is so very difficult for all of us. Yet once we learn what they knew, we can also peek outside the box.

Fourth: **Question the ideas others have embedded in our minds**. Never assume that every idea we have in our brain is correct, or even that the question we think we are answering is the right question. If you had not already learned an answer to the question; "*Take two apples from three apples...*" then the answer would be easier. That is one of the most important lessons of history and the most difficult to teach.

MISSION STATEMENTS IGNORE REALITY

Almost every college and university now include in their "Mission Statement" that one purpose of their mission is to *"teach students to think for themselves".* None of them do that, the statement is included because the colleges think that, when the auditors come to do College Accreditation, that will make the auditors think we are all on top of the issue. Not even close.

We could teach students to think for themselves, but we still teach rote memory. To teach students to think outside the box is not about having them write "opinion" papers or having them criticize someone else's ideas, it requires a real understanding of the extent to which every idea already embedded in our brains by the media, the school system, the press, the politicians, the preachers, our parents, our peers, our language, are determined by our unique experiences, not by reality.

> *"If you find yourself agreeing with the majority, stop and reflect."*
> Mark Twain

Thinking outside the box requires a real understanding of, not just ***what*** we know, but ***how*** we know what we know. Understanding the insights of Copernicus, Darwin and Einstein is a small beginning in understanding how to think outside the box. And this is why we need a strategy, *the scientific methods*, to be able to think outside the box.

The ideas embedded in our minds, like the language we speak, become our reality. Like words spoken in a foreign language, we cannot easily imagine or even understand ideas that conflict with the ideas already in our minds.

The ideas and beliefs others have put in our brains become the criteria by which we judge all things.

"Most illogical." Mr. Spock

If you take apart a human brain, examine the structure and diagrams of its connections; trace the components of the video apparatus, its CPU, the internal structure of the brain, you find nothing but cells; neurons, and glial cells. Even knowing everything we could possibly know about the brain would tell you nothing about the programs that could be fed into that computer. It is important to understand the structure of the brain, the DNA code, but even knowing everything there is to know about the biology of the brain, the code of the DNA, you would still know nothing about the human mind.

Inside, the brain is bloody, saturated with veins and arteries, squishy with nerve cells and glial cells, with no hint of understanding, void of the information we need to know to understand reality; *the real importance is in the learned programs embedded in our mind.*

The responses of a computer are much like the way the human brain works. Both depend on the information fed into it being accurate and adequate. Computer programmers have a term for this, "GIGO"; Garbage In—Garbage Out.

ON THE TRACK
OF LITTLE CAT FEET

There is nothing that is more subtle, nothing we are less aware of, than learning. We are only aware of being formally taught in school. In the real world we learn the language we speak, the meaning of words, the emotions elicited by words, in such a subtle way that we are never aware of learning as it takes place.

The critical question for psychology becomes; how is it possible to take something so subtle, so invisible, something we are completely unaware of when it is happening...and make it into something we can see? Because the most basic need of science is the need to make something we can't see, into something observable, so we can study it.

QUEST FOR THE MIND CODE
Spit and Death and Mind Control

From the dim mists of the Second World War comes a story of blood and death and mind control that defies most of our assumptions of what reality is. The story originated in the laboratory of Ivan Pavlov, long since dead. Hitler had invaded the Soviet Union in search of glory and lebensraum. His Panzer divisions quickly cut through the Russian divisions and surrounded them from the rear causing panic.

Russian forces, expecting only a replay of World War I, could not adapt to the new Blitzkrieg tactics and fell apart. Months into the invasion the captains of Panzer Group Center reported a bizarre experience in the moonlit night on the Russian plains. While waiting in their tanks for their next move, they saw two dogs hit the ground running. Not a surprise, dogs are usually terrified of tanks, the stench of diesel fuel, the roar of the engines, and the clank of steel on steel. Except these dogs came running directly at the German tanks, not away from them. The dogs had satchels attached to their backs. Were they messenger dogs? Supply dogs? Germans watched in amazement as the dogs picked out individual tanks, ran around the back of and under the tanks. A huge explosion followed, taking out the tanks from their soft underbelly.

How is this possible? Was it genetic? Had the Russians bred dogs for generations to come up with a tank-killing instinct; a desire to destroy tanks on sight? Was it brainwashing? Were the dogs so imbued with Marxist-Leninist Dialectic Materialism that they were willing to die for Mother Russia?

PSYCHOLOGY'S SPECIAL THEORY OF RELATIVITY:

Any Stimulus-Any Response

(Already wired into the Autonomic Nervous System).

"When you are courting a nice girl, an hour seems like a second. When you sit on a red-hot cinder a second seems like an hour. That's relativity." Albert Einstein

Einstein was being facetious, of course. Maybe.

What did the Russians see in Pavlov's work that others did not?

Our first hints of how the brain is programmed by the environment came from a seemingly meaningless observation.

Every psychologist has heard the textbook story of how Pavlov conditioned dogs to salivate to the sound of a bell. Generations of psychologists have grown up knowing nothing about Pavlov's work except what they read in textbooks. Yet the most important work is not in the textbooks, it is only found in the original Pavlov.

Pavlov already knew that any stimulus could be associated with food to trigger saliva. Repeated pairings of Bell followed by Meat and then just the Bell alone, would cause the dogs to salivate to the bell. After three pairings, Bell-Meat, Bell-Meat, Bell-Meat, an average of six drops of saliva appeared in the tubes. After six pairings they reached the maxim level of saliva. Purists will point out that Pavlov used a Metronome first, but Bell is so much easier to write than Metronome.

 Everyone thinks, "of course the dogs salivate; the dogs *knew* they were going to be fed." No.

The genius of Pavlov was that he realized that saliva was part of the Parasympathetic branch of the Autonomic Nervous System. Autonomic, means automatic. We have no conscious control over saliva; it is automatic when food touches the tongue. Now, simple learning had *reprogrammed* the biology of the

Autonomic Nervous System in the brain. Instead of salivating to food, a natural biological response, the dogs would now salivate to a bell, a learned response.

The stimulus could be anything; a bell, a tone, a metronome, a touch, a word, music, anything.

How about pain? Pain is a stimulus. Pavlov wanted to find out.

He started with a low level of static electric shock, about what you would get if you walked across a rug in winter and touched metal. He paired it with food: Shock-Meat, Shock-Meat, Shock-Meat, etc. Then the shock without the meat. The dogs slobbered. Not to the meat, but to the shock.

Not only do dogs slobber, but they also get excited, they wag their tail, they perk up when they know they are about to be shocked in anticipation of food! Fifty shades of the Marquis de Sade, he had discovered experimentally induced masochism.

He gradually increased the level of shock until it became very intense. Instead of struggling and trying to run away, the dogs would stand there, salivate and wag their tail. Not that the dogs enjoyed the pain, as some think of masochism, but they enjoy what was *associated* with the shock and had been gradually desensitized to their fear of the shock, by *gradually* increasing the intensity of the shock.

"Within a few weeks the dog would actually wag its tail excitedly, salivate, and turn toward the food dish in response to the electricity."

Instead of the natural, biological response of fear and escape, the "*Fight-or-Flight response"*, the dog's brain had been programmed to give a totally different response, one of pleasure. They had been gradually desensitized to the pain. They enjoyed what was *associated* with the pain. Yet textbooks only teach about Pavlov teaching a dog to salivate to the sound of a bell. Even PhD psychologists rarely know this. The most important work of Pavlov is left out of our textbooks, ignored perhaps, because it tells us something we do not want to know about how easily the mind can be controlled, and controlled to a degree that it overwhelms even the brain's own powerful defense mechanism; the Fight or Flight response.

People think of "conditioned" learning as a special type of training. Instead, what Pavlov was doing, using bells and saliva, was to take *learning*, something that was so subtle, so invisible, and make *learning* <u>visible</u>. It is the first rule of science, before we can study anything, we must first find a way to observe it.

Ivan Pavlov

If Pavlov had done nothing else, that alone would be a major contribution.

Pavlov had "rewired" the biology of the dog's brain.

The biological response of "fight or flight", which is so essential to survival, had been replaced with the learned response of saliva.

Learning can control our biology.

Learning can rewire the biology of the brain.

That is the real significance of Pavlov's studies. And that is lost in decades of textbooks that teach nothing except how Pavlov made a dog salivate to a bell. Textbooks are only a poor imitation of reality; they have become "*archivists of facts*".

Do not become archivists of facts. Try to penetrate to the secret of their occurrence, persistently search for the laws which govern them.
Ivan Pavlov

Pavlov had taken learning, something so subtle, so impossible to observe, and made it into something we could study.

Even to this day, we hear people talk about the malleability of the brain or about "neuroplasticity" without giving credit to where it was due. It is not what the textbooks tell you about Pavlov's discovery that is important; it is what was left out that is important.

Although Pavlov himself blew off emotions as only "generalized excitement" it would turn out that emotional conditioning is even more important than the learned reflexes Pavlov studied.

Some think that is a terrible thing to do to a dog, yet we do far worse to our children. Beginning even in middle school, coaches tell the children, "No pain, no gain." From high school to college football coaches' echo, "Hit 'em harder!" And "Don't be a wuss!", "Grow a pair!"; because the coach's high paying job depends on their motivating their "boys" to beat the other team, even at the risk of injury to their brains. More than a few of these boys have dropped dead on the field from heatstroke or suffered head trauma that may last for life.

Words, associated with emotions, rule.

LEARNED EMOTIONS RULE OVER CONDITIONAL REFLEXES

Words, *associated* with emotion, are all it takes to make children endanger their brains for the glory of sports.

Fellow team members echo that with, "Wow! Did you see the hit he put on that guy?" "Way to go!" Accompanied by back-slapping and grins of approval. The "roar of the Sunday crowd" rules their minds. They seek it with gusto. They revel in it. They salivate over it. Only in the last few years have we learned that pro football players and even high school players often suffer brain concussions that can plague them for the rest of their lives.

Some 5,000 former NFL players have been involved in a class-action lawsuit against the NFL for brain damage from playing football. The NFL settled this lawsuit quickly, for 675 million dollars, to keep it out of the press.

We hear about famous players that last for years and make millions. Little boys yearn to be heroes like what we present to all in our school's pep rallies and our glorification of sports on national television. Yet the average NFL player lasts only 3 ½ years before they are injured and cut or replaced by a younger, hungrier buck. This fuels the joke among players in the NFL that NFL stands for Not For Long.

HOW DID HOBBITS PLANT
MEAT UNDER THE GERMAN TANKS?

How did the Russians plant meat under the German tanks? Did they genetically breed Hobbits small enough to sneak under the tanks at night to plant the meat? Did they sabotage the tanks on the assembly line by smearing chicken grease on the underside of the German tanks? Did they learn the secret of mind control from Ancient Aliens on the History Channel?

What did the Russian's see in Pavlov's study? They took puppies from a very young age, fed them near a tractor with the motor running (to counter-condition the fear of tanks with the positive effect of food). Then, they moved them gradually closer to the running tractor (gradual desensitization). Finally, they fed them under the moving tractor with a food dish attached underneath the tractor. Later they switched them to training under a tank. It was all right out of how Pavlov conditioned dogs to salivate to pain, the fear of tanks being the same as the fear of shock. Finally, they strapped a backpack full of high explosives on the dog's back with an automatic detonator.

The meat was not planted under the German tanks. The meat was planted in the **mind** of the dogs.

The Russians have a video of the result of this *learning by association* with a German Shepherd dog, eagerly leaping toward running Panzers, while his master had to restrain him until the tanks had passed. A second dog wags his tail enthusiastically when he sees the German tanks.

The tank-killing dogs never turned the tide of battle, but the Russians claim the dogs killed over 200 German tanks. They do not mention how many Russian tanks the dogs killed by mistake.

But imagine the effect of stimulus generalization on the German panzer crews after they learned of these dogs. The word spread quickly. When, sitting quietly in the turret of their tank at night, out of the dark they hear a rustle in the bushes; an "arf arf" just from a local dog would send a chill up their spine, their heart would jump as adrenalin shot into their blood.

Just like Pavlov's salivating dogs, learning can control your biology. Humans, being smarter than dogs, only take one trial, using words, to learn fear.

Could this only happen with a dog? Are humans too smart to fall for this? Will free will save us?

Why did the Japanese Kamikaze pilot in WWII drive their planes out of the skies and dive them directly into the American battleships to die for glory in the process: Free will? Because he "wanted to"? This explanation would never satisfy any psychologist today.

There was no glory on the battleships. The glory was planted in the **mind** of the pilots. Instead, we need to know about the learned emotions embedded in his brain by the stories they learned growing up; of the Bushido Code, the Samurai Tradition; death before dishonor.

They were taught, "*Duty is hard. Death is as light as a cherry blossom falling from a tree.*" They were told stories of glory, of others who died for their Emperor, Hirohito, and those emotions became embedded in their mind. They cheered those heroes like we cheer our football team.

Dying was made heroic. The living glorify the dead. The dead, are never available for comment.

In the American invasion of Okinawa in WWII 3,000 Japanese Kamikaze pilots died taking out over 300 American battleships. Over 30,000 Japanese soldiers died in that battle on land, often in suicidal Banzai attacks. 8,000 civilians, mostly women and children, committed suicide rather than surrender to the Americans. The Japanese considered it a "holy war".

https://www.atomicheritage.org/history/japanese-mass-suicides

Humans are far easier to condition than a dog. All it takes is an emotion associated with a word, thought, or idea. Just pay attention to what is happening in politics in America today. The more we understand this, the less likely it is that we will be sucked into the same emotions.

NO TRIAL LEARNING:
72 Grateful Black-Eyed Virgins

On 9/11 fourteen terrorists died attacking America after hijacking four airplanes to attack a country they were convinced were infidels. Two crashed into the Twin Towers, one crashed into the Pentagon, and one crashed into a field. When the FBI investigated the materials they had left behind, they found jihadist literature resurrecting an old story that if a man died in a Holy war, a Jihad, they would go directly to heaven where 72 black-eyed virgins awaited them.

To this day, no one has ever been able to disprove that claim.

The glory was planted in the **mind** of the martyrs, it did not exist outside of their own mind. The ideas planted in our minds determine our very perception of reality, not just a response.

What can you say to a man who tells you he prefers obeying God rather than men, and that as a result he's certain he'll go to heaven if he cuts your throat?
Voltaire

Being willing to die for your cause does not make you right.

In a frightening event in the Middle East, a female suicide bomber wrapped herself in dynamite underneath her bourka and set it off in the center of a crowded market. As one of the first female suicide bombers, this created a sensation in the press. A journalist and CNN film crew were sent to the tiny village that she came from to find out why, why would she do this?

When they came to the center of her small village, they found a fountain. The fountain had been transformed into a shrine to the suicide bomber with garlands of flowers around it. Her picture had been enlarged and placed in the center of the shrine. Local school children had turned out to sing her praises.

When the journalist asked some children, "What do you want to be when you grow up?", the children replied enthusiastically, "I want to be a suicide bomber!"

The human mind is infinitely programmable, like a good computer. It matters not one binary digit if the programming is accurate. It all proceeds on the principle known to every computer programmer; GI-GO; Garbage In – Garbage Out. And the mechanism for programming the human brain--is the simple association between stimuli.

The preoccupation with finding evidence that our brain is something more than simple programming has led to decades of ignoring the most basic principles of programming our brains in favor of chasing the idea that we are a creature of reason. Yet for the vast majority of human thought, it is only after learning has occurred that we seek to find a rational reason to justify the Garbage Out produced by the brain.

The hard evidence rules, our opinions are just brain poop.

CONDITIONAL = REALTIVE TO THE CONDITONS

The inability of the mind to change on its own is dramatically illustrated by an incident in psychology. When Pavlov published his work on reflexes, he called this a work on *conditional* reflexes, the Russian word ***uslovnyi***, or ***conditional*** was mistakenly translated as *conditioned* reflexes. Pavlov considered the reflex to be *conditional*, or ***relative*** to the conditions under which it occurs. Conditional means it depends upon, or is relative to, certain conditions.

Hence, psychology's first Theory of Relativity.

But even though we have known about the mistranslation for about a hundred years, once the mistake was solidified in our textbooks it became impossible for psychology to change. Even knowing this, I find it hard to change. The Primacy Effect in action. Every single textbook continues to use this mistake. To this day, it is not just a mistranslation, but a mistake in understanding.

SPECIAL AND GENERAL THEORIES OF RELATIVITY

LEARNED RESPONSES V. LEARNED EMOTIONS:

Pavlov was most concerned with the association of a stimulus and response in the brain. I have called this the Special Theory of Relativity because it deals only with a very specific type of response, *relative* to Any Stimulus - Any Response (already wired into your autonomic nervous system).

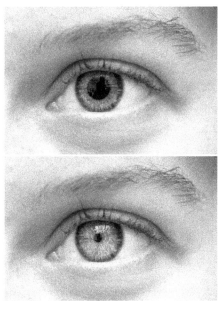

A simple experiment has been done to show that. Stare into a mirror at the iris and pupil of your eye and think; constrict, expand, constrict, expand. What will your pupil do? It will stare right back at you like you are stupid. This is part of the Autonomic (automatic) Nervous System; we have no conscious control over the pupil of our eye. It normally responds only to light.

Yet, go into a dark room. Have someone behind you with a bell and a light. At random, have him sound the bell, turn on the light. Your pupil will constrict to the light. Turn off the light the pupil goes back to normal. Repeat this a number more times. Then sound the bell *without* turning on the light, your pupil will constrict; not to the light, but to the bell.

Babies will often start crying to be fed as soon as they see their mother's face but not to other faces. Not that they "know" who their mother is, but they have associated their mother's face with feeding and maybe fun times. It is learning by association but it does not involve thinking. New mothers often report that after a while they will automatically start lactating as soon as they hear their baby's hunger cry. Thought is not required.

Pavlov's Special Theory applies to everything from hunger to sex. More on that later.

But Pavlov's idea was limited in its application. It could not explain why we behave as we do without experience, why we seek things we have had no experience with. Psychology's General Theory of Relativity, *relative* to what emotion is associated with what stimulus, is far more indicative of most motivation.

Instead of explaining simple behaviors such as typing or driving a car, the General Theory applies to the motivation that makes us seek *general* goals, such as what we like or dislike, what we seek to achieve or to avoid, and what stimuli make us angry or afraid, who we vote for or "choose" to die for.

The human brain itself is an emotion-driven machine, constantly associating stimuli (ideas, words, thoughts, etc.) with positive or negative emotions or anger. Constantly making value judgments of everyone and everything. This allows us to make our way in the world, more or less successfully. But it also produces the greatest prejudice; the willingness to destroy those who are different. Yet it all follows the basic paradigm studied by Pavlov.

Later we will see how permutations can change the very nature of learning, but these simple associations are the starting point for our exploration of just how far we can reduce the mind to its more basic elements before we run slam into a singularity; a point where general laws no longer seem to apply.

CONTROLLING THE BIOLOGY OF THE BRAIN:

Before we go looking for the Ghost in the Machine, let's see just how far simple association of two stimuli; *Stimulus-Stimulus* associations or *Stimulus-Response* associations can go in cracking the mind code that determines our behavior before we look for the ghosts of cognition.

Pavlov's work was important, not because he taught a dog to salivate to the sound of a bell, but because he glimpsed an understanding of how stimuli in the environment can control the biology of the brain; by rewiring the biology of the brain.

The evidence is all around us yet we are only vaguely aware of much of the evidence. Even if it is pointed out, few see its importance. People would still say, "But the dog salivated because he *wanted* to." Or maybe, "Your pupil constricts or expands because it wants to." If this were all a new discovery, it would be far more impressive than black holes in space or Einstein's theory of gravity. It is psychology's version of E=mc2. Yet its importance is barely realized.

The equivalent of the General Theory of Relativity began only when American psychologist John B. Watson studied Conditioned Emotions. Conditioned (sorry, *conditional*) emotions are a far simpler and more profound control over human behavior. Instead of requiring learning a chain of responses, like typing or playing a guitar, it only required a direction.

Emotion provides us direction, a goal, as we saw in the Kamikaze pilot. Emotion, associated with stimuli, also tells us what is good, what is bad, and what should make us angry: **Relative** to what *emotion* is associated with what *stimuli*.

New ideas in psychology seek to use a computer analogy to explain human behavior. It has the potential for giving us an understanding of some of the functions of the brain. Yet no computer model could explain the emotions that govern human behavior, because no computer has emotion to determine its behavior.

ANY STIMULUS-ANY EMOTION:
PSYCHOLOGY'S GENERAL THEORY OF RELATIVITY

The cow of all animals is most sacred. Every part of its body is inhabited by some deity or other. Every hair on its body is inviolable. All its excreta are hallowed. Not a particle ought to be thrown away as impure. On the contrary, the water it ejects ought to be preserved as the best of all holy waters – a sin destroying liquid which sanctifies everything it touches, while nothing purifies like cow-dung. Any spot which a cow has condescended to honor with the sacred deposit of her excrement is forever afterwards consecrated ground, and the filthiest place plastered with is at once cleansed and freed from pollution, while the ashes produced by burning this hallowed substance are of such a holy nature, that they not only make clean all material things, however previously unclean, but have only to be sprinkled over a sinner to convert him to a saint."

Sir Monier-Williams *Bramnism and Hinduism*

In India, cows are sacred. In America, we mulch them into burgers and eat them. We wear their skins on our feet. When McDonald's moved to India, they were greeted with wild protests, "Cow killers!", even though they were already serving vege-burgers. It made front-page headlines in India; it was ignored in America. It is all *relative* to what stimuli have been associated with which emotions. Then, that emotion *generalizes* to other associated stimuli.

Mahatma Gandhi offered a more modern version; cows are venerated, he noted, because they are *associated* with life-giving. All life is sacred.   But it is a matter of association. Words that have been *associated* with positive emotions are then *associated* with any other stimuli.

In our culture we may see the relics, the bones of a saint or a sliver of wood we are told is from the "original" cross, are treated with reverence and often believed to cure us from disease.

In America, politicians do the same thing, associating themselves with all things positive and their opponents with all things negative. And many believe their excreta are hallowed, even when the hard evidence shows their words to be puerile.

The fact that we can "feel" those emotions, that it tickles our limbic system, has created the illusion that those emotions reflect reality.

Words, associated with emotion, control the mind. It applies to our thoughts, our value judgments, our politics, our religion, our individuality. Few ever ask, "What is the hard evidence?" Even the press largely asks, "What is your opinion?" Unless we understand that evidence is vastly more important than personal opinion, we cannot control our own mind, we cannot do science.

"The obscure we see eventually, the completely obvious, it seems, takes longer." Edward R. Murrow

Chains of learned responses described by Pavlov control the practice of athletes. Constant repetition trains the cortex of the cerebellum to learn these chains to perfection. You see this in learning to type, or riding a bicycle, or playing sports. We also see it in driving a car; at first, we have to think about each move, every change of lane, every glance in a mirror, but after a few years, we get in the car in the morning and daydream all the way to work. When we finally get there, we may be amazed and not even remember all the turns, because our automatic mind would move, turn, and brake automatically, all the while we are daydreaming.

Yet most of human motivation is directed by emotion, not by chains of conditioned responses. We seek what is associated with positive emotions and avoid what is associated with negative emotions. An unknown poet put it well, an echo of Thorndike's Law of Effect; I wish I could give credit:

"No matter how high or lowly the beast,
we all do what pleasures most or pains least." Unknown Sage

The importance of psychology is in knowing that "what pleasures most or pains least" is not determined by reality, it is largely determined by the emotions *associated* with the words and ideas of others. Those words then determine our thoughts, our beliefs, and our very perception of reality.

And, can your mind anticipate what is coming next? The evidence is all around us, hidden in plain sight; obscured by the first ideas embedded in our mind; the ideas that we are rational, thinking, intelligent beings. Yet no one notices the evidence that we are saddled by the emotions others embed in our minds. The emotions seem so obviously correct.

What Pavlov did not realize at the time was that a stimulus associated with an emotion creates a General Theory of Relativity (Any Stimulus-Any Emotion) that does not require the learning of specific reflexes or chains of learned responses to explain behavior. Most of what we have talked about, from the Kamikaze pilot to the responses of high school football players, is based on emotions that set a goal, that does not require a learned chain of responses.

Yet there is a third variable, not so apparent: The biological effect of novel stimuli on our brain. From Donald Hebb to Harry Harlow the effect of novel stimuli has been shown to create a variable degree of emotion. A moderate degree of novel stimuli triggers a "curiosity" response. We seek to approach. A strong degree of novel stimuli can create a dramatic Fight or Flight response. Children show a marked degree of fear when lost in a supermarket. Intense and directed fear can create anger and attack directed against whatever perceived danger we encounter.

Every emotion we feel, comes out of our experience of stimuli associated with the fear, anger, and pleasure in the biology of our brain. Such a simple fact, yet no one notices.

After a while there *is no need to experience an actual emotion*, the brain computes the emotions, associated with words, in a way that determines what we like or dislike or what makes us angry, just based on our past associations.

THOUGHTS CAN CONTROL
THE BIOLOGY OF YOUR BRAIN

One of the most important studies ever done, both for understanding the mind and for understanding psychological problems of anxiety and depression, is a study that demonstrated how thoughts can control the biology of your brain. Neal Miller, who developed the concept of bio-feedback, has demonstrated that even the very thoughts in our brain can be controlled by emotional conditioning.

Miller wired volunteers to a machine that would deliver an electric shock. Then, he used a form of tachistoscope to present a simple symbol, a "T" or a "4" to the subject. Every time the "T" was presented, a shock would quickly follow. If a "4" was presented they received no shock.

He measured the fear reaction by using a GSR machine, part of what is used in a "lie detector". "Lie detectors" do not detect lies, they detect activation of the fear or anxiety response.

After a series of shocks, he now presented just a series of dots; *without any shocks.* The subjects were instructed to **think** "T" for the first *dot*, then **think** "4" for the second *dot*, and so on.

Even though no shocks were given, the ***thought*** of "T" was enough to trigger a fear response. The fear response was recorded by the "lie detector".

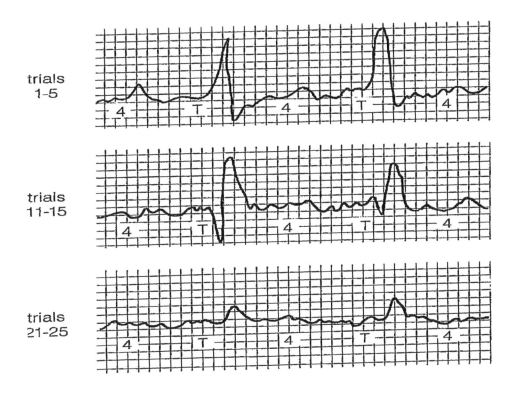

The subjects showed a fear response just to the ***thought*** of "T" that continued for 25 trials, *with no shock being given.* "Once bitten—25 times shy?"

This study should have been a bridge between behavioral psychology and cognitive psychology, although it was largely ignored.

More still, this is a demonstration of the environment controlling the brain in a way that applies to the origin of anxiety disorders and depression. We know that those who have problems such as PTSD or those who commit suicide have had as much as four times more negative experiences as those who do not.

THE HARD EVIDENCE OF THE PSYCHOLOGICAL CAUSE OF BIOLOGICAL EVENTS

Imagine this: you are in a car speeding along in the rain, and an 18-wheeler pulls out in front of you. You hit your brakes, you skid and skid... Then nothing happens; you do not hit the truck after all. What happens in your body then? Adrenalin and epinephrine shoot into your bloodstream; your heart jumps, and you breathe heavily; your heart rate goes over 120 beats a minute, and your hands get cold and clammy. Why?

Now, suppose doctors do a simple blood test on everybody who has or almost has a traffic accident. And they find overwhelming evidence that such people had 600 to 800 times more adrenalin or epinephrine in their blood. Does that prove that the presence of these chemicals caused people to have traffic accidents?

This is a fear reaction, triggered, not by biology, but by psychology—the fear of being in an accident. But that is a learned fear, triggered by learned associations between ideas in your mind. You had no accident—no physical damage to you happened. A learned fear of having an accident triggered the neurotransmitters. A simple psychological association between accidents and the emotion of fear triggered the adrenalin that shot into their blood.

The same is true of every finding that there may be a biochemical cause of a psychological problem. Psychology can control our biology. There is no reason to assume that depletion of serotonin or any other neurotransmitter causes a psychological problem. But that has not prevented the media from being certain that biology is more important than psychology.

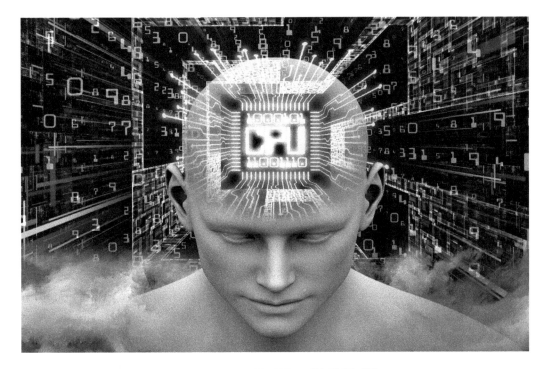

THE MIND CODE:
THE POWER OF ASSOCIATION
STIMULUS + STIMULUS = PERCEPTION

Learning at its basic is by a simple *association* between two stimuli. Some years ago, a vacuum cleaner company brought a new, space-age vacuum. Using sound-deadening materials along with baffles; they took their basic model and made it very quiet. They test marketed it alongside its standard noisy model, to prove it works just as well but was very quiet. Women would not buy it. Why?

Think about this, every time you rev the engine on your car, the more power it puts out, the more noise it puts out. The more noise it puts out, the more power it puts out. Every time you press 10 on your blender, the more power it puts out, the more noise it puts out. When you turn the electric fan on high, the more power it puts out, the more noise it puts out.

Power and noise are intimately associated. This is a Stimulus-Stimulus association that imprints on the mind so firmly that noise (S) = power (S), creates a new perception in the brain. Not just a thought, but an actual perception. Never in the entire of human history have we ever had motors until about a hundred years ago. Only within this short period has everyone born since 1900 had this learned perception imprinted on their brain. A vacuum that was not noisy simply was not *perceived* as powerful.

In my day when a teenager got his first car, he wanted to put a glass-packed muffler on it, because it gave it that deep-throated varoom, Varoooom, Varooooommm, Babala, babala, babala... Aaaah, that was so cool. It was the very definition of cool to a teenage male. The sound made it seem like it was putting out more power. But noise did not make the car more powerful, it only made it noisier.

Yet we were motivated to seek noise just because of our perception that noise = power. Stimulus (noise) + Stimulus (power) = Perception. Even before we got a car, we would take a clothespin, put it on the strut of our bicycle wheel, and attach playing cards to the strut, so that when the spokes went around, they would make a brrrrrrrr, sound. Noise is *perceived* as power by the human mind.

We do not "think" that *noise is power*, **we actually experience (perceive) noise as power. Stimulus + Stimulus = Perception. One step beyond Pavlov's learned responses or even emotional conditioning is the idea that simple associations of stimuli can produce a** *perception*, **not just a response; more on that in the next chapter.**

The fact that we can "think" has created the illusion that we do think. In fact, we mostly perceive instead of thinking.

The relatively high speed of neurons masks the associations and perceptions that the brain makes into what we call the conscious mind. This speed of associations and perceptions may be what behaviorists call stimulus generalization.

S+S+S+S + Stimulus Generalization = Perception.

PABLO PICASSO AS A NAME (S)
ASSOCIATED WITH MONEY (S) AND FAME (S)

In January 2010, at Sotheby's auction in London, a painting by Pablo Picasso sold for 54 million dollars. One year later, another of Picasso's paintings sold at auction for over 110 million dollars. In 2015, one of his paintings sold for 179 million dollars. Why? What makes a painting with Picasso's name on it worth more than a painting with your name on it?

"I never heard of this Picasso fella. Give me five bucks
and it's yours."

Decades ago, Pablo Picasso interviewed with *Life* magazine and said something so profound that I tore out the page and memorized it. I still have it. What he said was this:

"*...I have not the courage to think of myself as an artist, in the great and ancient sense of the term. Giotto, Titian, Rembrandt were great painters. I am only a public entertainer who has understood his times and exploited as best he could, the imbecility, the vanity, the cupidity of his contemporaries. Mine is a bitter confession, more so than it may appear, but it has the merit of being sincere.*" Pablo Ruiz Picasso, *Life* magazine

Picasso was being too hard on himself. But he was also being painfully honest. He took a CBS film crew on a tour of his studio in Spain. He showed them how every morning, his associates would set up a row of easels and canvas on one side of a grand hall. Picasso would start with the first canvas, go all around the room, and at the end of the day, he would sign each one. His signature on a painting made it worth a small fortune. My signature on the same painting would devalue the canvas it was painted on. They couldn't even give it away. Or, they would have to sell it at the flea market like damaged goods.

"Until doing this painting, he was a starving artist."

Picasso was honest enough that he told people, in no uncertain terms, in effect, "I mass produce this crap." And it still sells.

Early in his career, Picasso painted perfectly normal pictures, such as his classic "The Patient" but it did not sell. The more bizarre he made it, the more famous it became. People started paying attention. Its value increased. Fame has a value all its own. Much like in politics.

"A powerful statement of the artist's
hunger for recognition."

If you took a pair of thirty-dollar tennis shoes and put Michael Jordan's name on them, suddenly, they are worth many times as much. That is why companies pay celebrities millions of dollars to allow them to put their name on a product. If you go on eBay, you can find his older editions selling for hundreds of dollars. A simple association between a famous name, and any stimulus, even a shoe, gives that stimulus the power to control the emotions in the brain.

Not long ago there was a minor scandal associated with P-Diddy, the rap singer. He brought out a T-shirt with his name on it that sold for $40. Forty dollars? The media discovered that this T-shirt was being manufactured in Honduras by sweatshop labor using 14-year-old girls who worked 12 hours a day, six days a week, who were paid fifteen cents for every P-Diddy T-shirt they sewed together; Fifteen cents. Having a celebrity name on a product makes it worth more?

HOW MUCH IS YOUR SNOT WORTH?

Simple association between a name and fame makes that Stimulus + Stimulus association extraordinarily powerful.

A fan of Britney Spears spotted her and a friend walking around Hollywood one day. She watched Britney go into a Hot Dog stand and come out eating a hotdog. The fan followed her. When Britney dropped the wrapper into the trash, the fan picked it out of the trash. She sold it on eBay for three hundred dollars.

I mentioned that story in class one day and a student told me something similar had happened with Jay Leno. When Scarlet Johansson appeared on his show, shortly after the Britney hot dog story broke, Scarlet Johansson had a cold. Jay told her to sneeze into a handkerchief and they would put it up for bids on eBay.

After the student mentioned this, I Googled "Scarlet Johansson's Snot" on the computer in class. It was purely as a lark. I did not expect to find anything. It came back with page after page after page of hits on Scarlet's "snot". Wow.

Scarlet Johansson's snot sold in a white-hot auction on eBay for five thousand three hundred dollars; Five thousand three hundred dollars. Wow. How much is your snot worth? When I saw the $5,300 eBay sale of Scarlet's snot pop up on the screen in class, the only thing that popped into my mind is, "we are all going to hell in a handbasket". No doubt it would have to be a Gucci handbasket.

It was bought by a biologist in southern California. The word on the street was that he intended to use Scarlet Johansson's snot cells to clone her. Noticed anyone who looks like Scarlet? She seems to look different in every movie she is in. The proceeds from the sale were donated to charity.

Even Tiger Woods, the golfer who was virgin pure and a role model for all, got in on the action. He became the first billionaire golfer; A billionaire *golfer*? Not from playing golf, he made hundreds of millions of dollars in product endorsements because his name was *associated* with fame. In one ad, he was endorsing Buicks, the car. He is a golfer, what does he know about cars? It turned out he did not even drive a Buick; he drove a Cadillac Escalade. And apparently, he does not even drive that well, at least not with his wife beating out his rear window with a nine iron after she discovered some of his fourteen mistresses on his cell phone. He ran into a post.

Whose name is on your butt? Jordache? Calvin Klein? Guess? Bebe? Putting a famous name on jeans, shoes, purses (Gucci), perfume (ode de Octomom?) seems to make it worth far more. I have K-Mart on my butt.

Apparently, just fame alone is enough to sell jeans. There is a new pair of jeans out there called "True Religion" that sells for some three hundred dollars. Three hundred dollars? For that price, you should get a free pass into Heaven.

When the push began to get students in school eating healthier, a nutritionist did a study of what children eat or do not eat in the lunchroom.   She found that students routinely threw away most of their spinach. This was back when Superman was big in the theaters. So, she put a sign above the spinach that read, "X-Ray Vision Spinach", a takeoff on Superman's supposed X-Ray vision. Soon, the consumption of spinach went up 300%. Even after they made her take the sign down, the consumption of spinach was still up 40%.

Do you think only children would fall for this?

In Patagonia in Chile in South America, there is a fish called the Patagonian Tooth-fish. They call it a "Toothfish" because it is an incredibly ugly fish with rows of sharp, needle-like teeth. Fishermen used to consider it a "trash" fish and threw it away when it showed up in their nets. No one wanted to eat them.

Then, in 1977, Lee Lantz, a fish wholesaler, decided to rename the fish. He called it the Chilean Sea Bass. It quickly became a delicacy, its sales soared, and everyone wanted to try it.   The best restaurants in Europe and America hyped it as a rare delicacy; Amazing success story. What's in a name? A rose is a rose is a Chilean Sea Bass?

Left: Hake, a Japanese "Sea Bass". The next great delicacy? Or just another politician?

Alaska Blackfish was not a big seller, until they started calling it "Alaska Cod".

Reality cannot compete with words. Facts are ignored in favor of feelings. Politics is all about being a Chilean Sea Bass.

WHY WOMEN LOVE A MAN WHO LIVES IN A HOLE IN THE GROUND AND EATS RATS

At the end of WWII, some 15,000 Japanese troops in Southeast Asia refused to surrender for years. They could not believe that the emperor had ordered them to surrender. A handful of these continued living and fighting for some 30 years. One had lived on the American island of Guam for 30 years as B-52 bombers took off to drop bombs on North Vietnam in the Vietnam war.

Another, Hiro Annado, lived in the Philippines for 29 years in a hole in the ground; still killing Philippinos who he thought were the enemy. Living on rats and bugs for decades, he was finally convinced the war was over and came out of hiding.

On his return to Japan, he was given a hero's welcome; "*He received over 100 marriage proposals from awestruck women*" the media reported. Men have always wondered what it takes to impress a woman, now we know; you have to live in a hole in the ground for 30 years, eating rats.

Of course, it is more than this. He was revered by the Japanese people because he refused to surrender, an idea that was viewed with awe and respect by the Japanese people of his age. The Philippine people viewed him as a war criminal because he had continued to kill their people long after the war was over. The emotional response depends entirely on whether the words or ideas have been paired with a positive emotion or a negative emotion. Any Stimulus-Any Emotion.

WORDS CONTROL THE BIOLOGY OF YOUR BRAIN

Imagine you are an executive presenting an important paper you spent months writing, in a meeting with your boss and fellow executives. The boss briefly looks at the paper you just handed out, says "Idiot", and hands you back your paper in front of everyone. How would you feel? What emotions would flit through your brain? You would be hurt, you would be angry, your self-esteem would drop, and you would trash your boss behind his back.

Imagine you are a college student sitting in a class when the teacher is giving back your term papers. When he comes to your paper, he pauses briefly, looks at it, says "Idiot", and hands you back your paper. How would you feel? What emotions would flit through your brain? You would be hurt, you would be angry, you could lose some of your self-esteem, and lay awake at night going over and over what you should have said in response.

A word now has the power to control the biology of our brain, to elicit an emotional response from the depth of our autonomic nervous system, to tickle the neurons in our amygdala, to damage our self-concept, to change our behavior toward that teacher, to hijack our very thoughts. How did this come to be?

The term "genius" is perhaps the most recognized word in psychology, a term used by Alfred Binet. Genius is a term rarely used in intelligence testing today, it is absent from the two common tests, the WAIS and the WISC. Yet the name is so popular it has stuck in the public mind.

Most people, even psychologists, do not know what Alfred Binet and Henry Goddard called the individuals in the bottom two percent of the Stanford-Binet Intelligence test. It is missing from today's textbooks. Those with an I.Q. of a two-year-old were called *Idiots*. Those whose I.Q. was that of a five-year-old were called *Imbeciles*. Those who fell in the eight to twelve-year-old intellect were called *editea*, which became *Morons*, a term coined by the American psychologist Henry Goddard.

THIS MOST IMPORTANT QUESTION
TELLS US VOLUMES ABOUT THE MIND

Why? This is one of the most important questions ever posed to our understanding of the human mind. Why would Binet and Goddard have used such terrible words as idiot, imbecile, and moron to describe people of low intelligence? The answer to that question highlights one of the most important lessons in human history and perhaps, the single most important fact to understand for your sanity. It ties together all we have learned with a bow.

These words had little meaning in English until **after** they were used to describe people of low intelligence. It was the I.Q. test itself that made these words famous.

Then, human nature being what it is, people began beating their kid brother and each other over the head with words to trash other people's ideas with; "You Idiot, don't you know nothing?" We started calling people we disagreed with, "Morons". People we disliked were labeled "Imbeciles".

These words were associated with negative emotion*s in the tone of voice.*

Words, associated with emotions, now insured the words could tickle the emotions in the biology of your brain, your amygdala.

Imbecile is a French word, derived from a Latin word meaning "weak". The word "Idiot" is originally Greek and is used in our medical profession to this day. If you hear a disease or disorder referred to as "idiopathic" it means we do not know what causes the disease. It does not mean the disease is stupid, it means *we* are stupid.

We made words that had little meaning, into emotionally charged words. How? Simply by the *association* of the word, with a negative tone of voice. The word then took on the emotion attached to the tone of voice. And by associating the words with the idea of low intelligence, the word acquired the meaning it has today, quite different from what was intended.

If you look the word Moron up in Webster's Dictionary, you will find it came from the Greek word "Moros," or "m oros" which was made into a new word, Moron. It did not appear in the dictionary until 1910, two years after it was first used. The original dictionary definition is the same used in the original Stanford-Binet intelligence test; a Moron is someone who is functioning at the intellectual level of an eight to twelve-year-old child. So, if your eight-year-old calls your six-year-old a Moron, he is paying him a compliment. But don't expect he will take it that way, the only understanding we have of the word today is from the *emotion* associated with that word.

Today, psychologists no longer use words like Idiot, Imbecile, and Moron. They have been replaced by terms like, *Mentally Retarded*; Mild, Moderate, and Profound. Yet, human nature being what it is, it was not long before you began hearing, even on television, kids beating each other over the head with terms like, "…you *retard*!"

In 2013, the APA came out with a new edition of the DSM, the DSM-V, often called the Bible of Psychiatry and Psychology, and the term "mental retardation" is no longer in there. They took it out because the term "retarded" has now become a "bad" word. Now "retarded" has been changed to "Intellectual Disability". In more popular terms this has become "Intellectually Challenged."

Human nature being what it is, it will not be long before kids start beating each other over the head with, "He's *challenged*!" or even a caustic, *"He's disabled!"* It has already happened. Even kids who do not know what the word means or where it comes from are using the word to put others down because of the emotion they hear the word associated with.

Beginning in eighth grade, or even earlier now, we get tagged with words associated with emotion. Name-calling, put-downs, bullying become more common. Going through eighth grade is like running for President.

We do not need to keep changing the name; we need to educate people to understand how their mind creates value judgments based solely on the emotion *associated* with a word. This is a fact so powerful, so profound, that it affects our interpersonal relations with others, our politics, and our religion. We see it again in racial and religious prejudice, and in our politics of hate that has overtaken us without our understanding. And few have any awareness of its impact on our minds.

If you do not understand how easily words can control the emotions in your brain, you cannot control your brain. Such a simple fact…

This is no small thing. We routinely see children and adults using words to elicit an emotional reaction from others. In bullying, kids call each other names; "fag", "stupid", "fat" and much more, all because these words now have the power to control the biology of the brains of others, even to the point of making some kids laugh while others commit suicide. In America, nearly 5,000 teenagers and young adults commit suicide each year, every year. Yes, really. Not always for the same reason. Yet words are stimuli that can powerfully affect your mind, especially when you do not understand what is happening.

THE PAST IS PROLOGUE FOR THE FUTURE:
Education is the Key to Changing Our Future

Simply giving young people an understanding of how this occurs is empowering, it gives them a bit more control over their minds. Instead of teaching them to understand their mind, we dump them into a world of value judgments and let them sink or swim. Then we are surprised that so many sink.

Our mind is shaped and controlled by the words of others. If you do not understand the forces that shape your mind, you cannot control your mind. Understanding this, helps us to become desensitized to such words, much as Pavlov desensitized dogs to pain.

Yet we still teach nothing of this in our schools, parents understand nothing of how to protect their children. Our societies, our prejudices, our schools, our politics, our understanding of others, all seem to change at the speed of dirt.

The human brain is an emotion-driven machine, not a thinking machine. The fact that we can think, that we can manipulate stimuli with our minds, obscures our most basic emotions. We invent rationalizations to excuse what our emotions dictate.

Observe any baby. If the mother looks sad, sounds sad, sings a sad song, then the baby's face puckers up, becomes sad, they even cry. If the mother laughs, giggles, makes faces, the baby laughs. It takes very little to trigger a major emotional reaction.

Teenagers and adults may seem more sophisticated than a baby; we do not always react with an emotional response, but that is only because we have learned a few more intervening responses; *"never let them see you sweat"*.

Even adults are hotbeds of emotion, just pay attention to politics. Emotions control our thoughts, our fears, our beliefs, what we will die for, even who we vote for.

CAN STIMULI, ASSOCIATED WITH POWER, DETERMINE WHO IS PRESIDENT?

Hot dog wrappers and snot are just a bunch of fluff. The real power of simple association is seen in something far more important. Answer one question. Who was governor of California for eight years at the beginning of this century? Who?

Why? Why did people elect Arnold Schwarzenegger governor of California for eight years at the dawn of the millennium? Superior intelligence? Intellectual genius? Vast experience with how to deal with budget deficits? Alien intervention? Could only something as powerful as Alien intervention possibly explain this?

He was The Terminator. He was a B grade Hollywood actor with no other experience except weightlifting. In his movies, he hardly had any lines. His most famous lines were, "I'll be back." and "Hasta la vista, baby." He campaigned using the slogan, "If you elect me, I will terminate the deficit." Yes, really. How did that work out?

When Arnold was elected in a landslide, California was twelve billion dollars in the hole, in debt. Republicans were talking about amending the United States Constitution so that Arnold, who was born in Austria, could run for President of the United States. They were not worried about the "birther" issue then.

Four years later California was 24 billion in debt, and they re-elected him. Seven years after he was first elected, California was 42 billion dollars in debt and the state treasurer Bill Lockyer said the state had 77.8 billion in outstanding general obligation bonds; triple what it was seven years earlier. The cost of payments on the debt was three times what it had been when Arnold was elected. California was firing schoolteachers and public employees, increasing college tuition, cutting back on services, to help avoid bankruptcy.

He was elected because his name (S) was *associated* with power (S) and fame (S). He was elected because he was a celebrity who got the constant attention of the press while other, more qualified candidates, were ignored by the press.

"The cornerstone of Democracy rests on the foundation of an educated electorate." Thomas Jefferson.

Does anyone seriously believe that George W. Bush would ever have had a chance to be elected President of the United States if his dad had not been President? He had been a "C" student and a cheerleader before. Being the son of the President gave him name recognition and the entire Republican Party apparatus behind him.

Does anyone seriously believe that Hillary Clinton would have had any chance to run for the Democratic nomination for President if she had not been married to President Bill Clinton? That gave her name recognition and the press followed her everywhere, embedding her name in everyone's brain.

Four years before Barack Obama ran for the Presidency nobody had ever heard of Barack Obama. The Democratic nominee for President, John Kerry, picked Barack to give the keynote speech at the Democratic National Convention. It was a very good speech. The press was amazed at his speech. After that, the press followed him around, gave him public exposure, and gave him a platform. His name was embedded in everyone's brain. He had only served two years as a United States Senator before he was chosen to be the Democratic nominee for the Presidency of the United States.

Can anyone grow up to be President of the United States? That depends on what the press covers and what they choose to ignore. In the Democratic Party, the front-runners for the position in 2008 were Joe Biden, Hillary Clinton, and Barack Obama. Joe Biden was a Senator with decades more experience than Clinton and Obama put together. In Congress for 37 years, he had chaired important Senate committees; he had passed dozens of bills through congress. Obama had recently been elected to congress. Hillary had been married to President Bill Clinton and had been elected senator from New York. Yet the press gave all of its attention to Clinton and Obama. The press had anointed them with celebrity status.

One member of the press said of Joe Biden, "He has no sex appeal." Huh? They meant of course that he was not "exciting" enough to bother covering. It is all about stimulating your limbic system; grabbing the biology of your brain using words associated with emotion. That grabs our attention and that is the drug the news media push.

In the election of 2016, the Republicans had 16 candidates running for the nomination. Yet 400% more media coverage went to Donald Trump than any single Republican candidate. Trump got 236 minutes compared to Jeb Bush (56 min), Ben Carson (54 min.). Hillary Clinton, the main Democratic candidate, got 117 min. Trump sucked all the oxygen out of the room.

https://money.cnn.com/2015/12/06/media/donald-trump-nightly-news-coverage/index.html

Why? Because he kept saying controversial things, kept calling his opponents "idiots" or "liars" or "crooked"; words that triggered an emotional reaction because every stimulus out of his mouth grabbed the limited attention of the press.

Just about the only attention the other 15 Republican candidates got was when they were asked to react to a name Trump called them. "Little" Marco Rubio, or "Lying" Ted Cruz. Or "Crooked" Hillary Clinton". Every time Trump rang a bell, the news slobbered. The airwaves became his wet market. Those words tickled our amygdala, hijacked our thoughts.

Every politician today tries to associate himself with stimuli associated with all things wise and wonderful and all things associated with positive emotions; God, motherhood, patriotism, and apple pie in the old days. More recently; cutting taxes, putting people to work, guns, and, of course, religion and patriotism. Each tries to *associate* his opponent with all things negative and bad; to portray them as weak on crime, drugs, the economy, and terrorism.

These are just words, words associated with negative emotions, but words have the power to fire our amygdala all out of proportion to reality. Words become our reality. Those who are unaware of this have no real control over their minds, but don't try to tell them that.

> *"The victim of mind-manipulation does not know that he is a victim. To him, the walls of his prison are invisible, and he believes himself to be free."*
> Aldous Huxley

The media were constantly putting emotionally charged words and ideas in front of all else. Hard evidence was ignored by many. The politics of fear and smear dominate. The emotions triggered by the politics of hate control the minds of vast numbers of people who watch, just as effectively as name-calling controls the minds of eighth-grade children on the playground.

The fact that we are free to vote, has created the illusion that we are free to choose.

One of the most effective mind control methods in politics is a promise to "pay you money" if you vote for them, by giving you a tax cut. Everyone likes a tax cut. Everyone likes money. It does not cost a politician anything to make the promise, they do not even have to follow through on the promise, or they can give the greatest tax cuts to themselves and their wealthy campaign contributors, and few will notice.

In the great tax cut of 2017, the average American family of four got $870 per year or $22 per individual per month. Some media covered it, but few people noticed, as long as the politicians kept talking about the great "Tax Cut". The biggest tax cut went to wealthy corporations and the rich in the top 10% and another 100% tax cut for the very rich to pass on their money and property without tax at all after they die. The top 10% own 89% of the stock market wealth in America. Do the math.

> *"A household earning $1 million or more would get an average cut of $69,660, an income bump of 3.3 percent. Compare that with the tax cut of $870, or 1.6 percent, for the average household earning $50,000 to $75,000."*

> https://www.npr.org/2017/12/19/571754894/charts-see-how-much-of-gop-tax-cuts-will-go-to-the-middle-class

> *"Top 1% Of U.S. Households Hold 15 Times More Wealth Than Bottom 50% Combined."*

> https://www.forbes.com/sites/tommybeer/2020/10/08/top-1-of-us-households-hold-15-times-more-wealth-than-bottom-50-combined/?sh=75c824a85179

> https://www.cnbc.com/2021/10/18/the-wealthiest-10percent-of-americans-own-a-record-89percent-of-all-us-stocks.html

"If you don't vote, you have no right to complain" is a common refrain, used to shame people into voting. Really? How has that worked out? In states like

Texas, and many other states, it does not matter one iota if you vote for a Republican or Democrat for President. Every single one of Texas 38 Electoral College votes always go Republican; every single one. They are not distributed equally among the politicians who are running; it is winner take all. Texas has not gone Democratic, except for Jimmy Carter, since LBJ, a Texan and a Democrat, ran for President some 60 years ago. Texas Republicans complained that LBJ was so popular that people would rise up out of their graves to vote for him. They are still making that complaint, when they lose.

Even if every single Texan voted in the national election, that would not change anything. Every single one of the Texas Electoral College votes would still go Republican. There are many such "red" states or "blue" states. In national elections, Al Gore beat George Bush by a half-million votes; half a million votes. Who became President? How did that work out? Hillary Clinton beat Donald Trump by just under three million votes; three million votes. Who became President? How did that work out?

Our illusions overpower reality. Our high school civics classes deny reality. Why is it so hard to tell the truth? Do the math. Start your own "orgy of free-thinking".

Inevitably, people will eventually vote out one party. Then people will say, "See, your vote counted!" No, what counted was what the press covered, or failed to cover, words, associated with emotional stimuli, that determined who would vote for whom, or against whom. Dogs pay little attention to words. You have to reward a dog to get them to do what you want... but humans?

Words, associated with emotions, have become more powerful than reality.

"Human beings act in a great variety of irrational ways, but all of them seem to be capable if given a fair chance, of making a reasonable choice in the light of available evidence... But today, in the world's most powerful democracy, the politicians and the propagandists prefer to make nonsense of democratic procedures by appealing almost exclusively to the ignorance and irrationality of the electors.

Aldous Huxley

That is power. Stimuli, and what they are associated with, determine our destiny. They determine whom the press will anoint. They determine whom we will be allowed to vote for as President. They determine far more than this. They determine the very religious beliefs we hold sacred. Religions compete to see who can embed their ideas in the minds of youth first. Our beliefs sound obviously correct to us. Yet we have only the vaguest awareness of how stimuli, associated with something positive or negative, affect our perception of reality. Politicians are in no hurry to see this change. Schools are afraid to teach the truth. People would be outraged. Ideas would be burned.

Of course, not everyone considers the same stimuli to be positive because we all grow up in slightly different environments, with different emotional conditioning and different "reasons" for why, whatever we were told to believe, is absolutely correct, and those who believe differently are mistaken, or misled, or downright evil.

Some politicians are far more wrong than others, but we are not allowed to say who, because that would violate the illusion that we have to be "fair and balanced" to both sides, instead of being honest. If you doubt the power of stimuli to control the mind, all you have to do is pay attention to politics in America.

"Politicians and diapers should be changed often, for the same reason."
Mark Twain

Everything we have been talking about, the election of a Governor or a President, the determination of whom we will be allowed to consider, attempts to trade money for political advantage, is all happening in plain view for everyone to see. Yet unless we are forced to consider the associations between these stimuli, we have little conscious awareness of what is happening; much less can we do anything about this. Like learning the language we speak, it has happened so subtly, we cannot imagine any other reality. Other beliefs sound like Chinese to us.

The evidence is hidden in plain sight. And no one notices?

A DISTURBANCE IN THE FORCE:
The Power of Knowledge

"Weak minds are powerless against The Force," said old Ben Kenobi in *Star Wars*. It was Hollywood poetry. There is no such thing as "The Force" in any sense used by Ben Kenobi. But it is no small truth that the forces in the environment that leave their track on our minds become *The Force* that shapes or determines our lives. And until we come to understand how these forces impact our minds, we will be helpless in their grip.

Only by coming to understand the subtle forces that shape the human mind can we possibly acquire the knowledge that will allow us to change our psychological environment as effectively and rewardingly as we have learned to change our physical environment.

In greater or lesser degree each of us becomes trapped in the programs fed into our mind by our society, as Einstein realized early on. Sometimes these programs benefit us or others. Or they may lead us into posturing and pretense that may be destructive to ourselves or others. Yet the basic principle still holds: As long as we are unaware of the mandate these forces impose on our minds, we can do nothing to prevent it or to change for the better.

But more than this; when we become aware of these forces it then becomes possible to consider their effect. Knowledge requires contrast and comparison. Is it true? Does the hard evidence support it? Is the result what we really want? Is it helpful or harmful? Only when we reach that point is it possible to change our behavior, to prevent our past from dictating our future. That requires a commitment by people to learning the hard evidence, to valuing the facts more than our own opinions, to valuing reality more than our personal feelings.

We require our children to learn algebra before they are allowed to get out of school. Yet how many people in the world will ever have an opportunity to use algebra in the entire of their life? We do not allow them to learn more than a superficial smattering of psychology; even though understanding how we think, or don't think, might benefit them far more in the real world.

Psychology today is as controversial as Copernicus in his day or Darwin's biology even today. It may be another one hundred years before psychology is allowed to talk of heavy ideas instead of salivating dogs. Artificial Intelligence scholars talk about the danger of machines becoming "sentient" or aware. It may be another four hundred years before the average person becomes "sentient" or aware of how their mind works. Those who understand this may have an advantage in life over those who do not. Those countries that teach their children to think will blow past us in the years to come.

There is no Nobel Prize for psychology; it was barely around when the Nobel Prize was created. Without fame and attention, the press never noticed. "Where are the droids we are looking for?" How can we find them if our minds cannot see what is in plain sight?

If psychology had only recently discovered what Pavlov learned about how easily we can rewire the biology of the brain, taking the brain's natural Fight or Flight response and turning it into a salivary response, this alone would rank as one of the most important discoveries in human history. The fact that this learning, associated with emotion, can produce a genius, a Kamikaze pilot or a 9/11 terrorist, ranks alongside Einstein's E=mc2 in its impact on our future, for it is the human mind that can "decide" whether or not to unleash an atomic war that could take out much of humanity, or who will be elected President. Yet this discovery has been so diluted by the criticism from those who insist on "free will" or "cognition" as the dominant player in the human mind, that its real importance has been ignored.

Psychologists have a wealth of real-world knowledge hiding in plain sight. If astronomers or paleontologists or historians or even physicists had a fraction of the real-world evidence that psychologists have, they would be thrilled, yet psychologists have ignored the simple evidence in favor of textbooks full of nothing but experimental studies to make us look more "scientific".

Generations of budding psychologists have suffered from textbooks that leave out so much of reality, natural observation, to force it to fit into an experimental paradigm, to make psychology into something that would offend no one. Reality suffers.

Psychology itself has become so dependent on the idea that psychology can be a science only if everything is reduced to experiments. We have forgotten that the great discoveries of Hippocrates and Copernicus and Darwin and Fleming and Einstein and Jane Goodall, Margaret Mead, Clyde Klukholn, were based on the simplest scientific method, *naturalistic observation*, not experiments. Systematic observation, which has served so well in the history of science, has been ignored by psychology textbooks.

"No, these aren't the droids you are looking for." O Be Wan Kenobi

Students sign up for psychology courses in greater numbers than any other elective. They desperately want to understand how our minds work. Students could memorize all 6,000 experiments in our textbooks and come away with little understanding of the mind. They leave our courses disappointed, with little to show but rote memory of sterile facts, devoid of understanding.

Only within the last century has a scientific understanding of the mind became apparent: That the human mind is as profoundly shaped by our experience in our environment, as our human evolution was shaped by our physical environment. Understanding reality will empower us far more than wishful thinking. Stay with me again as we go deeper into our minds in our search for the footprints that life leaves on our minds.

Not only can we read the mind code, we can rewrite it.

Like a good computer, the human mind is infinitely programable.

One question still lingers that must be disposed of before we go into the dark looking for the Ghost in the Machine. If the human mind is not the cauldron of seething DNA energy described by the media, if it is not just the biological template of our genes envisioned by the socio-biologists, if it is not the free will described by others, if it is not just the chains of conditioned responses described by Pavlov, or the emotional forces within the mind, then what is it?

PEEKING OVER THE EDGE

THE ORIGIN OF REALITY

If we are to understand our minds, we must first learn to read the language that our experiences write into the mind of each of us, the mind code that determines our very perception of reality is not just a simple stimulus but in an entire perception.

Perception as The Basis of Our Reality

Psychologists Combs and Synyg tell of two graduate students who were speeding along a lonely highway late at night when the headlights of their car fell upon an object, about two feet in diameter, in the middle of the road. Both saw the same object. The driver kept right on going toward the object. The passenger, seeing that the driver was going to hit the object, suddenly grabbed the wheel of the car and tried to steer it around the object. The driver fought just as hard to keep the car going straight into the object.

Why? Both saw the same object. Both reacted quite differently. The passenger was from the Rocky Mountain States and the object he saw on the highway was a boulder. If you know Colorado, you know this is not uncommon. The driver was from the plains states and the object he saw on the highway was a tumbleweed.

The moment of truth comes, of course, when you hit the object.

I have been driving along the highway at night in New Mexico and had the headlights fall on a tumbleweed in the middle of the road. It looks absolutely solid, until you hit it.

BUMPS AND DENTS:

How can you see in Three Dimensions When there is No Third Dimension?

If you think this could only happen at high speed at night, consider the following picture. Are the large impressions in the picture bumps or dents?

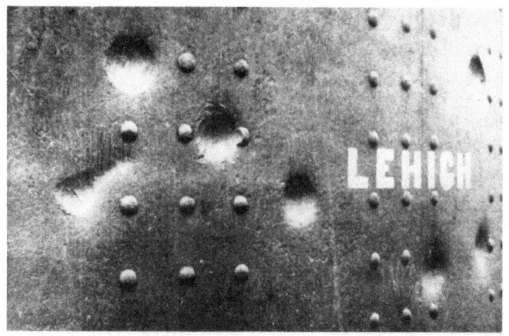

Clearly, the large impressions are dents. In fact, they are cannonball impressions in a steel plate. You can see one of the rivets has been dented by a cannonball. They cannot possibly be anything except dents. Now turn the picture upside down and look at it again. Now, what do you see?

How is it possible that the same picture appears to be dents one way and bumps upside down? What does your mind cue on?

No conscious thought is required. No conscious thought can prevent it. Your automatic brain presents this to your conscious mind.

Yet your conscious mind can sit back and observe how your brain works, quite independent of your conscious awareness, to create reality.

We do not just "think" there are bumps or dents; we actively *perceive* them as bumps and dents.

Whether you see bumps or dents does not depend on reality. In fact, you are seeing neither bumps nor dents. What you are seeing is a flat, two-dimensional picture. It has no depth. Yet, even though there is no depth in the picture, the brain actually "sees" (perceives) this as three dimensional because of our past experience with light and shadow, in much the same way as the people saw a tumbleweed or a boulder. How is this possible?

The sudden change between bumps and dents is identical to the sudden change in we saw in Darwin and others, having a *sudden* insight where the brain automatically triggered a new perception in their mind. The sudden association of two ideas or thoughts or perceptions produced a new insight.

Instead of an association between two stimuli, we have an association between two perceptions. Unlike what many psychologists think about genius, conscious thought is not required to produce the association; all that happens may be no more than the association of two perceptions (or concepts) in our mind.

By turning the picture from one position to the next, you can observe what I think is a most important and unique phenomenon: You can consciously observe the brain operating in a way that is quite independent of your conscious mind. Textbooks all say that we have no way to study the conscious mind directly, so we study a chapter on "Altered States of Consciousness". Yet, here is a way to observe with our conscious mind, how our automatic mind works. Why does it work?

All of our lives we have learned one basic fact about light. Light always comes from above. Even indoors, the light comes from the ceiling. If the objects were a bump, and the light was coming from above, the top of the bump would be lit and the bottom of the bump would be in shadow. On the other hand, if the object were in fact a dent, the top of the dent would be in shadow and the bottom of the dent would be lit.

The brain *perceives* them as bumps or dents, *not* because they *are* bumps or dents, but only because the shadow is at the top of the impression or the bottom.

But the remarkable thing about the effect is that it does not depend on reality at all. Our past experiences have so influenced our perception we find it difficult to see the photograph any other way. Even though you consciously **know** the picture is flat (in 2-dimensions), your brain will still *see* them as dents or bumps (in 3-dimensions).

This is not "just an illusion." It is a demonstration of how our experience changes the brain so completely to determine our most basic perception of reality. If I were to show you something that looked like a dent, and was a dent, such an illustration would tell us nothing about how that perception came to be. What is important about this effect is that it takes the subtle, less obvious impact of our experience and makes it more obvious, more apparent, than it would otherwise ever be. It makes the hidden influences of our experience into something we can begin to see, something we can begin to understand.

Thus, two things are important here. Our experiences can completely alter even our most basic perception of reality, and second, this effect can exist without the slightest conscious awareness of its influence. Even what we mentioned about noise associated with power makes us perceive noise as power. We do not just think it; we *experience* it as power.

Not only is no thought necessary, but thinking cannot easily change the perception written into your brain.

Some might raise the question whether the effect might not be innate, and biological, instead of learned. The way to find out is to simply raise two groups of children from birth in two separate environments: One group in which light comes *down* from the ceiling and one group where light comes *up* from under a glass floor. Brilliant, but hardly practical. Mothers would object. Codes of ethics would be violated. Babies would cry in the night. Yet Eckhart Hess of the University of Chicago devised a simple and ingenious way around this.

Hess reared chicks from the moment of hatching in cages where the light came from below, through an opaque glass floor. This meant grain placed in their cage would have a shadow on top of the grain and the bottom would be lit. A second group was raised the traditional way, with the light coming from above. The grain placed in their cage would have a shadow on the bottom, as it would normally be.

When the first chicks were later shown photographs of grain with the shadow at the top, they spent the vast majority of their time pecking at the photo of this "grain" rather than at the grain in an ordinary photograph where the shadow was on the bottom; just the opposite of normally reared chicks.

WHAT THE CONSCIOUS MIND
CANNOT SEE
OUR VERY PERCEPTION OF REALITY

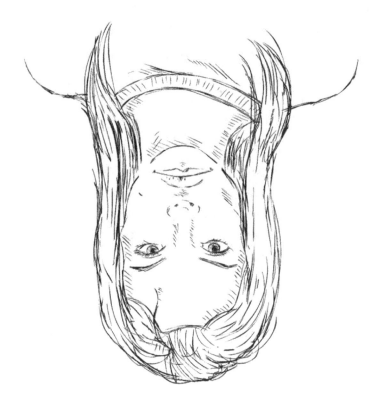

What is it your conscious mind cannot see? Look at the image above until you are certain of what you see. Then, turn the picture upside down to see what your conscious mind cannot see.

First demonstrated by Peter Thompson of York University with an actual picture of Margaret Thatcher. It works with other pictures as well.

Why? Why is your conscious mind unable to see reality? We all have no imprints in our brain for what people look like upside down. All we know is what she should look like right side up. So, when we see the above image, her mouth is actually right side up. When we turn it right side up, then we see reality.

The first ideas or images embedded in our mind become the template by which we judge all reality. Our ability to perceive reality, like our ability to answer a question like, "Take two apples from three apples, what do you have?" depends entirely on our previous experience. Our automatic mind, the Google scan, presents this to our conscious mind.

Perhaps more than any example in psychology, this illustrates how tightly the conscious mind is controlled by our past experiences. See chapter IV on beauty.

HOW THE BRAIN SEES 3D OUT OF 2D

To see a remarkable example of how an artist can use light and shadow to create a flat 2-D page to make our brain see it in 3-D see the following examples from youtube.com. The artists use only light and shadow to produce this three-dimensional effect, well worth seeing:

https://www.youtube.com/watch?v=Z3wAHpYcZNA&list=PLfOBr97D W53nIkACVWauclryi5-bFMTPY&index=3

https://www.youtube.com/watch?v=TnVv3hO8vE4&list=PLfOBr97D W53nIkACVWauclryi5-bFMTPY&index=1

https://www.youtube.com/watch?v=h6pE1wOs1pA

In the next picture the footprints appear to rise above the sidewalk, as Three Dimensional, even though it is only painted on the walkway. The use of light and shadow give the appearance of three dimensions, looking as if the footprints were raised above the surface, even though the page has only two dimensions. Leonardo da Vince, and others, helped to perfect this technique.

NEUROPLASTICITY

CAN THE BRAIN ADAPT TO AN UPSIDE DOWN WORLD?

Studies by psychologists George Stratton, Ivo Kohler, P. K. Pronko and others have taken normal college students and fitted them with goggles with a prismatic lens that flips the world upside down.

Students volunteered to wear these goggles all day for a week. At first, they had great difficulty adapting to such a distorted world. The desk in front of you appears upside down and when you reach for a cup, your hand comes in from above.

The simple act of reaching for a glass of water was hazardous. Pouring water from a jug into a cup was incredibly difficult, and they spilled water everywhere.

The jug and glass, which were on the lower right side of the desk, now appeared to be on the top. Like a baby in a study by Piaget, they had to learn how to guide their hand to the jug. Slowly they adapted. They became as skilled as if they had normal vision. After one week, they had adapted so well that some could even ride a bicycle around campus.

The evidence is strong that human perception of reality is profoundly malleable.

We have only touched briefly on the overwhelming impact that our environment has on our behavior. We must go on to track the limits of its imprint on our minds. It is important to take the rest of this chapter to explore just how complete is the effect of our experiences on our mind before we look for clues about the cues that affect us all.

THE HIGGS BOSON OF PSYCHOLOGY:

The "Footprints and Shadow" in the Mind

No one can observe the brain as it processes information. Yet what we will see in this chapter is psychology's equivalent of the CERN Hadron supercollider that is looking for the famous Higgs Boson, nicknamed the "God Particle". Rob Roser who led the research at Fermi lab in Chicago noted that they cannot directly observe the particle, but they can observe the track it leaves behind. "*You see the footprints and the shadow*" of the Higgs boson and you know you have found a great clue, like an anthropologist finding the fossilized footprints of Lucy, an ape that walked on two feet, you know you have something important.

Our perceptions of reality are the tracks of past experiences embedded in our minds. We must search for the clues left behind by our experiences. To understand the nature of the mind, we must follow these tracks as far as they take us. Like snowflakes falling on paper, they leave a trace so light we can hardly see, yet they affect our lives all out of proportion to the track we can see.

What is the code that experience writes on the brain? How does this determine whom we like and dislike? How does our environment set our motivation into play? Before we go into the night to search for the tracks in the snow, please bear with me while I take you on a brief tour of just how total is the control of the environment over the mind.

THE BRAINS OF COLLEGE STUDENTS
NO LONGER SEE REALITY AS IT IS

One of the first insights into the question of the origin of human knowledge was provided by one of the all-time greats in psychology Gordon Allport, author of two of the most readable and valuable books ever penned by a psychologist; *The Psychology of Rumor* and *The Nature of Prejudice*.

Gordon Allport and Thomas Pettigrew showed a simple geometric design to a group of college students. The design was that of a trapezoid, the Ames window illusion. That is an object that is similar to a rectangle but is dramatically shorter at one end than at the other. A wire through the center of the object was connected to a motor that would slowly turn the object around in a circle, always in the same direction. Go to youtube.com and search for the "Ames Window" or the "Ames room", another trapezoidal illusion.

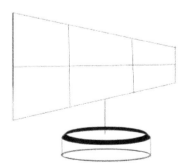

Now, this was a simple, straightforward observation. Yet when college students in America are asked to draw the object they are looking at, they do not draw it as a trapezoid, which it is, but as a perfect *rectangle*. When they are asked to describe what the object is doing, they will tell you, every one of them, that the object is *flapping back and forth*, not going around in a circle.

Thousands of miles away in the heart of Africa are the remains of the proud Zulu nation. These stoic warriors were once prized for their ability to run at a steady pace day and night and still be ready to fight, twenty miles away, on the next day. Only the advent of the Enfield rifle brought about their defeat at the hands of the British during the period of colonial expansion.

When the descendants of those Zulu warriors are today asked to look at the same geometric figure the college students saw, they draw it as a trapezoid, which is exactly what the figure is. When they are asked to describe what the figure is doing, they do not say that it is flapping back and forth. They see it as it is, as going around in a circle.

How could there be such an incredible difference between how American college students see a simple figure and how it is seen by African natives?

Do the natives have superior genes? Is it the result of centuries of biological selection that has honed their senses to the peak of perfection? Are they just genetically more advanced?

What about our college students? Why are they incapable of seeing reality? Are their senses so jaded by years of smoking weed that they can no longer see what is in front of their eyes? Is this your brain on weed? Have their brains turned to mush from the millions of cell phones attached to their ears? Are they the result of a decadent evolutionary backlash in which their senses are no longer capable of perceiving reality as it is?

Why the difference in perception? Allport and Pettigrew found that if these same images were shown to the Zulus living in the city, with the identical genetic background to those living in the wild, that these Zulus who grew up in the city saw the same distortion of reality as the citified American college students. They drew it as a rectangle. They saw it slowly flapping back and forth.

Genetics was not the answer. The reason lay in the environment. Zulus in the wild grew up all of their lives without seeing squares or rectangles or signs or windows or even lines. They lived in round beehive huts with rounded roofs and doors. They tilled their soil in contoured furrows that clung to the rolling hillside of their fields.

But when Zulus were raised in the city, surrounded by rectangular windows and signs and doors in a world of western architecture, their brains began to see reality in the terms of their new sensations. Their exposure to rectangular signs and windows so biased their perception in favor of seeing rectangles that it was impossible to see it as it really was. Instead, they saw it the same way American college students saw it.

This trapezoid effect is no small illusion. I have shown the actual illusion in front of classes of students and I have always been amazed at how complete the effect is, not just on students, but also on myself. When I showed it to students, I was sitting where the students were in a fully lit classroom.

The effect was total. It looked to me as if the object were flapping slowly back and forth instead of moving in a circle. Even though I knew well in advance what to expect and why, even though I knew the motor that powered the machine could not possibly do anything but take the figure in a circle, I found it impossible to see the effect as it was. If you see it in three dimensions, it is even more striking than the bumps and dents effect.

Again, no conscious awareness is necessary at all for the effect to work, and no conscious awareness seems to prevent it from working. Even consciously trying to see the trapezoid as going in a circle did not seem to help, it still looked as though it were flapping back and forth.

To see an exceptional example of the trapezoid illusion in 3-D, even though the film is only 2-D see this exceptional example by Veritasium:

https://www.youtube.com/watch?v=dBap_Lp-0oc

Nor was this the only case where our college students were incapable of perceiving reality. Many more have been found. Unfortunately, the trapezoid effect

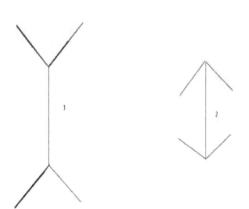

does not work in two dimensions on the printed page. You would have to see it in real life or the above example, to experience the effect. But one that does work is famous as the Muller-Lyre illusion. If you look at the figure below, you find that the center line (1) on the left appears to be longer than the center line (2) on the right.

But if you measure both lines, you find that both are exactly the same length. If you take the same illusion and show it to the Zulus, they will not be fooled by it. Most will see the two lines as the same length. This effect is not as pronounced as that of the trapezoid but it is easier to show on the printed page.

The fact that most of our perceptions are accurate means nothing. The accurate perceptions are formed in the same way as the "illusions" we have seen. Yet seeing these illusions tells us volumes about how we learn to perceive reality.

MAKING THE CODE VISIBLE:

What the Conscious Mind Cannot See

What kind of environment could lead to such widely different effects as the Muller-Lyre effect and the trapezoid effect? What elements of the environment lie encoded in our brain?

The key to decoding the Muller-Lyre effect was suggested by the Dean of perceptual psychology, Richard L. Gregory, professor of Neuropsychology at the University of Bristol. The angles provide the clue (and the *cue*). In the Muller-Lyre illusion, you will see the same angles present on the corner of a room or ceiling or buildings or in the inside of a book when the binding is facing toward you or facing away from you.

The Muller-Lyre illusion is based on a very similar distortion of angles, as you see in the trapezoid. The mind "reads" the angles at the end of the line as though they were the corners on the inside of a building or the edges of a box. This is what Zulus raised in the city saw that Zulus raised in the country did not see. Both lines in the center of the figure above are equal in length. Note the similarity to the trapezoidal windows.

In art, this would be called "perspective". Leonardo da Vinci used this masterfully to create the feeling of depth in his two-dimensional paintings. That was the real da Vinci code.

These effects have one thing in common. Whether the angles of the Muller-Lyre illusion, or the angles of the trapezoid, all involve experiences that we have with boxes, buildings, signs, and angles that are remarkably unique to our modern civilized environment, and often completely missing from the environment of our more primitive ancestors. Yet, within the space of a few years, a child's brain will adapt so totally to this new environment that their perception of the very stuff of reality is changed forever.

It is happening again. The dramatic changes brought about by computers, television and smartphones have created a generation that learns in a way that is quite different from previous generations. Learning by studying words in a book is going out the window. Students today expect to be entertained. They need immediate feedback. They need fast-moving information. Any educational system that fails to change to meet the novel way the human mind works is going to fail. We cannot compete with the glamor and flash of television and youtube.com unless we change how we present education to students.

Recently a student came by looking for a colleague whose office was next to mine. The colleague was not in. The student whipped out her cell phone and took a picture of the closed office door. For a moment, I was astonished; it made no sense to me. She told me she was actually taking a picture of my colleague's Office Hours that were posted on the door because that was easier than remembering them. Coming from a different reality, I had no clue.

ONLY WITHIN THE PAST 12,000 YEARS COULD WE SEE THESE IMAGES. WHY?

In our search for the origin of the mind, these images are much like the track of an electron or neutrino on a photographic plate or a bubble chamber to a physicist. They are the track of a vanished reality, the imprint of experience that has touched our minds and forever altered how we experience reality.

Consider the two-dimensional Necker cube.

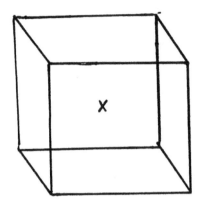

Is the X in the picture on the cube in the inside of the box or the outside of the box? Move your eyes around the cube for about thirty seconds or so, and you can make the cube go from inside out to outside in and back before going on.

You will find that the brain seems to automatically switch back and forth from one "insight" to the next without the slightest conscious effort.

As with bumps and dents, it is as if *you can step back and observe your brain functioning quite independent of any conscious effort on your part.*

Again, we are seeing in three dimensions even when there is no third dimension.

It is unlikely that Zulus living in the outback could see this effect. Only those who have lived in an environment full of boxes, angles, signs, and children's building blocks could see this effect. However, once you have learned it, it becomes almost impossible to see it as *just* the two-dimensional collection of lines that it is. Like the bumps and dents effect, it seems to be "three-dimensional", like a hologram imprint in the brain, read by our mind.

All the books on perception describe the Necker cube as an "ambiguous" figure. Richard Gregory suggests that the brain makes two "hypotheses" about what the cube is and switches back and forth between the two. But I do not think the hypothesizing theory is necessary. This is not the ambiguous figure it has long been considered. The brain cues on very specific stimuli, just as the bumps and dents effect is triggered by whether the shadow is at the top or the bottom. Can you guess what it is in the Necker cube that cues the mind?

From your experience in reading this book, you may have guessed that it is the angles that cue the mind. But that only part of the picture. The brain takes its cue from the sides. Try this experiment; First look at the *top* "side" and switch to the *bottom* "side". Now go back and forth between those two. You find that merely by looking from top to bottom, you can change how your brain sees the figure just as turning the bumps and dents picture up or down changed whether you saw bumps or dents.

Ah, but why should this be? What does the brain see in one view that differs from the next? The brain sees the side you are looking at as being the side *closest* to you. *This is exactly the way the brain would see the side of a "real" box in "real life".*

The brain has made a generalized model of an actual box, vaguely analogous to a hologram, and uses that model for contrast and comparison to allow it to interpret any new experiences.

On Insight: The sudden change in perception we see when we change our focus from the bottom of the Necker cube to the top of the cube is remarkably identical to the sudden change noted by Darwin and others when they saw an immediate change when reading Malthus, On Population or Crick in seeing the double bannisters of the spiral staircase and immediately associating that with the structure of DNA.

The brain itself seems to make the association, the insight, without the need for thought. It requires, of course, a background of ideas that make the association possible.

It is not "just an illusion", in fact, our experiences have made biological changes in the brain, in the neurons themselves. Changes so profound that it is as if it were biologically programmed into our genes, as if they came from our DNA. These changes do not come from our genes, they are clearly learned. Yet the effect is as dramatic, as total, as if they were present at our birth.

The human mind is as totally controlled by our learned experiences as it is by the biological propensity created by our DNA. In the most important ways, our beliefs, feelings, and personality, are far more dependent on learning than on any built-in biological response.

We have the capability of going beyond the controls. We can come to control our own minds. Yet one thing is overwhelmingly clear, we cannot control our own minds, we cannot go beyond the prison of our perception, if we are unaware of why we believe as we do.

Next, the combination of the Necker cube with light and shadow again create a three-dimensional effect on a flat two-dimensional surface.

PERCEPTIONS NEVER BEFORE SEEN
IN HUMAN HISTORY

Remember, no Cro-Magnon, no Neanderthal, no Australopithecine in the entire of human history had *ever* seen a *box*. None exist in nature, none in the baskets, pottery, or even huts and tepees of primitive people, none have been mentioned in the catalog of thousands of prehistoric cave paintings from Lascaux or Altamira or elsewhere.

The first known boxes were the apartment-style houses of Jericho and those surrounding the circles at Gobleki Tepe, both from about twelve thousand ago. We can trace their evolution from round huts and centers into squares and rectangles. Even a straight line is rare in nature. To a lesser extent, the same is true of bumps and dents, although they would undoubtedly have learned the basic "shadow" principle from watching the shadow fall on ridges or trees or shallow depressions in the rocks.

No Neanderthal in the bush, no Cro-Magnon with his cave drawings of charcoal and ocher, no nomadic herdsman wandering through the entire of our history could ever see the reality you have seen in these line drawings. They are unique to modern society, and we see reality in a way that is slightly, yet profoundly, different from the way they did… not because of any change in our genes, but simply *because of the change in the environment in the life of a child in the space of a very brief time.*

This imprint on the brain changes the brain itself. And that, changes what the mind sees.

Cultural experience cuts both ways. As long ago as 1886 in Laws' work, *Woman's Work in Other Lands*, Laws found that the work of young Malawi girls who were brought in to work as domestic servants for Europeans turned out to be very difficult when they had to adapt from their round huts and stools in their environment to the square one of Europeans. For example, in setting out the dinner table, Laws notes:

> "...at her home the house is round; a straight line and the right angles are things unknown to her and her parents before her. Day after day therefore she will lay the cloth with the folds anything but parallel with one edge of the table, plates, knives, and forks are set down in a corresponding manner and it is only after lessons often repeated and much annoyance that she begins to see how things ought to be done and tries to do this.

Marshall McLuhan tells of a native Maoris woodcarver from New Zealand who executed a woodcarving so skilled that the crowd watching broke into applause at his talent. Yet this same woodcarver spent days trying to put two pieces of wood together at a right angle to make a box to ship the carving. McLuhan reports that he gave up. It is not for lack of inborn intelligence or ability, but for lack of experience. "All knowledge is from experience."

All perception is from experience.

All of this should have obvious implications for intelligence testing. Individual tests such as the Stanford-Binet or Wechsler use "block design", "picture completion", and "puzzle" fitting subtests that depend strongly on such abilities. Often thought to be "culture-free" it is apparent that such tests may be as dependent upon learning as their verbal subtests.

OUR VANISHED REALITY:
The Track of a Neutrino on a Photographic Plate

Every textbook in psychology has a chapter that says, in effect, "Here is a bunch of illusions. Aren't they cute? ". This is not just a bunch of cute illusions; this is a footprint of our past, a profound bit of evidence of how our experiences shape our minds. These are clues left behind by a vanished reality; the footprint of a dinosaur, the track of a neutrino on a photographic plate.

What has not been so clear, even to psychologists, is that these are not just illusions, not just distortions of reality. They are examples of the most basic process of learning. The learning that takes place in our environment is normally so subtle, so totally obscured because conscious awareness is unnecessary, that the process of learning is not clear.

Learning does not just give the brain information to use in processing as a computer; it changes the brain itself so completely, that it creates reality in the brain. From this reality, our conscious mind "sees" what the brain has been programmed to see.

Only when one contrasts the effects of learning in one environment with the dramatic difference of how others see reality in a second environment, can the subtle and delicate origin of the mind become apparent. For all its low-key, soft-spoken origins, learning has such a dramatic effect on the human mind that it must be understood as its most basic.

These changes in perception seem to represent the most basic of all forms of learning. It suggests that even the classical conditioning of Pavlov and the operant conditioning of Thorndike are not separate forms of learning, but may be seen as simply another aspect of this far more basic form of learning.

Not that all illusions can be explained as learned effects. Illusions often have quite different origins. Nor is the point that biology is unimportant, for that is not true either. The point is simply that the experiences we have in our environment can affect every area of our lives, even our most basic understanding of reality.

PSYCHOLOGY'S POTSHARDS
OF OUR PAST

The illusions of our mind are not unlike the potshards that Archeologists examine to inform them of the past by observing the remains of pottery for evidence of how they were fired, similarities in markings, even writing or record keeping from a vanished civilization.

The illusions give us insight into how memories are formed, what the conscious mind is, and most importantly, how the brain itself is constructed out of the bits and pieces of reality we are exposed to in our culture.

PSYCHOLOGY'S MIND CODE:

The Simplicity of the Complex

Morse code is the simplest code you may have seen. Simply using dots (.) and dashes (-) we can assign every letter of the alphabet a series of dots and dashes, like S-O-S (... --- ...) and one telegrapher can tap out on a key an entire book and send it a thousand miles away and another telegrapher can reproduce the entire book from just dots and dashes.

The complexity of genetics masks the underlying simplicity of only four base pairs that make up the entire of the DNA code. Each rung on the DNA ladder is made up of different variations of either adenine-thymine or thymine-adenine or cytosine-guanine or guanine-cytosine; usually written as ATCG. Yet a complete human being can be constructed from such a basic combination of only four letters. We think a human being is too complex to be reduced to a four-letter code, yet…

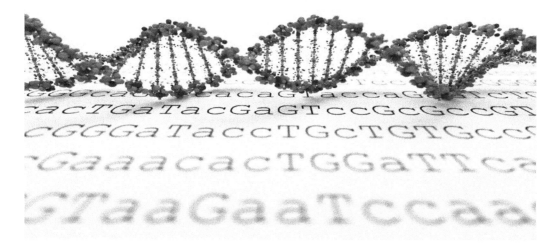

Complex computer programs mask the overwhelming simplicity of the machine language, the coding, on which all programs are based… two binary digits, ones and zeros; 10010110. If you press the W key on your computer, it does not send a W to the screen, it sends a series of eight binary digits, ones and zeros, to the video processor that creates a W on the screen.

If you have a CD with music on it, there is no music on that CD; there is only an infinite series of ones and zeros that the processor transforms into every conceivable variation of the human voice, tempo, music, and language.

If you have a DVD with a movie on it, there is no movie on that DVD. There is only an infinite series of binary digits, ones and zeros, that the central processor uses to control every pixel on the video screen to produce motion, sound, music, and more.

As with that DVD, the fact that human behavior has so many possible permutations masks the underlying simplicity of the mechanism involved. The simple stimulus-stimulus connections and perceptions embedded in our brain, that determine our reality are not immediately obvious. Despite their utter simplicity, they have a dramatic effect on the mind.

As with the DNA code or the binary digits of computers, the stimulus-stimulus code that experience writes into our mind produces something far more impressive than those basic codes would ever predict.

Cracking the human genome was an extraordinary achievement. Yet you can know everything there is to know about the DNA of an individual and still know nothing. The media is so "irrationally exuberant" about hi-tech, that they have missed a far more important point. *The only way to find out what these genes do is to go back to lo-tech, to compare the DNA of a given trait or disorder in one individual to the DNA of others who have a different trait or disorder. Hi-tech tells you nothing by itself.* Yet the news media is so awed by hi-tech it ignores how essential this lo-tech is.

Can a human being be created with only four codes (base pairs)? The 20,000 + genes (instructions) seem too paltry to account for the complexity of nature. The complexity seems impossible, yet it happens. The genes are coded in only four base pairs that carry the entire DNA code.

Can psychology be reduced to nothing but Stimulus-Stimulus or Stimulus-Response associations and Perceptions? Are simple S-S or S-R connections that are read into the brain the raw material that becomes perceptions that are acted on by the conscious mind? Like the "Singularity" in Artificial Intelligence, it can do far more than we know.

We think our minds are too complex for something so simple; yet…

Still, there is reason to believe that S-S and S-R associations are not the most basic elements, but a part of learning that comes out of our more basic sensory experience.

REDUCTIONISM AND SCIENCE: THE SINGULARITY

All of science is based on reductionism. In physics, the subject is *matter*. Matter is reducible to molecules. Molecules are reducible to the elements in the periodic table. These are reducible to the structure of atoms. Atoms are reducible to electrons, protons, neutrinos. These subatomic particles are reducible to quarks and maybe strings…

In biology, the subject matter is *living matter*. Living matter is reducible to organs; heart, lungs, liver, brain. The organs are composed of organized groups of cells. All of the organs are composed of cells. Every part of the human body is composed of cells; Neurons in the brain, the Isles of Langerhans in the pancreas, bone marrow cells, cells that secrete protein to make fingernails, hair, bone. Cells are reducible to mitochondria, RNA, DNA, and the four base pairs of chemicals in the DNA code…

In psychology, there has been no easy agreement, yet we see similar reductionism. The subject of psychology is the Mind. The Mind is reducible to Concepts (Ideas or thoughts, schema, learning sets, cognitive maps) which are reducible to perceptions, which are reducible to associations (S-S, S-R).

SUBJECT	Reduces to:	Reduces further to:
Physics (Matter)	Elements------------Atoms--------------Subatomic Particles	
Biology (Living Matter)	Organs--------------Cells-----------------DNA, RNA, etc.	
Psychology (Mind)	Concepts-----------Perceptions--------Associations (S-S, S-R)	

Yet are S-S or S-R associations the beginning of ideas? Or is there something more basic than the simple associations? What we have seen in this chapter suggests that sensory impressions may be even more basic to learning than these simple associations. How can the seeming difference between perceptions and associations be explained?

Which came first; the chicken or the egg? Even the very interesting new addition to Cognitive Psychology, the computer analogy, cannot explain what we have learned in this chapter about how the mind works. The question is not as simple as it seems.

The evidence presented in this chapter suggests that Sensory Impression comes first; S-S or S-R associations come second. Adding Stimulus-Stimulus associations then create Perception. Stimulus + Stimulus + Stimulus Generalization = Perception.

The "singularity" in Artificial Intelligence is the idea that, as memory power and computing power increase exponentially, it may eventually reach a point where it can no longer be contained, it goes beyond control, and it becomes "self-aware". Here it is used to describe how simple associations combine exponentially until our mind becomes capable of doing far more than the simple S –S connections could predict.

Most of the seemingly complex aspects of reality can be reduced to a few basic underlying principles; DNA reduces to four base pairs, Computer language reduces to Ones and Zeros, neurons in the brain reduces to *on* or *off* and graded potentials. In physics, gamma rays, cosmic radiation, x-rays, visible light, infrared,

TV, radio waves, radar, and more can all be reduced to different frequencies of electromagnetic radiation, just as changing the channel on your radio dial will give you different frequencies and different radio stations. Psychology, at its most basic, is likely to be the same. Magical-mystical thinking has not been productive.

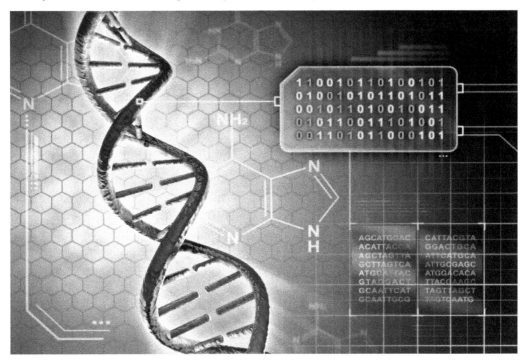

THE CRITIQUE OF S-R ASSOCIATIONS:

Critics of the S-R, S-S approach have pointed out problems that they say cannot be explained by this simple approach.

- Consider a "flashbulb" memory. Almost everyone can remember where they were the first time they heard of the Kennedy assassination or the attack on the Twin Towers on September 11. I can not only remember the event; I vividly remember the road I was on when I first heard of these events on my car radio and exactly where I was when I saw it on television later. It is not just a stimulus-response memory it is like a general impression of everything going on at the time. An image is implanted in my brain. It is like Darwin saying, "...*I remember the very spot in the road whilst traveling in my carriage...*" when he had his great insight. What kind of memory is a flashbulb memory? Is Sensory Impression the most basic form of learning?

- Studies show that we do better on exams if we take the exam in the *same* room we study in instead of a different room. Why?

- Edward Tolman noted we learn by what he called "Cognitive Maps" and "Latent" learning. How?

- We can condition an adult to fear a word in a laboratory, by giving a mild electric shock associated with that word, yet he will not fear that word outside of the laboratory. Why?

- You cannot teach an adult to fear a furry animal as easily as you can a child. Why?

ESTES STIMULUS SAMPLING HYPOTHESIS:

How Nothing becomes Something

Robert Estes did not start out to solve the problem of the century in psychology. He wanted to explain something more simple. Why did it take Pavlov's dogs six pairings of Bell-Meat, Bell-Meat, before they reached the maximum level of saliva? Why did the dogs not learn this simple response in one trial?

The question of one-trial learning was once a significant issue in psychology. Estes provided a remarkably simple answer to this profound question that also applies to the issue of "which came first, the Stimulus Impression or S-R learning". Imagine a dog in Pavlov's laboratory. The Bell sounds. He perks up his ears, a curiosity response. But it is not associated with anything yet.

What Estes realized is that the bell (S) is not the only stimulus going off just before the food is presented. Other dogs may be barking (S). Pavlov's assistant may be sneezing (S), the door may be creaking (S), the wind is blowing outside (S), people may be talking nearby (S), anything that catches his attention (S, S, S).

As trial follows trial, most of these stimuli gradually drop out. The Bell will still sound, dogs may still be barking, the wind may still be blowing... but no sneezing, no squeaking door.

As trials continue, the one constant stimulus is the Bell associated with the Meat.

Many studies in psychology that never before made sense now suddenly makes sense; For example, we know that if you study for a test in the same room in which you take that test, you will remember much better than if you take the test in a different room. We do not just learn the material; we learn the material as part of a complete Sensory Impressions of everything that is going on at the time. Many of the other stimuli present at the same time are learned, along with the initial impression.

I remember my grandmother going into the other room to get something, and then forgetting what she went in for. Then she had to come back into the room she came from, with all the stimuli present at the time she started out, to be able to remember what it was she forgot. I find myself doing the same thing. Somehow, just being in the same room you started from, with all the original stimuli, makes it much easier to remember.

When we have a flashbulb memory, it is a Sensory Impression on the brain. We are not learning just one S-S connection, but every impression that is going on at the time, even brief bits of a recording of everything going on at the time. Vision, sound, touch, sometimes even taste and smell, all stimuli may all be recorded at the same time.

What this also would illustrate is that Sensory Impressions, as in Bumps and Dents, is the most basic form of learning. Then, only after the initial impressions, do Stimulus-Stimulus associations (light and shadow) develop.

Finally, Perception develops out of the associations. So, the confusing part; stimulus-stimulus associations can become a perception, but out of many perceptions, perception can then become a concept or even a stimulus by itself. Something in-between "which came first, the chicken or the egg?" and Schrodinger's cat. Out of many perceptions, those perceptions can develop into concepts, ideas, schema, learning sets; whatever you want to call it.

Yet terms like "schema" or even "information processing" are in danger of falling victim to the "word magic" of the word "instinct" some one hundred years ago. Psychologists were convinced that just calling behavior an "instinct" explained something. Nothing of the kind. There is little in the way of hard evidence to tie these words to the ideas they are supposed to represent.

"Just because your doctor has a name for your problem, doesn't mean he knows what it is." Franz Kafka

The concepts of Sensory Impressions and S-S associations provides a hard-evidence bridge between the most basic of learning and our perceptions of reality.

TOWARD A
UNIFIED FIELD THEORY
OF PSYCHOLOGY

Mind is reducible to programmed responses or organized programs, what we call concepts (or schema or learning sets or cognitive maps or patterns of experience or sequences of experiences, or information processing), which are formed by associations (S-S or S-R) or trial and error learning, which is also learned by associations that come from *sensory impressions*. So, the reductionist sequence would be:

MIND = CONCEPTS--- PERCEPTIONS ---ASSOCIATIONS ---SENSORY IMPRESSIONS (MORE)

The **MORE** would include some of the permutation effects already mentioned; Selective Attention, the Prime Experiences, the Order of Experiences, and the Timing of Associations, Stimulus Generalization, Discrimination or Contrast and Comparison, patterns of experience, novelty, attention, Trial and Error, Information Processing, Approach-Avoidance stimuli, and how all of these eventually become associated and organized in the brain.

As in physics, with its interest in vast numbers of subatomic particles; neutrinos, gluons, weak and strong forces, Higgs Boson, up and down quarks, and multi-string theories, much of psychology has been devoted to understanding how these variables, and their permutations, interact to produce the mind.

> "*If I could remember the names of all the particles,*
> *I would have been a botanist.*"
> Einstein

PERMUTATION EFFECTS:

When Learning does not Work as Predicted

Watson taught little Albert to be afraid of furry animals by banging two pieces of steel behind his head every time he looked up and saw a furry animal. Loud noise = fear reaction.

Furry animal + loud noise + stimulus generalization = fear of furry animals.

Now, just the sight of any furry animal would frighten Albert. He looked "bug-eyed" even at a piece of cotton. But some have tried to repeat the experiment and failed. Why? Adults cannot easily be taught to fear furry animals the same way. Why? Does age change the brain as Piaget and Developmental psychologists say? Or is there something wrong with the S-R paradigm, as some suggested?

If little Albert had many positive experiences playing with friendly furry animals, before Watson tried to teach him to be afraid, it would have been almost impossible to teach him to fear furry animals. That is the *Prime Experience*:

whatever experiences we have *first*, changes the very nature of learning the next time we are exposed to similar stimuli.

This is one of an infinite number of permutations that make it seem as if learning does not work the same for everyone. It also makes it difficult to see the effect of learning because there are trillions of different experiences that make us respond to stimuli differently. That is why behavioral psychologists started out studying rats and pigeons. We can control their entire learning history so we can be sure we are seeing a more basic form of learning, without the thousands of extraneous variables changing the nature of how we respond to reality.

"The difference between rats and people is that rats learn from experience."

B. F. Skinner

The difference between rats and people is that rats learn about reality from experience, not words. No rat ever killed another rat because someone told him the other rat believed in the wrong politics or the wrong religion. For better or for worse, words take on more power than reality; one more extraneous variable that makes it difficult to see reality.

The prime experience changes how we will react the next time we are exposed to a similar experience. Since we have all had trillions upon trillions of experiences, it should be no surprise that others may react differently, even to the same stimuli; as in tumbleweeds and boulders.

PERCEPTION AND THE INVISIBLE SQUARE:

Generalized Perception: Beyond Past Experience

Can the brain really leap the gap between the bare outline presented by the Muller-Lyre illusion and our past experiences with actual buildings and boxes?

Psychology has a significant bit of evidence that it can. Consider the following:

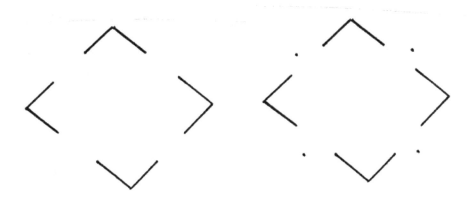

Simply adding four dots to the figure on the right above creates an "invisible" square in the center. The brain automatically "sees" a square, as if each dot were the corner of a square, even though no square exists. *The brain automatically connects the dots*. Compare the two figures until you see the effect.

The brain *generalizes* from experience with squares to connect the dots or "fill in the blanks." It is almost as if the brain creates a hologram from our experiences. The same type of *Perceptual* Generalization is basic to the Stimulus Generalization of Behavioral Psychology, and perception is the basis of both.

Stimulus Generalization itself seems remarkably similar to the same process that allows the brain to switch back and forth between the top of the Necker cube and the bottom, as the brain presents different perspectives to our mind.

Some might call such generalization "intuition." "I just *knew* it was a square." Or even extrasensory perception "I had a feeling..." but such intuition or ESP is usually based on the brain's *generalizing* from experience based on cues like the bumps or dents. It is unlikely that the Zulu's in Allport's experiment would see any "invisible square" in this picture.

The brain generates its own semi-holographic *perception* of a square, deeply hidden in the ruts and curves in the neurons of our cerebral cortex. It is created simply out of our history of sensory experiences; no magical-mystical origin is implied.

So, who in psychology is right; Pavlov's Stimulus-Response paradigm, or Piaget's Schema, or Harlow's Learning Sets, or Tolman's Cognitive Maps, or Perceptual psychology, or Cognitive psychology? All of them are right in significant parts. All of them are wrong in specific parts. Getting psychologists to agree is like "herding cats". Yet each of them provides a vital piece of the whole picture.

CHASING SCHRODINGER'S CAT:
The Conscious Mind and the Brain

Textbooks in psychology note that we have no way of studying the conscious mind. We have no idea what the conscious mind is, so instead, we study "altered states of consciousness"; specifically, sleep, drugs, and hypnosis. Yet we have already seen a new way to study the conscious mind, by our conscious reaction to how the brain tries to interpret bumps and dents based on shadow or the Necker cube or the Muller-Lyre illusion, based on angles, etc.

Psychologists could never agree on what consciousness is, but one idea seems to stand out as better than any other. Consciousness is related to the scanning waves of the brain in ways that defy the magical-mystical ideas of how the mind works.

How do we know what Schrodinger's Cats are doing when we are not looking? How can we get Schrodinger's Cats to stand still long enough to figure out what consciousness is?

HERDING SCHRODINGER'S CATS:
Consciousness as a Google Scan

There is one thing that seems to be critical to the idea of the conscious mind. That is the scanning waves of the brain that rapidly scan across the surface of the brain. Using an Electroencephalogram (EEG), we find that the nature of conscious awareness changes dramatically between conditions such as sleep, dreaming, wakefulness, and an alcohol-induced feeling.

Alpha waves rule the brain when we are awake and relaxed. They cycle across the brain at 9 to 13 waves per second (cps). Beta waves are fast frequency waves that kick in when we are awake and *focusing* our attention on a problem, cycling at 15 to 30 times per second. Delta waves are the special type of very slow frequency wave that is common to being asleep, cycling at about 2 waves per second. REM waves show dreaming with spindle bursts of up to 12 cps.

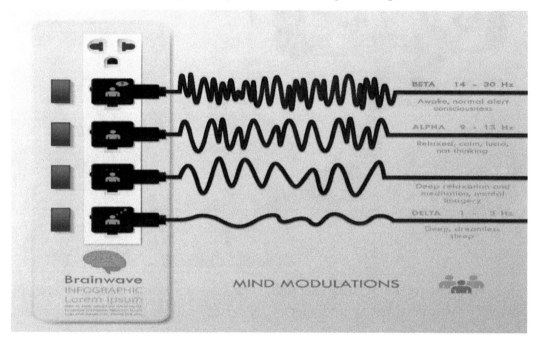

Think of the Beta wave as similar to a Google search engine, scanning through the brain, touching whatever stimuli or images were embedded in our brain by learning, trying to *associate* the stimuli you see, with the perceptions in the brain.

If we drop the frequency of this wave down, we lose focus and eventually, consciousness, as in deep sleep or drug use or hypnosis. Only when this wave is working at the Beta level, do we have *focused* conscious awareness.

The high speed of waves cycling across the brain at 14 to 30 times per second, associating every encounter with patterns or stimuli with past experiences, allows us to navigate through our environment with relative ease. Like the Bell with Pavlov's dog, the high speed of associations allows us to anticipate what is coming next, out of our past associations.

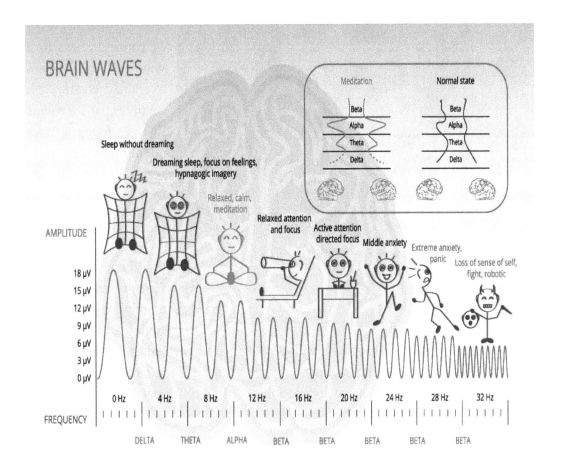

Consciousness is a product of the brain itself, not an alien artifact. Most animals seem to have this. It is not clear to what extent the brain waves create consciousness or are an after-effect of the consciousness mechanism of the brain; most likely both. One way or another, they are tied like a bow to our conscious awareness.

The professionals at Alphabet, Google's parent company, are working on an Artificial Intelligence that can mimic the human brain. We can only hope it can do better than that.

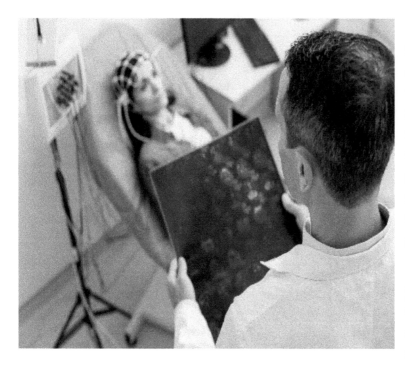

The brain itself creates this wave of consciousness in a way that we cannot explain; clearly, it involves the waves that focus our attention. Yet, it is somewhat separate from the memories stored in the brain.

The programmers at Google have noted that, by way of a close analogy, the conscious *Mind* is like the Google scanning mechanism. The rest of the *Brain* is like the information stored on the internet. We have a built-in, biological scanning program in the brain that functions independently of the information storage part of the brain, although it is also a process of the brain itself.

The scanning is at such high speed that the process is not visible, giving us only the dimmest awareness of the effect of that scan. When we look at the bumps and dents, or even when we consider why we perceive noise as power or consider why we vote for whoever for President, our conscious *mind* can observe our *brain* operating at a level that is usually quite beyond our conscious awareness.

The conscious mind is not the great mystery of our science, instead, it is our ability to render experiences into symbols (words, etc.). The problem of understanding our dramatic ability to transmit experience and ideas through symbols (words, etc.) is far more difficult than the issue of consciousness.

Most animals seem to have consciousness. The real mystery is how the biology of the brain can give us speech. No single subject is as important as that. Yet that is a topic for another chapter.

One thing that gets lost in the textbook treatment of Pavlov is the fact that his primary interest was never in psychology, he was only interested in the biology of the brain; how associations between neurons in the brain are associated with thought. The title of his paper was in fact; *"Conditioned Reflexes: An Investigation of the Physiological Activity of the Cerebral Cortex".*

If we could look through the skull into the brain of a consciously thinking person, and if the place of optimal excitability were luminous, then we should see playing over the cerebral surface, a bright spot with fantastic waving borders constantly fluctuating in size and form, surrounded by a darkness more or less deep, covering the rest of the hemisphere.

Ivan Pavlov

Pavlov described beautifully, poetically, the result we would see using Positron Emission Tomography (PET scans) or functional Magnetic Resonance Imaging (fMRI) nearly 100 years before we developed a way to see what the scanning waves of the brain looked like. We "think" with our cortex, about a ¼ inch of gray matter, non-myelinated neurons, surrounding the surface of our brain.

LOSS OF CONSCIOUS AWARENESS

If the cortex is damaged, we lose conscious awareness of what we are experiencing, as in "blindsight". Individuals who have had their visual cortex damaged may still be able to walk around a chair in the middle of the room, even though they cannot consciously tell you there was a chair that they walked around and will insist that he sees no chair.

All of this scanning happens at such great speed that we are unaware of what is happening. It is a constant flow of consciousness based on the stimuli the mind is attending to at the moment. It equally depends on the ability of our brain's *selective attention* to ignore all the irrelevant stimuli and focus on just what is important at the moment. This is no "unconscious" mind envisioned by Freud and others, it is an automatic process that happens so fast, we are simply not conscious of what is happening. We could not get Schrodinger's cats to stand still long enough to observe.

We cannot see inside the brain as learning occurs. It is most unlikely we will ever be able to trace a single thought in the brain. Yet psychology, sociology, and anthropology provide a way of studying how the brain is programmed, as it is being programmed; how motivation works, how emotions become attached to stimuli, and what emotions can do to control our thoughts. We must study the programs written into the brain as it is happening; the stimulus-stimulus connections that create the code in the brain that our mind reads. That is the track we must follow if we are to grasp what has made us what we are.

By this analogy, the brain is the computer, programmed by experience, and the mind is the conscious awareness produced by selective attention and the scanning mechanism of the brain itself. All of which depends on our past experiences.

Yet the latest information suggests that something even more dramatic is happening. The brain itself cannot develop normally without this experience. We have always assumed that the brain is determined by our biology and that psychology (experience) only affects the brain after it is formed; not anymore.

BEFORE THE EVENT HORIZON
The Brain Itself is Molded by Experience

Until recently, it was widely believed that genes determine the development of the brain, quite independent of experience. The brain springs forth able to see, hear, and feel just out of the force of our DNA. Even in psychology, no one thought that experience would turn out to be essential before the biology of the brain itself would develop as it does. This is certainly one of the most dramatic discoveries in the history of psychology, and one of the least noticed.

ASSEMBLY REQUIRED:
The Biology of the Brain is Shaped by Experience

Hubel and Wiesel won the Nobel Prize for their work showing that there are neurons in the visual cortex in the brain of a cat that respond only to lines moving across the retina in one direction or another. By touching an electrode to an exposed area in the back of the brain, they could hear those cells firing.

Some cells respond only to vertical lines. Some cells respond only to horizontal lines. They called these cells, "edge detectors" or line and motion detectors. It was brilliant work, but more remarkable work has since been done that questions the origin of these line and motion detectors.

If you keep your eyes steady, and move the above picture around, you will see a fluttering from the firing of the line and motion, or edge detectors, in the back of your visual cortex., without the messy need for brain surgery.

Blakemore and Cooper found that even the edge detectors discovered by Hubel and Wiesel may not develop without experience. They raised kittens in a box that had only *vertical* stripes. When they attempted to test how they responded to similar lines in Hubel and Wiesel's study, they found these kittens seemed to have no horizontal line detectors, only vertical line detectors. When they held a pencil horizontally and moved it toward their eyes, the kittens ignored the pencil. When they moved the pencil vertically toward their eyes, the kittens immediately blinked and reacted to its movement.

The second group of kittens was raised in a box that had only horizontal lines. Their cortex seemed to have developed only *horizontal* line detectors, not vertical ones. They flinched only when a horizontal pencil was moved toward their eyes. They did not react to a pencil moved vertically toward their eyes. They seemed to have no vertical line detectors. They found only horizontal line detectors in the cortex of cats reared with only horizontal lines, and only vertical line detectors in those reared with vertical lines.

The implication is astonishing. It means that the line and edge detectors discovered by Hubel and Wiesel do not exist in the biology of the brain; they only develop out of the experience of the brain with lines and edges!

Just as the Necker cube and the trapezoidal illusion could not be seen by the brains of Zulu raised in the outback, we can only see certain elements that our brain has already been programmed to see.

All of this is supported by the previous illusions, from the Necker Cube to the Trapezoidal Illusion to the "invisible square".

THE BRAIN
CANNOT DEVELOP
WITHOUT EXPERIENCE

The most exciting new study has been largely ignored by our textbooks. Cataracts are a clouding or distortion of the lens that focuses what we see onto the retina of the eye. Today, a simple procedure restores normal sight by replacing the bad lens with a clear plastic lens. It is remarkably successful.

Recent studies of human children show just how dramatic the effect of experience can be on the brain. There is a rare condition where a human baby is born with a cataract in the lens of only one eye. The other eye is normal. Although rare, some 200 children have been treated with this defect. The Nobel Prize-winning philosopher John Paul Sartre seems to have had this problem. He describes himself as a child, "...one eye, already gone bad..." as giving him a "walleyed" appearance, one eye looking off into space.

Surgeons have found that this cataract must be removed within the first three months of life, or the visual cortex of the brain served by that eye will never develop. Without stimulation in the first few months of life, the brain itself will never develop an ability to see with that eye, *even if the eye and the brain are both perfectly fine*.

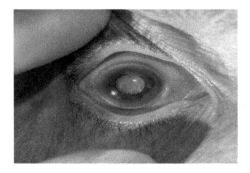
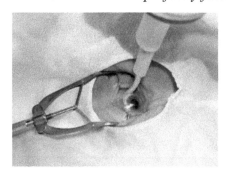

Cataracts are a clouding of the lens inside the eye. It commonly occurs in the elderly as above, but some 200 cases have occurred at birth in only one eye. The lens can be surgically removed and replaced with a plastic lens, or, in young children, with a contact lens, because their eyes will continue to grow.

More than this, after removing the cataract in the poor eye, the good eye must now be patched all day long for many months, even years, to force the poor eye to develop neural processes in the visual cortex. If it is not patched, the stimulation from the good eye will grab all the brain's *selective attention* and the brain will simply ignore the input from the poor eye. Unless the brain is forced to ignore the good eye, the poor eye will never develop the cortical mechanisms it needs to become a good eye. The brain would ignore the poor eye.

Imagine Arnold Schwarzenegger. Now imagine Arnold Schwarzenegger naked. Now imagine what Arnold Schwarzenegger would look like naked if he had the left side of his body taped up as a child so he could not exercise it. All of his early years he could only exercise one side of his body. The tied side would quickly give up trying. That is roughly analogous to what would happen in the brain if the brain *failed to attend* to the stimulation coming from the poor eye. In the brain and vision, experience is even more important, our experience determines what we may see, or even if we can see.

For a visual example of the cataract studies in babies see the PBS Public Broadcasting Station series on *The Secret Life of the Brain*; *A Baby's Brain,* near the end of the video:

https://www.youtube.com/watch?v=U0L0mYi_ftc&t=87s

Again, without experience, the brain itself cannot develop normally. Our experiences change the very nature of the biology of the brain. These experiences determine what we may see, even what we can understand. This, is what the studies of Blakemore and Cooper showed, as well as the studies of the Trapezoid illusion and the Necker cube when seen by Zulus raised in the outback.

The brain is even more of a Tabula Rasa, a Blank Slate, than the critics of that idea ever imagined.

The ease with which the environment molds the brain itself raises important questions about many issues. For one, there is the old worry about the impact of television or motion pictures on the minds of young children; and what about adults? The ideas adults and society imprint on the mind of children has a profound effect. We imprint our ideas of people, childrearing, politics, religion and much more into the brains of our children. Do most adults have the ability to go beyond the ideas others embed in our mind?

This is an important issue not just from the standpoint of morality, it cuts much deeper. It questions the impact of our school systems, peer group pressure, our religious teaching, our ability to choose in politics, and our child-rearing practices themselves. Once ideas are embedded in the brain, the ability to change is markedly reduced.

Unless... the first ideas in the brain teach us to be willing, even eager, to learn new ideas, even to learn ideas that contradict what the brain already believes.

Once any perception becomes embedded in our brains, it becomes incredibly difficult to change that idea. We saw this in how our minds perceive Bumps and Dents, the simple lines in the Necker cube, the upside-down woman. We have seen this over and over again in what happened to Socrates, Bruno, Galileo, Darwin, and in the problems of witch hunts, slavery, women's rights, religious opinions, and in our invasion of Iraq for weapons of mass destruction that never existed, except in our imagination. We see it in the judgmental attitudes of name-calling and bullying in school and even in the political hate machine in our politics and presidential campaigns.

We do not just "think", we actively *perceive* a different reality.

No one wants to consider that their view of reality is wrong. Instead, we hear self-serving clichés, "*Stand up for what you believe*" or "*Fight for what you believe in*". We never hear, as Einstein learned early, in effect, stop believing what you are told and find out for yourself what the evidence shows. We are as prisoners in a box of our own creation. Words become the box.

The fact that learning proceeds so subtly, so without our awareness, must raise questions that have never been asked. We have studiously ignored the great implications of these questions. Can we have freedom of speech or freedom of belief if we can only judge reality by the images embedded in our minds as a child by others? Can we have free will if we do not understand that the ideas embedded in our minds are the very criteria by which we judge all reality? There are few areas more important than learning how our environment has changed the mind of a child and how that determines the perception of the adult.

In a classic treatise, John Stuart Mill wrote in *On Liberty*, that we must always be concerned for freedom of speech and freedom of belief. But he went further than most in calling out the "tyranny of the majority" today echoed in the concern over bullying in schools and even in political correctness.

But what has gone unrecognized is the tyranny of beliefs; the ideas embedded in our minds when we were children by parents, peers, society, Hollywood, religions and our educational system that have a hold over our minds, that make it difficult or even impossible to see how our own minds have been shaped by others. This colors our politics, our personal opinions, our religions, our wars, and our perception of reality.

WILL WE WILL
OR WILL WE WON'T:
Free Will and the Forces of Life

We want to believe that we make our own decisions through the force of our own will. We *decide* what we think. We *decide* what we want to believe.

But answer one question; can you remember how old you were when you first *decided* to speak English instead of Swahili? Do you have the ability to *decide* to understand what people who speak Swahili are saying? By the same token, it is extremely difficult to understand how other people think or even to understand that there is any reality outside the reality of our own mind.

The content of our brain is far more determined than we want to believe. Yet we can step back and look at the contents of our brain and determine if that content is accurate or needs to be changed. Before we can do this honestly, we must first make a commitment to go wherever the evidence leads us. That is a difficult commitment to make. You can see just how difficult by judging the reactions of Democrats and Republicans on the evidence in the impeachment trial of Donald Trump. Or how religious beliefs affect our opinions on issues of abortion and politics.

The more we understand about how our mind works, the more control we gain over our mind. Potentially.

Reducing the idea of "will" to an either/or question is not accurate. It is largely a matter of degree. The more we understand about the mind, the more control we have over our behavior. Potentially.

HARDWIRED BY EXPERIENCE

From our language to our behavior, we are all "hard-wired" to behave as we do. Not by our genes, but by our environment. Only new experiences, new ideas, new environments can change the outcome. We all can go beyond our wiring, but only if we learn to understand how our mind works, and value evidence more than the ideas others have embedded in our brains.

We are also "hard-wired" by experience with a learned paradigm on how to organize and understand reality. Those who are wired to think in terms of "anything is possible" or a magical mystical view of reality are going to learn quite different information and to think differently than those who think in terms of the methods of science that have brought us such success.

Those who think in terms of "teach 'em a lesson" are going to raise their children differently than those who think in terms of democratic ideals or who believe we are here to assist them in growing up. Those who think in terms of "law and order" are going to think differently than those who think in terms of "reaching our potential".

They not only think differently, they pay attention to what supports that point of view and ignore all else.

Learning does not just give the brain information to use in processing as a computer; it changes the brain itself so completely, that it creates a new reality in the brain. From this reality, our conscious mind "sees" what the brain has been programmed to see.

Again, there is no Nobel Prize in psychology. So, the greatest discoveries in psychology have gone unheralded and there is no one to trumpet the importance of the new understanding of the human mind. And without a trumpet, the media never noticed. When the media never notices, the public cannot learn. Perhaps in another four hundred years…

Each of us grows up believing that the world revolves around our unique perception of reality. The new knowledge of the mind cuts deep into every raw nerve of our illusions of reality and we are not well prepared to learn to control our own mind, because we have the illusion that we already do.

Learning is so profoundly important that it changes the biology of your brain. The biochemical and neural changes that occur tend to be permanent. We can learn new connections, but it is often not easy.

In a way, this is perhaps the most important chapter in the book, although it is not the most exciting. It lays out the psychological basis of the human mind, the building blocks on which all else hangs, the genesis of the mind, the quantum theory of psychology.

The most important point of the mind code is that the experiences of our lives become the fabric of our lives. They are written into our memory just as we write code into a computer. They are so deeply imbedded in the mind of the individual that they become reality. The individual sees no reality beyond that of their own mind. To the extent to which this accurately reflects reality, this is useful in guiding us through life. To the extent to which it is an illusion, it may be harmful. Garbage in--Garbage out.

What else do we need to know before we can reach the point where we may gain control of our minds? How much of our personality is written in our DNA and how much is determined by the forces of life? What determines our opinion of what is beautiful? Why did men in China consider tiny feet as sexual for over one thousand years? How can words that are written on white paper trigger a sexual response? How do our perceptions affect the most basic interpretation of reality?

For most of reality, the mind does not "think", we *perceive* reality; based on our experiences.

Our brain has the ability to process stimuli relatively rapidly, thus allowing us to "*consciously*" make our way through the stimuli in life by anticipating what we will encounter next, in much the same way that Pavlov's dog's brain could anticipate what would come next, after the bell rang.

Anticipation and stimulus generalization are the basis of much of what we call the *conscious* mind. This much comes from the biology of the brain itself.

Next, we go into the "real world" applications of what we have learned.

Any Stimuli—Any Emotion--Any Perception... It is all relative.

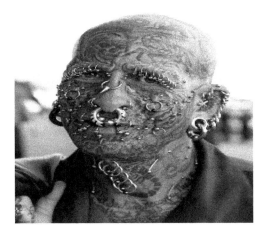

4

CULTURE AND ATTRACTION

THE "WOW" FACTOR:
ANY STIMULI—ANY PERCEPTION
THE HARD EVIDENCE

I can remember sitting around a psychology class when I was a sophomore talking about what kind of things parents had a conflict with their teenagers over. Back then, one of the critical issues was how old should a girl be before she got her ears pierced. You don't hear that much anymore. Now, girls are getting their ears pierced when they are born.

Today, both girls and boys are getting everything pierced. Boys wear an earring in a pierced ear. Girls pierce their tongue, navel, labia… Back then, no one got tattooed except a drunken sailor on a Saturday night. Today even girls are getting tattoos. The secretary where I once worked had little running cats tattooed around her ankle. It was cute.

A few years ago, Angelina Jolie appeared on the Jay Leno show. She was talking about her four tattoos. One was a tattoo of her boyfriend's name. Does anyone remember who her boyfriend was back then?   It was Billy Bob Thornton. Can you imagine having Billy Bob Thornton tattooed on any part of your anatomy? Did you know that more college students know her boyfriend was Billy Bob Thornton than know who was the second man to land on the moon?

Later she married Billy Bob and about a year after that, she got a divorce from him. I remember thinking at the time that it will be much easier to get rid of Billy Bob than it will be to get rid of that tattoo. It took her four laser treatments. And she had a Cambodian verse tattooed on top of it.

As you make it through life, try, try, try to avoid the impulse to have your boyfriend's or girlfriend's name tattooed on your butt. Yet some are getting tongue rings and lip piercings and labia piercings. Boys wear earrings, muscle shirts showing their tattoos, and some are getting their tongue pierced. Is it just to freak out their parents? Or is something more basic involved?

Today, tattoos, tongue piercings, nose piercings, and more have become an accepted cultural expression of individuality. Except by the older generations—The Primacy Effect in action.

HOW CAN A TEENAGER LIVE WITHOUT AN UMBEPO?

Every generation seems to up the ante on the next generation. Parents are often unable to guess what will happen next. By the time kids today have teenage sons and daughters what will they think is cool? Parents can almost hear it now; "Mom, dad, I gotta have an Umbepo. All the other kids in school have an Umbepo, why can't I have an Umbepo?"

The Zoe natives of South America all have Umbepo's, males as well as females. This is a six-inch long, one inch in diameter piece of wood they have stuck through a big hole in their bottom lip. They start their children early by poking a hole in their bottom lip and gradually enlarge the hole until they can take the full Umbepo in their lip. Why?

Why? Because *"they consider people without the Umbepo to be unattractive".* This original video can be found, along with many others, on YouTube. Go to the following site, it is well worth it.

https://www.youtube.com/watch?v=XMLbCYCMp2w

If you look at the video above, about 1/3 the way through, you see the Zoe dancing around naked while singing chants. Some of the people in the picture are drinking Cepe', an alcoholic concoction that makes them throw up. It is a lot of naked people dancing and throwing up. Just like Spring Break in College.

The repeated episodes of drinking and purging are actually from the oldest medical theory of disease on the planet. Our ancestors learned long ago that if you eat tainted meat, you get sick; you throw up; you may live, you may die. If you eat certain fruits or berries, you get sick; you throw up; you may live, you may die. If you eat certain mushrooms, you get sick; you throw up; you see colors. This became the "Poison" theory of disease. Just like Americans one hundred years ago, they use purgatives to get rid of the imaginary poisons in the body.

Go by any American pharmacy today and you will still find one of the oldest medical treatments, the Colon Cleansing Kit. It flushes the poisons out the other end.

Most doctors will tell you that your body is quite capable of taking care of most toxins, unless you actually drink poison, and this method does nothing to help. Yet colon cleansing sells. How can an ancient remedy, with no scientific evidence behind it, still be so commonly sold at otherwise respectable stores? How could people still believe this? Are Ancient Aliens responsible?

But how does anyone decide what is attractive and what is not?

If you travel to the Surma society of Africa, you will find a different version of what is attractive. A National Geographic Special, *Riddles and Rituals*, gives a profound glance into the mind of a different culture. Here you will find Olikori, the son of a wealthy herdsman. Among his people, he is considered an attractive dude. He has enlarged holes in his earlobes to hold wooden fittings about one and a half inches in diameter, where you might find a pierced ear in America. His upper and lower teeth have been knocked out because that is considered "cool" in his culture.

All the girls think he is a good catch because he is a jock, a champion stick fighter.

Then you see Nadaju, his bride to be. This teenage girl has had her lower lip enlarged, in a process that takes six months. Starting with a small sharp stick and gradually increasing its size until the lower lip can hold a lip plate an astonishing five inches in diameter. It sticks out of her face, distorting her appearance dramatically.

Why do the girls do this? Their mothers are the ones who make them do it, because, without a lip plate, they would not get a good husband, and the family would not get the obligatory bride price, thirty cows.

As one Surma man says, "*Here a girl must do it. Here it is valued. I'd marry a girl with a big lip plate. We don't like girls without lip plates.*" Sorry ladies, without a lip plate you are only worth two cows.

In the process of enlarging her lip Nadaju's lip broke. The lady doing the enlargement stuck it back together and wrapped it in place. It grew back together. So, Nadaju says, "*Olikori loved me again.*"

Above, a different tribe, the Mursi also practice the use of lip plates, in this tribe using the upper lip.

And what did Olikori say about this? *"I only want her with a big lip. If it had ripped, I wouldn't marry her."*

Nadaju herself says, *"Only old men or fools would marry a girl with a broken lip."*

"Ugly girls get ugly men," says another Surma male. If you don't have a big lip plate, you get an ugly guy.

And what do the girls value in this society? Olikori says of his bride Nadaju, *"She only wants me because I'm a champion stick fighter."* Sorry guys, to get a girl you have to be a jock.

Birth control is also taught by the peer group. As one older male says, *"...when the moon is full, a girl can't get pregnant. When the moon tilts, that is when she can get pregnant"*.

Now you know all you need to know about birth control.

In still another Mursi tribe, a woman without a lip plate would be considered unattractive. The "Duck billed" women of Uganda pierce both lips.

Do we do anything like this in America? Of course we do. The noted plastic surgeon, Maxwell Maltz, said that in America in the 1920s, the "roaring twenties" the flapper era was in. The dress style was straight up and down. Back then, Maltz says, girls would bind their breasts to keep them from showing. If they went in for cosmetic surgery, it was breast reduction surgery.

Today, after forty years of Rachael Welch, Dolly Parton, and Pamela Lee Anderson, they want .44 magnums.

The Surma girls have seen westerners without lip plates and, like Einstein, now they are rebelling against the wisdom of their elders. They no longer want to endure the painful six-month process of enlarging the lip. Their complaint, though, is not about the size of the lip, but about the pain and suffering of the process.

I am willing to bet that Pamela Lee Anderson would not have had four breast surgeries if it were not for anesthesia and antibiotics.

WHATEVER A SOCIETY CONSIDERS GOOD, WE RATIONALIZE WHY THAT IS

But surely these are exceptions. Right? Not really. There are tribes in South America where both males and females wear lip plates. There are others in Africa, the Duck-Billed Women of Uganda, who wear lip plates in both their upper and lower lips, giving them a dramatic appearance. Other tribes in the Philippines, Thailand, and Africa put rings around the neck of young girls. As they grow older, the number of rings is increased, until their neck is stretched nearly a foot above their shoulders. They cannot now remove the rings because their neck muscles are unable to support their head.

These "long neck" adornments are considered beautiful by men and women alike.

Below, children are started at the age of five or six. Each year another ring may be added, stretching the head as much as a foot above the shoulders.

Below a lady from Thailand's hill country.

Left, a Pandaung woman from the Philippines also wears the same long neck rings that are found in Africa and Thailand.

There are tribes where, at puberty, males have the foreskin cut away from their penis, a practice we in America routinely practice, but only as a birth rite. Once a practice is adopted, we invent rational explanations to justify it. It is said that circumcision helps reduce infection. Maybe, but nature probably put it there for a reason, to protect the penis. Natural selection would have eliminated it from the breeding pool long ago if it was a serious problem. We invent reasons to justify our beliefs.

BEAUTY IS DETERMINED BY THE SIZE OF YOUR FEET

But if you want to understand how an entire culture can come to believe that a practice is not only beautiful, but sexually exciting, look at the case of Chinese foot binding. This is a practice that was the norm in China for over one thousand years. It was finally banned by the government just about one hundred years ago. Although there are a few who still practice the art in secret.

National Geographic did a remarkable show on Chinese foot binding which showed the barbarity and the "beauty" of the practice. When they are about two to four years old their mothers wrap their feet tightly in bandages, often sewing them on because the pain was so great the girls would often secretly remove them at night. Today there are hundreds of older women still alive who went through this process.

Daughters were told that no one would want to marry you if you had big feet. The Chinese had a standard of beauty based on the size of a woman's feet. The most beautiful, have three-inch-long "Golden Lotus" feet, if your feet were four inches long you had "Silver" feet, and you had "Iron" feet if they were five inches long. One woman who had her feet bound notes that, back then, a mother would be laughed at for failing to do her duty as a mother if she did not bind her daughter's feet.

This was the criterion on which men based their appraisal of a woman's beauty. National Geographic noted that a matchmaker would not ask about the beauty of a woman's face, but only how big her feet were.

Amazingly, they were still able to find some women today who still bind their feet secretly, even though the practice is now outlawed. She was extremely proud of her bound feet and considers this to be the thing that gave her a good marriage. Her husband too is proud of his wife's feet and says, "I considered them good looking back then, and I still do."

A woman's beauty was rated on a scale of one to three, based on the size of her feet. Three-inch feet were the idealized Golden Lotus, four-inch feet were Silver, five inches were Iron. The greatest standard of beauty was the three-inch Golden Lotus, the ultimate for a grown woman, about the size of the feet of a three-year-old child today.

Not only were tiny feet considered attractive, but they were also considered sensual. They say, "A man did not consider a woman sexually exciting unless she had bound feet." Only a couple of hundred years ago a Chinese magazine was printed with articles on men's erotic thoughts while playing with women's tiny feet. It was sort of an early Playboy, except instead of a fold-out woman in the middle, the magazine included cutouts of women's tiny shoes. Yes, really.

Why were tiny footed women in China sexually attractive to men? Every culture rationalizes why it does whatever it does. The Chinese said that if a woman has tiny feet that makes her vagina tighter, leading to a supernatural sexual experience for the male. Along with ground-up rhino horn, this was the Viagra of the day in China. Science has found no evidence of either having an effect.

Ok ladies, you get to vote. Are men stupid or what?

Duh, we already knew that. But women don't get off the hook either. It was the women among the Surma who insisted their daughters have lip plates.   It was the women among the Chinese who forced the foot binding on their daughters for over one thousand years. Why? Because they too believed it was beautiful, they too

were caught in society's box.

Even in our recent past, we see dramatic differences in what the western world considered beautiful. Just over one hundred years ago in America women were expected to be plump. Look at the nudes of this period, they had none of what we think of today as models, they were plump.

Left, the Venus of Willendorf, named after the village in Germany where it was first found, approximately, 26,000 years old.

This is the oldest known representation of a human figure dating from 29,000 to 16,000 years ago. One hundred and forty-four of these figurines have been found from Norway to the Check Republic to Catal Hoyak in Turkey, the most recent, dating from 8,500 years ago. All but a very few are overwhelmingly similar in appearance, with dramatic amounts of fat and clearly different from anything we would find in magazines today.

Left: Czechoslovakian Venus dating 25,000 to 29,000 years old. No, she is not pregnant. Those are her breasts hanging down. Way down.

The 19th century explorer, Sir Richard Burton, wrote in his books of encountering a tribe in Africa where women were being kept in cages and force-fed goats' milk and fruit. These were the future brides of the chief, and they had to be quite plump before they would be acceptable.

There is no agreement among archeologists as to what these one hundred and forty-four, 4 ½ inch figures are intended to be; a fertility symbol, a lucky talisman, the Mother Earth goddess, an idealized woman, an amulet, or even some prehistoric porn. No one knows.

In America, young women may pad their bras to make their breasts look more appealing. In Haiti, women pad their behind to make them more attractive to men.

ANY STIMULUS-ANY RESPONSE

(Including emotions and sexual responses)

What would explain how this could happen in the first place? Why was almost every single representation of the female figure plump? They were not just fertility symbols, which anthropologists believe, they were what our society considers "morbidly obese". How is it possible the tongue studs, lip plates, tattoos, tiny feet, big breasts, and more could come to have such a different emotional reaction in so many different cultures? The answer to that question is one of the most important in the history of psychology. The issue dates back to the origin of the great Nature-Nurture debate.

Any Stimulus---Any Emotion. The answer is identical to the question of how is it possible to have over seven hundred named phobias. There are at least 450 named paraphilias, sexual attraction toward objects that are not sexual. Could there be a gene for each of those seven hundred phobias? Or the 450 paraphilias? Of course not. Any stimulus, associated with any emotion, will cause those stimuli to elicit that emotion, whether it is a fear reaction or a positive emotional reaction, or even a sexual response. Not just an emotion, but a complete perception is formed in the brain.

In a striking experiment, psychologists took 10 pictures of men and 10 pictures of women and asked Americans to pick the most attractive. Most picked the same picture, which was not a real person, but a computer-generated composite of the other 9 pictures.

It suggests a built-in ability of the brain to generalize from past experiences. Stimulus generalization in action?

Again, it suggests that if you are "beautiful", it means you are average.

The "WOW" factor, whatever the peer group, society, or Hollywood gets excited over, becomes embedded in the mind of the child. From sports to sex, it all happens with the same subtle method with which we learn the language we speak; Simple Association and Psychology's General Theory of Relativity.

It is all relative.

And it is relative to a degree that our conscious mind cannot easily comprehend.

5

THE GREAT NATURE VS NURTURE CONTROVERSY

In the vast span of human history, we have long believed that our destiny was determined by our stars, as in astrology, or by how we were born; our genes. Until perhaps one hundred years ago, almost everyone on earth believed that nature ruled. If a person were a good musician, he was said to be a "born" musician. If he were a good doctor, he was said to be a "born" doctor. If a superb athlete, he was labeled a "born" athlete. If someone went over to the dark side, he was said to be a bad "seed" as in a tree that failed to grow straight. In the 1800s, books by Hawthorne and others used the term bad "seed" to label those who were bad, as if that explained it. Today, that has not changed; it has only been replaced by "it's in his DNA".

In the 1930s the American psychologist John B. Watson made a dramatic pronouncement that ushered in a new paradigm, a new way of looking at nurture. He said;

> *Give me a dozen healthy infants, well formed, and my own specified environment in which to raise them, and I guarantee to take any one at random and make of him any type of specialist you might wish; doctor, lawyer, merchant, chief, yes even beggar man or thief, regardless of his talents, penchants or the race of his ancestors."*

> Watson went on to say*, "I'm going beyond my data and I know it, but others have been going far beyond their data with considerably less data for far longer."*

Watson is criticized by others who note that we still do not have all the answers to what makes for success in life, but his statement was a bold pronouncement of the new era of study of how learning determines behavior. When he made this statement, most of America was quite racist. We believed that the race you were born into determined what you could or could not do. He dramatically contradicted what most people believed in saying race had nothing to do with it," ... *regardless of his talents, penchants or the race of his ancestors."* That was nearly 100 years before the rest of our society began to catch up with him.

Sadly, Watson later came to see himself as a failure at raising his own kids. There are too many variables to be certain what works and what does not work.

Around the 1960s, a new way of looking at the nature-nurture controversy caused a new shift in our paradigm. Now it became popular to say it is not nature or nurture but an interaction of the two. If we are talking about learning, we have to have a brain, or else we cannot learn. Of course, this is true, but saying it is all an interaction is unlikely to explain anything today. We still need to know how much is nature and how much is nurture and how do they interact.

Nothing is more important to ensure survival than how to find food and sex. If you really want to find biological programs in the brain, start with those behaviors that are most essential to survival. What do we find if we start with one of the most instinctual animals on earth and go up to the most intelligent?

SEX, CHOICES, AND CULTURE
ATTACK OF THE LESBIAN COWS:

Go to youtube.com and simply type in "lesbian cows"; you will find dozens of videos of "lesbian cows": Cows with udders attempting to mount and mate with other cows with udders. It seems to go on forever.

Eventually, it morphs into lesbian sheep, lesbian dogs, lesbian cats… it is as if, once farmers got hold of a video camera, they had nothing better to do than take pictures of lesbian farm animals. No wonder food costs so much.

Why is this important? Because the media itself is consumed with the first biological explanation for what causes sexual attraction, homosexuality, and sexual behavior. And their conclusion, and that of many biologists, is that hormones or genes make us male or female.

This idea is based on early studies that found that if you take female rat pups at birth, and give them a single, massive injection of testosterone, the male sex hormone, then at puberty those female rats will pursue, mount, and attempt to mate with other female rats. That is taken as evidence that sexual preference is dictated by our hormones or perhaps born into our genes.

Are those really lesbian cows? No. They are normal cows. Did they "choose" to become lesbian cows?" Hardly. This was once palmed off as "dominance behavior" by cows to avoid any conflict with our cultural values. But this behavior occurs during the mating season, which in most mammals is associated with the scent in the air and the estrus cycle.

Studies of the Bonobo Chimpanzees in the wild have found that fully half of all sexual behavior is homosexual, usually genital rubbing. Other chimpanzee groups show quite different behavior.

The fact that this is occurring so commonly in mammals shows that the earlier studies that concluded that the behavior of female rats at puberty after receiving an injection of testosterone at birth, determined their sexual orientation, may have been misleading. Yet that study has had an impact on what we hear from the media, all out of proportion to reality.

You can find much more on youtube.com, there are videos of animals having or attempting to have sex with other species; dogs with cats, a wiener dog with a sleeping lioness, a cat with a turtle.

In one, a farmer is filmed bending over to pour a bucket of food into a trough, when a bull comes up behind him, jumps on top, and begins thrusting. The farmer fights him off, tries again, and the bull again attempts to mount him.

Why are there so many such videos out there?

And who needs scientists when we have farmers with video cameras?

Why does such behavior exist in cows, and dogs, and many species? Why would female cows behave like male cows? In humans, males have nipples. Why? What do they use them for? It is simply an artifact of the fact that there is no difference between a male and female fetus early on. It is an artifact left over from early on in fetal development. Most likely, this is true of cows and dogs.

INBORN KNOWLEDGE? Why Frogs Eat BBs

If you want to find proof of inborn biological programs of behavior, look at those areas most essential to the survival of a species. And the most important of all skills to ensure the survival of the species is the ability to find food to allow the individual to survive and sex to allow the species to survive. If he dies of starvation, not knowing what food is, he could hardly be able to survive to reproduce. If his type did not reproduce, they would go into extinction. So, what do species know about what to eat?

Start with the most instinctual of animals first. Zoologists who study frogs tell us that frogs are born with an inborn, genetically determined, feeding mechanism often called a "fly-catching mechanism". If a bug or fly comes within range of a frog, it will automatically flit out its tongue, grab the insect, and swallow it.

They do not live long enough to learn this; it has to be inborn. Those same zoologists tell us that if you roll a BB across in front of the frog, the frog will flit out its tongue and swallow the BB.

This frog has a biological program in the brain for catching insects. It works quite well in the wild because, in nature, there are very few scientists rolling BBs across in front of the frog. But does he "know" what food is? Does he even "know" what he is doing?

If you keep rolling BBs the frog, it will keep eating BBs until it croaks. This mechanism is so powerful, that even a painful tummy ache may not stop it.

So, frogs have an inborn fly-catching program in the brain. But just as clearly, they do not "know" what they are doing. They do not "know" how to stop.

What about puppies? Do puppies "know" what to eat? What does a puppy chew on? Everything! He will chew on your table legs, he will chew on your shoes, one puppy on a TV vet show started chewing on a sock. He could not back it up. He swallowed the whole sock and had to be operated on to save his life.

I had a puppy that chewed the bindings off of all the books on the bottom shelf of my bookcase. More than this, puppies will eat their own poop. They have no "knowledge" of what food is.

What they are born with is a biological program in the brain that says, "Chew on

everything" that will help them learn what food is and what food is not. This is nature's way of ensuring that they will learn what food is and what food is not. The fact that they tear up everything into pieces, ensures that they will know what to do with a rabbit to get to the meat. Oops. Too much reality?

They say it takes about a year before this behavior goes away and is replaced by a more "learned" version of what food is (in my experience, more like a year and a half). In the meantime, you will have to "puppy proof" your home, because you can't teach it out of them.

If you yell at a puppy for chewing, the puppy will look ashamed, but as soon as you leave the room, it goes right back to chewing; like the frog eating BBs. You may make the puppy afraid of you, but it does not change the behavior.

The same is also true of human children. Two-year-olds are famous for getting into everything; often called "the terrible twos". This is simple curiosity. It is nature's way of ensuring that it will quickly learn everything it can to survive. You cannot and do not want to punish this out of them. The best we can do is to "childproof" your home or at least one room so they can explore without getting in trouble.

What about primates? Surely at the higher end of the phylogenetic scale there must be some inborn, biologically determined, understanding of what food is and how to find food?

A couple in South Africa adopted an orphaned baby baboon. They raised it in their home like a pet. But baboons are not tame animals, and once they hit puberty, they not only have big canine teeth, but they will use them to bite your kids and eat your dog. They realized early that they were going to have to get rid of the baboon.

They took him to a hill at the Serengeti National Park near where there was another troop of baboons. He was surrounded by all the foods baboons normally eat. They figured he could join the troop of baboons and would have plenty to eat. But they didn't just drop him off and leave. They sat back and watched.

Before the first week was out, this baboon was starving to death. He was surrounded by all the food baboons eat, but it meant nothing to him. Food to him was served up in a dog food dish twice a day.   He had no idea what baboons eat.

If he had grown up in the wild, he would have followed his mother around and watched as she dug in the ground for roots and tubers. He would have imitated her behavior and dug alongside her. He would have watched as she ate the shoots of young trees and the fruit from trees. He would have imitated her behavior. He would have watched as she killed and ate small rodents and learned to do the same.

Having none of these early experiences, he did not know what food is, much less how to find food. They finally placed the baboon in a local zoo.

In the wild this baby Hamadryas baboon would learn what to eat by following its mother around, *imitating* her digging in the ground for roots and tubers and chewing on everything.

From a few years ago there was a movie called *Free Willy* and a sequel. The Orca that played Willy in the movie had also been captured in the wild and raised in captivity. After his Hollywood career was over, his owners decided to actually "*free*" Willy. They had to teach him what food was. He was used to having frozen fish, thawed out, and tossed to him in his tank. They put live fish in his tank for him to eat. He nosed them, tossed them up in the air, but did not eat them. They taught him to eat the fish, presumably by tossing live fish to him.

They took him to Puget Sound off the coast of Oregon and let him loose next to a pod (a herd) of Orcas like him. Maybe he would join the other Orcas. The Orcas have their own "song" characteristic of their pod. They sang. Willy squeaked. But he didn't have the rhythm, and he didn't have the beat. They ignored him. He ignored them. He was not doing well. After a month they rescued him and brought him back into captivity.

They tried again to "Free Willy" later, taking him to the Fiords of Norway, I'm not sure why, maybe he was captured there. But he died within a month. Unlike the television version, it did not have a happy ending.

Even modern humans do not have the skills we take for granted in our primitive ancestors. In the famous TV series *Survivors*, the second show, they took a bunch of modern humans and put them in Africa surrounded by lions and other wild animals. They had a corral built of thorn bushes for protection. But they had no fire. Using something like the Boy Scout manual on how to build a fire, they spent four hours rubbing sticks together, making a "bow and drill" and failed miserably.

The actual skills which make this easier for primitive people are not taught in the Boy Scout manuals. You have to pick the right types of wood for the bow and drill. You have to pound dry twigs or dry grass into shreds and powder to make it easier for a coal to catch when the friction heats it.   But without the skills learned growing up in a primitive society, they could not succeed. They built a fire only after one of the group figured out he could take a lens off the end of a pair of binoculars and use it to focus the light of the sun to start a fire. Not exactly what our ancestors would have done, but it worked.

So, what do we know from all of this about how much we "know" is innate and inborn and how much is learned?

There are biological programs for survival in the brain. But these programs are incredibly general, and not at all specific, even in lower animals.   The overwhelming masses of information we need to know to survive have to be learned. Virtually nothing of what humans would call "knowledge" is present in the brains of any mammal. Virtually everything important is learned.

What Food Is?

	INBORN BEHAVIOR	**KNOWLEDGE**
1 FROGS:	Fly catching behavior	No knowledge of food.
2 PUPPIES:	Chewing behavior	No idea what food is.
3 PRIMATES:	Chewing and imitation	Not a clue.
4. HUMANS:	Sucking reflex	Not much else until imitation kicks in.

Also inborn are Taste buds (sweet tastes are generally good, bitter taste is often poison)

HOW MUCH OF THE SEXUAL RESPONSE IS BIOLOGICAL? HOW MUCH IS LEARNED?

Almost everyone has heard about the "sexual revolution" in America. Almost no one is aware of just how dramatic that change has been. The following is a description of what American mothers were told about sex in infants in 1914. When I first saw the U.S. Government's publication Infant Care, I thought this must be some far-out, one-of-a-kind publication. No, this is listed in the Book of Lists, as one of the top ten most widely distributed publications of all time, right alongside the Bible. Martha Wolfenstein describes the U.S. Government's description of the sexuality of infants:

... the infant appeared to be endowed with strong and dangerous impulses. These were notably autoerotic, masturbatory, and thumb sucking. The child is described as "rebelling fiercely" if these impulses are interfered with. The impulses "easily grow beyond control" and are harmful in the extreme: "children are sometimes wrecked for life." The baby may achieve the dangerous pleasures to which his nature disposes him by his own movements or may be seduced into them by being given pacifiers to suck or having his genitals stroked by a nurse. The mother must be ceaselessly vigilant; she must wage a relentless battle against the child's sinful nature. She is told that masturbation "must be

eradicated... treatment consists in "mechanical restraints". The child should have his feet tied to opposite sides of the crib so that he cannot rub his thighs together; his nightgown sleeves should be pinned to the bed so that he cannot touch himself." Similarly, for thumb sucking, "the sleeve may be pinned or sewed down over the fingers of the offending hand for several days and nights," or a patent cuff may be used which holds the elbow stiff.

Even in the 1960s, it was not uncommon for males to be told, usually by gym teachers or each other, "masturbation causes insanity" or "...will make hair grow on the palms of your hands" or "it will make you go blind". The latter became a foil in a 1970s motion picture titled, *"Can I Do It Till I Need Glasses?"*

Today, it is almost impossible for us to imagine that this was taken seriously, but it was. Now, in the aftermath of AIDS, masturbation is sometimes known as, "safe sex".

The fear of sex was so dramatically embedded in our society that it could not publicly be questioned or even discussed. Through the 1960s even married couples such as Rob and Laura on the hit TV series The *Dick Van Dyke Show* could not be seen sitting on the same bed talking. They had to sit on separate twin beds. Otherwise, it would be "too suggestive" for the censors of television. Using a word like "pregnant" was considered too grating for television; you had to say "in a family way" instead.

When Elvis Presley first appeared on the Ed Sullivan Show, the camera crews were given strict orders to only film him from the chest up, lest he might wiggle his hips, which many considered sexually seductive and grossly obscene. Today, rock stars wiggle everything they have. And we think nothing of it.

The hysteria over sex in our society may have begun as a rational attempt to prevent unwanted pregnancy. Whatever the "rational" reason may have been, like the reason for Chinese foot binding, this quickly disappeared and we were left with only a hysterical fear response that pervaded our culture as surely as foot-binding pervaded China for one thousand years.

You can see how devastating this can be in a moment of candor by Oprah Winfrey. She describes how she became suicidal at fourteen, feeling "I'm just going to have to kill myself." She describes how she had been sexually abused at the ages of nine, ten, eleven, twelve, and thirteen. At fourteen, she was pregnant. Her mother sent her to live with her father in another state. Her father did not know she was pregnant but immediately told her the rules of his house, that he would rather see a daughter of his floating down the Cumberland River (dead) than to bring disgrace on this family by having an unwed pregnancy.

Today, Oprah is one of the most successful and self-confident women on earth. Her honest discussion of her own experiences helps to desensitize many women to the shame society has embed in their mind.

Not just Oprah, but millions of teenagers were told something similar. It did enormous harm, making people terrified of sex and, like Oprah, making them feel terrible about themselves if they were pregnant out of wedlock. That created feelings of depression and suicidal ideas in Oprah and many more.

 But societies never admit to the harm they do by their ideas, and we never say we are sorry about the horrors we write into the minds of our children. Society is only good at holding others responsible for their behavior, there is never anyone who can hold society responsible for the harm by society's judgmental attitudes, witch hunts, prejudice, or wars.

PAVLOV AND SEX

One of the great mistakes of our society is to confuse sex with intercourse. These are two different phenomena. Sex triggers a biological response in the brain, one of pleasure. Intercourse is what makes babies. We are caught by our definition.

Nature has made sex extremely pleasurable to insure that, eventually, in the process of having sex, we will get around to having intercourse; thereby insuring the survival of our species.

For centuries, our society has made sex into something to fear, presumably as our culture's crude form of birth control. Society has also put most of the burden of fear, shame, and guilt on women. The peer group has had just the opposite effect on males, making it something they consider a success.

Our society has done for sex, just the opposite of what Pavlov did for pain. Pavlov made pain into something pleasurable by associating it with the pleasure of food. Society has taking something biologically extremely pleasurable, sex, and made it into something to fear for women in our society. Fear, shame, and guilt became common for women in our culture. Maybe this is changing. Stimulus desensitization in action. Any Stimulus-Any Emotion.

This is no unconscious process described by Freud, it is that the brain functions totally independently of any conscious awareness of why we see or feel as we do. Yet the function of the brain overwhelms our conscious mind. We cannot readily will our mind to see bumps when our brain sees dents.

Our unique reality is a total perceptual experience. It includes every stimulus, every sensation, every perception we have attended to in our lives. It weaves through our minds with a network of interdependent thoughts, experiences, beliefs.

People who think that this is all just an illusion are missing the point. This is no small power. Our collective illusions become our culture, our reality.

Our society today, equates sex with intercourse. Yet, we have no more inborn knowledge of how to engage in intercourse than a frog. We have only the pleasure centers and the basic moves; known as thrusting and lordosis. All else is learned. Like dogs and frogs, even the species to have sex with is learned.

Today, with graphic pornography available on every teenager's cell phone, we are entering into a different reality which no one ever discusses and no one can predict the outcome. The next generation will grow up in a reality, unlike anything we have seen.

ALONG CAME KINSEY:
The History of Sex--Reality vs. Culture

In 1948 Kinsey published *Sexual Behavior in the Human Male* followed in 1955 by *Sexual Behavior in the Human Female*. Kinsey was immediately condemned from the pulpit, in radio talk shows, in newspapers. Kinsey found that 92 percent of males and 65 percent of females say they masturbate. Few in the public arena wanted to believe it. The statistics were opposed to what we had been teaching about the evils of masturbation. Many said it could not possibly be true. Yet as decades have passed, and his original study still stands. Today, the figures are about 95 percent for males and 85 percent for females.

Although many were delighted that Kinsey had exposed the hypocrisy, it still took decades before society itself would change. Once a perception is embedded in the mind, you almost have to have the older generations die off before new perceptions become accepted.

Even today, America is the only western, industrialized society on earth that still has schools that teach "abstinence-only". There is nothing wrong with abstinence. If it works for you, fine. But the highest teen pregnancy in the western world is in America, and the two states with the highest pregnancy rates are Louisiana and Texas, also among the few states that teach "abstinence-only". What works for you depends on your history of experience, not on someone else's.

But abstinence simply does not work for most. Half of our teenagers say they have had sex by the time they get out of high school; about as many females as males. America has the strictest controls over what we teach in sex education courses in the industrialized world and the highest incidence of premarital pregnancy, more than twice that of the next runner up, England.

Yet society blames the individuals if pregnancy results. "You should have listened". Yet we have failed to teach them about peer group pressure, historical changes, and the very knowledge of their bodies to be able to protect themselves from pregnancy.

If you want to find out just how dramatically our views of sex have changed, read the Bible. Jacob was married to two sisters, each of which competed with each other to see who could give Jacob the most children (Genesis 30, KJV). They even used drugs (mandrake root) which was said to increase fertility, to have more children.

When Leah could no longer have children, she gave Joseph her handmaid to have children by in her name. When Rachael could no longer have children, she did the same. Needless to say, we do not encourage this today.

In the Book of First Kings, King Solomon is credited with having 700 wives and 300 concubines, and innumerable children. Some scholars think that was an exaggeration to make Solomon look more virile.

All of this is censored from the Sunday School version of reality that we teach today, along with a great deal more. We are ashamed of our past, because of our present; Any Stimulus - Any Response. So, adults grow up thinking they know what is in the Bible, when all they know are those censored bits and pieces that they were told to believe as children.

THE BIOLOGY OF SEX:
Hormones and Pheromones

In most mammals, sexual behavior is controlled by the estrus cycle. Estrus is a cycle of sexual periods that determine when sexual behavior will occur. Deer tend to mate in November, the rutting season. The does become pregnant then, carry their offspring through the winter, and the young are born in early spring, just when grass and leaves are beginning to show. This timing ensures that the young will have a better chance to survive. If the young were born in the winter, their chance to survive would be far less.

If you go by the sporting goods section of any store in November, you will find bottles of "Buck Lure" on sale. The Lure is made from the urine of female deer, which contains chemicals, known as pheromones that female deer emit in estrus. The males scent the females and are attracted to the scent. Males also emit scents, which may attract female deer, but send other bucks into attack mode. Like a direct wire to the brain's amygdala, the center of fear and aggression, the buck's scent triggers an aggressive response in other bucks. The bucks attack the scent, much as the Robin attacks the color red in mating season.

You see the same scent control over sexuality in our dogs and cats. Although they may have a mating season, several times a year. It is not just curiosity that causes them to sniff each other's behind.

These are biological programs written into the brain by the DNA code. No learning is required. No understanding is necessary.

French perfumes were famous for a similar function in males. By adding pheromones from the scent glands of mammals, these perfumes would supposedly attract human males to whoever wore the perfume. In the 1970s this led to the near extinction of the Tibetan Musk Deer, whose scent glands were highly prized.

Many studies have been done that supposedly find similar pheromones in human sweat. Females are reportedly attracted by the scent of t-shirts worn by men, presumably sweating testosterone, and vice versa. One of the first things that is apparent when you hear of these studies is that they never say how often this works. Yet it is reported, uncritically, by the press. Are all females or males attracted to the scent of the opposite sex? Or only one percent better than a placebo control? Do they even do a placebo control?

The pheromones in sweat are exaggerated in humans. The human ability to smell is so dim that you are more likely to be chased by a rabid Chihuahua.

There may well be a residual scent in humans that has some effect, but the evidence for this is scant. In humans, the estrus cycle no longer functions. It has been replaced by the menstrual cycle. The only control over human sexual behavior is found in what the culture glorifies, we glorify sex, and what the culture damns, we condemn sex too.

APPROACH-AVOIDANCE CONFLICT

Anything a little bit good is greatly exaggerated as all things wonderful, by the peer group, by Hollywood, by television. Anything that is potentially a little bad like sex, is condemned as all things bad, by preachers, by politicians, by the culture. Sex has the rare distinction of being both exaggerated as all things wonderful, and exaggerated as all things evil at the same time in our culture; Any Stimulus-Any Emotion.

When something has both positive and negative emotions attached to the same stimulus this creates an Approach-Avoidance conflict that most teens will go through in their lives. One may want to have sex (*approach*) but be afraid of the consequences our parents and others warned us about, (*avoidance)*; pregnancy or "what will other people think", syphilis, gonorrhea, chlamydia, HIV, genital warts.... Yet we have failed to prepare them to understand what they need to know to control their mind; understanding peer pressure, what they need to know to protect themselves...

HOW MUCH OF OUR SEXUAL BEHAVIOR IS DETERMINED BY THE CODE WRITTEN INTO OUR GENES?

Konrad Lorenz was able to imprint graylag geese to himself, instead of their own species. But there is a discovery he made that is never mentioned in the textbooks. Male graylag geese have an inborn, biologically programmed, courting instinct. When a male goose reaches puberty, it will go out and find a nice, fat juicy grub worm, bring it back and stick it down the throat of its intended. Like chocolates on Valentine's Day?

When the males who had imprinted to Lorenz hit puberty, they went out and found a juicy grub worm, came back, and tried to stick it in Lorenz's ear.

Even the *species* we may want to have sex with is learned.

Do you remember the frogs who could not tell the difference between eating flies and eating BB's? Every time you roll a BB across in front of the frog, it would flick out its tongue and swallow the BB. The same zoologists who told us that frogs do not know the difference between a BB and a fly, also tell us that, when the male frog reaches puberty, it will attempt to mate with anything that moves; *"from a dead leaf blown by the wind, to the human hand"*. Just like college freshmen.

What does a male dog do when he reaches puberty? Like a puppy who chews on everything, he attempts to "hump" anything, including your leg. That behavior is built into their brain. Does that dog "know" what to have sex with? Hardly. Although they respond to the scent that is in the air at mating time, *they do not even know what species to have sex with*; it is all a matter of trial and error.

What about humans? Are we born knowing who to have sex with? Are we born either heterosexual or homosexual? Is it in our genes? Is it in our hormones?

DO GENES DETERMINE SEXUAL BEHAVIOR?

A classic series of studies done in the 1960s began the current theories of what causes sexual preference in humans. The study was done on rats, not on humans, but it has commonly been applied to humans.

The researchers took female rat pups, shortly after birth, and gave them one single, massive injection of the male sex hormone, testosterone. When these female rats hit puberty, they began to behave like males, not females. They would pursue and mount other female rats in estrus, a response normally triggered in males when they scent females.

The films of these studies look dramatic. You see male sexual behavior in the females who received a single injection of testosterone. This led to the currently most popular theory of why some of us are heterosexual and some are homosexual; it all has to do with hormones.

THE STORY OF DAVID REIMER:
Born Male, Made Female

The current theory of gender was cast in cement by the sad story of David Reimer. David was born a male, one of two identical twins.   While he was being circumcised, a bolt of lightning struck the hospital and burned off his penis.   What do you do now? The authority at that time was Dr. John Money, who recommended that David be raised as a female and receive surgery to make him into a female. Although David's circumstance was unique, Money had worked with many individuals who were born with "ambiguous genitalia" and the best view at the time was that they should be assigned a sex, based on whatever their genitals were closest to, and raised in that gender.

The book about David Reimer is sharply critical of John Money's recommendation to have David reared as a female. Why would Money even make such a suggestion?   The reason is not hard to find. In America, anyone who is different in any way becomes a target for abuse by the other kids in school. If their name is funny, if they look different, if they are a minority race, that makes them a target for name-calling, bullying, jokes, and worse. If the difference is sexual, the abuse is even worse.   Money knew this, and this was the basis of his recommendation. He even insisted to David's parents that they never tell him that he had been born a male. This too, is because the ideas he picks up from his peer group, that disparage and joke about anyone who is different, would have a profound effect on his own self-concept if he found out.

Despite the attempts to raise him as a female, David said he never felt female, he felt male. He looked male. Years later, after a difficult puberty, he found out the truth about what had happened to him. He set out on an attempt to turn himself back into a male. He even got married, though that did not work out well. David never felt good about himself.   The story has a tragic ending, he committed suicide.

Did David commit suicide because of what John Money did to him as the book suggests?   Or did he commit suicide because John Money was right about never telling him what had really happened? If he looked more male than female, what would the other students have done? Once he learned he was male, all of the conditioned emotions he picked up from the peer group, slamming those who are different, would have created an approach-avoidance conflict within his mind, possibly creating a very negative self-value.

It is easy to see how the peer group labels anyone who is different as someone to make fun of, an object of ridicule. It is also sadly true, that even the medical profession labels people who are different as "abnormal" a powerful condemnation in one's own mind, even if the professionals do not see it. It is difficult to know for sure what really happened in David's mind.

The David Reimer story hit psychology and the media like a bomb. There was a sudden and dramatic change in what we had long believed about gender and sex. Everyone started talking about gender being born in our genes, determined by our hormones. Even Anderson Cooper of CNN did an hour special on, *"Children Born into the Wrong Bodies"*.

Overnight, one hundred years of what we knew about sex and gender were thrown out the window. Suddenly everyone was talking as if that were the last word on the issue. It was all in the genes. Soon, no one dared to suggest that the environment is a factor. I have heard psychologists angrily respond to the suggestion that gender is determined by experience by saying, "Don't you know about David Reimer?"

Was this the last word in gender and sex? Rarely in the history of psychology has a single study had more influence and created more damage than the book about Reimer. Rarely has any book been more wrong.

PSYCHOLOGY, SEX, AND GENDER:
The Other Side of the Coin

Laura, a strikingly beautiful woman emerges from a swimming pool wearing a bikini. No one would mistake her for being a male. Yet this exceptionally beautiful woman has male genes (XY chromosomes) in every cell in her body. She had internal testes that produced the male hormone testosterone. Genetically she was destined to be a male, but a genetic mutation made her body fail to respond to the male hormone, testosterone. The disorder is called Complete Androgen

Insensitivity. About one in every 800 people has some type of genetic disorder that produces some changes in their sexual phenotype, often called "ambiguous genitalia".

All of her life she was raised as a female. She is into make-up, clothes, glamor pictures, and has never felt male. Even after being told she had internal testes, she never thought of changing her orientation. Her mother says, "…she is quite happy being a girl" and never seems to have felt any conflict over this. Although she says she thinks she should have been told earlier. After puberty, she had to take female sex hormones to fill out her body, and she still does.

How are we to reconcile her experience with those of David Reimer? We may never know all of what went into making them what they became. But we can still look at other hard evidence.

Once again, Learning does not just give the brain information to use in processing as in a computer; it changes the brain itself so completely, that it creates a new reality in the brain. From this reality, our conscious mind "sees" what the brain has been programmed to see.

WHAT STIMULI TRIGGER
A SEXUAL RESPONSE IN MEN?

There is a remarkable caricature of this from the college student's favorite time of life, Spring Break. The story starts with three men wildly excited about spring break. On the beach, they spot two girls lying on their stomachs sunbathing. One of them has long black hair, a bikini bottom, and no top. After giggling about this, one of the males decides to go over to the girls to see if he can get a response out of them.

"What's up ladies?" he says, not exactly an original line. The girl in the bikini bottom with no top suddenly turns over to see who is asking.

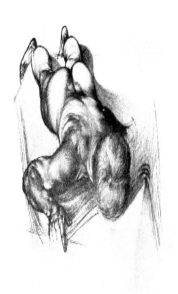

Instantly, her long black hair and bikini bottom are punctuated by a black beard and no breasts. She was a he. The spring breaker turns away with a shocked and embarrassed expression on his face. The other boys razz him about the mistake. "Did you get her number?" You might still find this on youtube.com (search for Spring Break Mistake).

What is remarkable is not that the boys are shocked by the exchange, so is anyone who is watching the film. We respond to the stimuli just as they respond.

What were the stimuli the young males were having a presumed erection over? The bikini bottom (S), the long black hair (S), no top (S), fantasizing about her turning over (S)? All of these stimuli create a perception that triggers sexual responses in the brain, triggering a perception that she (he) was an attractive young lady with no top, even though she was a male all along.

Even our most basic sexual responses are tripped by stimuli that create a perception in our brain, like the other illusions. It is all a matter of learning by association. This will be more significant later when we discuss how the sexual response itself comes into being.

HOW A LEARNED SEXUAL RESPONSE
BECOMES HARDWIRED INTO THE BRAIN

In a classic study, right out of the studies of Ivan Pavlov, Rachman, a psychologist, laid out the simple way in which a sexual response becomes embedded in our brain. Again, using male volunteers, he would show each one a series of slides. Some of the slides were of scenery. Some were of a woman's high heel boot. Some were of a naked lady.

Immediately after every picture of a woman's high heel boot, he would follow it with a picture of a naked lady.

After a series of slides, he would then test them by showing another series of slides without the naked lady; but with the high heeled boots.

He used a phallo plethysmograph, a small blood pressure cuff that goes around the penis, Look up "Penile plethysmography" on Wikipedia.com or just Google it. Be sure to spell it right. Rachman found that just seeing a picture of a woman's high heel boot would now elicit a sexual response.

Bell-Meat? Males would now salivate, figuratively speaking, to a high heel boot.

This is not as uncommon as it sounds. A man in New York the police called the" Foot Bandit" would walk around until he saw a woman sitting on a park bench or bus stop by herself. He would run up behind her, grab one of her shoes, and run off with the shoe. When the police caught him, they found over 1,000 half pairs of woman's shoes in his apartment. He would use them to masturbate with. Perhaps an escapee from Rachman's experiment?

In Florida, a school police officer was arrested for secretly taking pictures of women's feet. Who knew that was illegal?

A student of mine was a woman who volunteered to do religious ministry to prisoners in the Texas prison system. She had been doing this without problems for many months. One day she walked into the prison wearing open toed sandals. The officers stopped her. She was told she was not allowed to go into the prison because her shoes were too revealing. She challenged them to show her where it said that. They did. It does. Who would have guessed?

Throughout most of human history no one could read. Today, *words* written on white paper can elicit a sexual response. How? It is likely to be a chain of Pavlovian responses to sex. In the 1950's D.H. Lawrence's classic book *Lady Chatterley's Lover* was banned in Boston for being too sexual. Today, it is too tame to even make it on to a woman's soft-porn soap opera on television.

Novelist Kurt Vonnegut noted that when he was a desperate, starving writer, he would write prose for the "Panty" magazines that were then popular among men. They could charge big money for magazines that only showed women wearing panties. Today, you cannot even give away these magazines.

Stimulus desensitization in action.

But what determines our sexual interest in the first place? Most likely, what the peer group emphasizes; the "WOW" effect. Vonnegut notes that the only poem preteen males ever learned in his generation was like:

I see England

I see France

I see Suzie's

Underpants

Boys then considered the idea of seeing a girl's underpants to be exciting. Probably the same reaction you might get from Surma boys over a woman's big lip. This led to the once popular "panties" magazines.

In primitive societies, where women routinely do not cover their breasts, there is no sexual association with breasts. In our culture, breasts are considered so sexual, they must, by law, be covered up. Curiosity along with taboo, seem to be associated with increasing sexual interest.

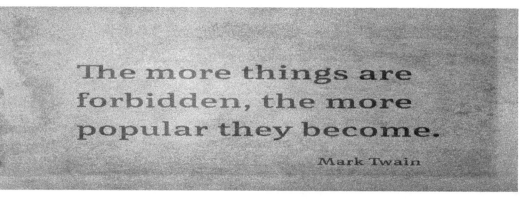

The more things are forbidden, the more popular they become.

Mark Twain

One young woman commented that she had a sexual reaction to the scent of her boyfriend's cologne. Whether it is cologne or boots, or breasts or spanking or open toed shoes, or words written on white paper, it is like the 700 named phobias or the 450 paraphilias, it is all about Psychology's Special Theory of Relativity; Any Stimulus-Any Response, even a sexual response.

The first experiences we have at puberty with the idea of sex, seems to set a permanent or semi-permanent reaction in our brains that can last a lifetime. It does not seem to require an actual sexual experience. The combination of puberty, excitement, and imagination all may play a role, along with the giggling of the peer group.

WHAT WILL OTHER PEOPLE THINK?

Determines Much of our Sexual Behavior

In a classic study of modeling behavior by Albert Bandura and Richard Walters, they used male college students to study how we are influenced by what we think is "normal".

They told the student volunteers, one at a time, that they were going to be attached to an "eye marker camera" that fit on their head that would record what parts of a picture they were looking at and how long they spent looking at it.

Next, the students were shown a series of pictures; some with scenery, and some with scenery with a naked woman in it. Then they recorded the results of the eye marker camera.

Incredibly, the male students were split down the middle. Half spent most of their time looking at the scenery, and only occasionally glanced at the naked lady. The other half spent more time looking at the naked lady and only occasionally glanced at the scenery.

Why? Were some of the students pure as the driven snow Divinity students and the other half raunchy psychology majors?

The only difference between the two groups is that before the study began, all of the males were shown an example of what other students had done. But in half of those examples, they were shown that students spent more time looking at the scenery and not the naked lady. For the other half, the example they were shown, the students spent more time looking at the naked lady, and not the scenery.

The males followed the example they had been given of what other students had supposedly done.

All of us know from our past experience, that if we are put in a situation we are not familiar with, we tend to look around to see what others are doing. At a formal dance, we may look to see what others are wearing, to see if we dressed up to haughtily or down to lowly. We compare ourselves to others. If we go to a formal dinner, we may look to see what the others are doing with the tiny little fork. Etc.

THE BIOLOGY OF SEX
Pleasure Centers of the Brain

In a remarkable discovery of the biological programs of the brain, psychologists Olds and Milner were attempting to drop an electrode into the hypothalamus of the brain of a rat. They missed the area they were aiming for but discovered a spot on the hypothalamus that, when electrically stimulated with a tiny current, produced a profound response in the rat.

When Olds rigged an apparatus that allowed the rat to press a bar to self-stimulate the Nucleus Accumbens in his brain with the small electrical stimulus, he found the rat would not stop slapping that bar. The rat would ignore food, water, and friendly rats to continue pressing the bar.

When he required the rat to cross an electric grid to self-stimulate that area of the brain, he found the rat would cross more powerful electric shocks to get to the bar than a hungry rat would to get food. The rat would never satiate to the pleasure, it would continue to press the bar for hours and hours, to a point of exhaustion.

The Nucleus Accumbens is directly adjacent to the olfactory or scent part of the brain in humans and rats. In most mammals, the scent emitted by the opposite sex during estrus, the mating season, is directly associated with seeking sex.

At Tulane, Dr. Heath carried this one step further, attempting to alleviate severe depression in patients. With electrodes implanted in humans into their left anterior and right mid-septal areas he found that humans would continually stimulate their own pleasure center. One woman described it as sexual. One man...;

> *"...stimulated himself to a point that, both behaviorally and introspectively, he was experiencing an almost overwhelming euphoria and elation and had to be disconnected, despite his vigorous protests."*

Unlike a normal sexual response, which has an automatic turn off switch at orgasm, rats and people do not easily satiate if the stimulation bypasses the "turn off" switch or refractory program in the brain. This discovery quickly became a model for understanding sexual behavior and also addictive behavior with heroin and cocaine.

There is more than one such "pleasure" center in the brain and other sites are considered basic to food seeking as well as pleasure.

The United States DOD, Department of Defense, devised a method of controlling the behavior of a rat with such an implant and a remote-control device that would allow an operator to remotely control the rat's behavior, determining if he turned right or left and more.

Exactly what the DOD planned to use these methods for is unclear. It is also unnecessary, as the use of words is just as effective with people, without the messy need for brain surgery. Yet all of this goes back to Pavlov's discovery that Any Stimulus could come to elicit Any Response, already wired into the Autonomic Nervous System.

THE PSYCHOLOGY OF GENDER:
Learning Gender Differences

Suppose your neighbors down the street just had a baby and you learned they just painted the baby's room pink. What do you know about the baby? Female? Male? Why? Why would pink be for girls and blue for boys?

In fact, the color for males used to be red. Red was the color of the British army uniforms for centuries. In America, we called them the "Redcoats". When America rebelled against England, we picked blue for American uniforms, when we could afford uniforms. In America, blue came to the color for males.

When Paul Revere made his famous ride, he did not say" The British are coming!" They were all British. He said, "The Red Coats are coming!", meaning the British Army.

Take a look at the profile of George Washington, the father of our country, on a quarter. What is strange about George? You have seen thousands of quarters but you may have never noticed this. He is wearing a powdered wig. Out of the back of the wig is a ponytail. On the ponytail is a ribbon tied with a bow.

If you look at the old nickel with Thomas Jefferson on it, he looks like he is also wearing a wig, but it turns out it is his real hair. Jefferson too has a ponytail with a bow on it. They censored this on the new Jefferson nickel.

On the one-hundred-dollar bill is Benjamin Franklin. He has hair down below his shoulders. They never told us this in High School, but all our founding fathers were gay.

No, of course not. This was the fashion of the day. Men wore lace ruffles on their sleeves and around their neck for formal occasions. In France, men not only wore powdered wigs, but they also wore pancake makeup and lipstick. In the court of England, the justices wear hideous curled wigs that look like mops and that come down to their breasts. In 2009 they voted whether to abandon the wigs and become more modern or to keep them. They voted to keep them.

What would happen today if you sent your ten-year-old son to school wearing a ponytail with a bow in it? If he were not beaten up, they would certainly make fun of him. We have failed to teach the *relativity* of reality, the truth of our history. Children grow up to become adults with absolutely no idea just how relative our concept of male and female can be.

LEFT, Verban in full wig.

Below: British Scientist Robert Boyle

Societies inject their own ideas into the minds of children. In a series of studies by Sadker, he went into first, second, and third-grade classrooms to observe differences between boys and girls. He found that the teachers, almost all female, reacted differently to children, depending on their gender. If a little girl were to hurt herself and run crying to the teacher, the teacher would sympathize with her and bandage her injury.   If a little boy were to hurt himself and run crying to the teacher, the teacher would bandage his injury and say, in effect, "there now, that didn't hurt, did it?" Or maybe "you're a big boy". The unstated implication being that big boys don't cry.

The idea that "big boys don't cry" is further conditioned by the peer group who may make fun of other males for being "yella" or "a scardy cat" or "chicken" or a "crybaby". The conditioning of the peer group, by the peer group, is powerful.

By the time they get to college, the die is set. In one study they took college freshmen males who volunteered for a simple experiment. They were told that they would be connected to electrodes and given electric shocks. The shocks would start very mild, and gradually work up to increasing levels of shock. They should tell the experimenter immediately when the shocks became painful and they would stop the experiment.

When they came in, one at a time, there was an old psychologist there to run the experiment. He connected the electrodes and began the shocks. They would go up to a modest level and, when they reported the shock was painful, the experimenter immediately stopped the shocks. Then the psychologist excused himself and left the room. Shortly after, a young attractive female about the same age as the subject would come in and ask to redo the experiment. They found the males would take whole bunches more shock for the young female than they took for the old man.

Were the males so distracted by the young female that they failed to notice the shocks? Was testosterone shooting into their bloodstream to make them less sensitive to pain? No, the males would take about as much shock if the experimenter were a young male their own age as if it were a female. What were the males doing? They were trying to live up to the cultural image of what a male should be, a tough guy, not a crybaby. And they were more concerned about what their peers thought of them than what an old man thought of them.

Any psychologist or psychiatrist will tell you that seventy percent of their patients are female. Males rarely come in for treatment. Is it because only females have problems? Or is it because males are supposed to be tough guys, the ideas of showing weakness is a powerful fear that prevents men from seeking help even when they need it. This came to the fore recently because of the Gulf War. A Pentagon study found that 39 percent of the soldiers returning from the second Gulf war would come down with either major depressive disorder or Post Traumatic Stress Disorder. Yet the soldiers who needed treatment would rarely come in for treatment. Admitting a mental problem was considered too unmanly, in a very macho culture.

You can see the difference in how males and females respond to problems. If a woman has a problem, what does she do? She calls her mother, she calls her sister, she talks to everyone at work about the problem.   If a man has a problem, what does he do? He "slips on down to the Oasis, where the whiskey drowns and the beer chases those blues away, it'll be ok." Garth Brooks.

This idea of the difference between men and women is so deeply ingrained in our culture that there even a joke about it, called the "Five Flies".   As the story goes a woman awakes in the middle of the night to noises coming from the kitchen. The noises go, Bop followed by a Ding, then a Bop and another Ding, then a Bop.

She goes into the kitchen to see what the noise is and finds her husband standing in the kitchen with a fly swatter. She asks, "What are you doing?" He says, "I'm killing flies." She asks, "Did you get any?" He says, "Yeah, I got five; three males and two females." She asks incredulously, "How do you know if a fly is a male or a female?" He says, "Easy. Three were on a beer can, two were on the phone."

"This is my first Male Awareness Weekend. Where's the frig?"

That quickly summarizes the cultural idea of the difference between men and women; men are drinkers, women are talkers. Of course, not all men are drinkers and not all women are talkers. The stereotype may be changing. A recent survey of high school students about drinking found that 25 percent of males and 26 percent of females say they have had a drink in the last month. It is hard to know what that result means, but it is interesting.

YOU DON'T WANT TO BE A SISSY, DO YOU?

Suppose, ladies, that your husband comes home one day and finds his two-year-old son on the floor playing with his sister's dolls. What might he do? "You don't want to play with that, that's sissy stuff. Here's a nice shotgun, play with that".

What can girls do that boys can't do? Play with dolls or other "sissy (sister) stuff". It is an idea impressed upon the mind early. Even if parents do not put their sons down for this, the other boys will. They make fun of any other male that might seem sissy. Even if they do not believe that another boy is a sissy, they still commonly use that as a cudgel to beat each other over the head.

So, males cannot play with dolls, unless… unless we re-label them as ACTION FIGURES; Arnold Swartznegger dolls, or half naked Sylvester Stallone dolls or toy soldiers. That makes it all right for males to play with dolls.

Does it hurt for males to play with their sister's dolls? Well, yes and no. It does not make them gay, but in our culture, it guarantees that the other boys will make fun of them.

The idea of what a male should be has changed dramatically within our lifetime. In a previous generation, the "tough guy" image held up to our youth was John Wayne. As a cowboy hero, he was tough, emotionless, and unsentimental. It used to be said that in his cowboy role he would save the damsel in distress, then kiss his horse and ride off into the sunset. In actual life John Wayne was tough and unsentimental; he was married three times and divorced three times.

The change from one generation to another can be seen in another male of his time, the award-winning actor Henry Fonda. In his day, men were also not sentimental. His son, Peter Fonda *of Easy Rider* fame, tells of never having heard his father say, "I love you" growing up. It was not something men were supposed to say. After his father was much older and becoming frail, Peter Fonda tells of a conversation he had with his father. At the end of the conversation, Peter told his father, "Dad, I love you."   His father was so dumbstruck by the sentiment that he could not speak, he stammered and stuttered, trying to say something, but then just hung up.   He had no experience with a male saying something like that to another male and he could not respond.

One of the findings of the Sadker studies is that boys in the age range of four and one half to six- and one-half years old spend *eleven times* more time playing with other males than with females.   Why? It could be that males prefer to play with "male" toys and girls prefer to play with "female" toys, but any look at how kids think at this age shows something quite different. The emotionally conditioned idea that "sissy stuff" is bad is so firmly embedded in the minds of males at this age that they think girls are "yucky" that girls have "cooties" or worse.   They actively avoid any contact with girls.   They tease other boys by saying, "Bobby's got a girlfriend" as a putdown. Bobby feels he has to deny having a girlfriend, just to keep from being associated with the negative emotions.

All of this comes from the emotional conditioning of the peer group, by the peer group. It is all done with words (S) associated with emotions (S). Stimulus + Stimulus = Perception.

So, when males hit puberty, and start to notice girls, what do they do to show a girl they like her? They pull her hair, make fun of her, tease her, be mean to her, all guaranteed to make her dislike him, because boys still have no idea how to react to girls. Some say we never learn.

JUDGMENT BECOMES AUTOMATIC

After a while, our behavior and beliefs may become so natural to us that we continue to behave in such a way, or judge others, without any conscious awareness at all of what we do or why. Thought is not needed. It all becomes as automatic as our perception of the Necker cube or bumps and dents.   And it may be just as likely to be wrong. Yet we may not see any other reality.

The ease with which the environment molds our minds raises important questions about many issues. For one, there is the old worry about the impact of television or motion pictures on the minds of young children. And what about adults? This is an important issue not just from the standpoint of morality, it cuts much deeper. It questions the impact of our school systems, our religious education, and our child-rearing practices themselves.

The fact that learning proceeds so subtly, so without our awareness, must raise questions that have never before been asked. We simply do not have a science that has ever studied these questions in the depth that they deserve. And there are few areas more important than learning how our environment has influenced the mind of a child and how that, in turn, determines the perception of the adult.

Those of us who were high school students in the John Wayne era can remember the impact of experience on our perception of reality if we stop to think about it. It was an era of short haircuts, button-down collars... neat slacks, and good manners. And in the generation that followed, anyone who deviated from that view of what a "good American" should be, met with severe criticism from society. Teachers patrolled the halls with rulers to make certain that the dresses of girls came to 2" below the base of the kneecap. And in the generation after that, they applied a similar ruler test to boys whose hair length seemed too long to the older generation. Dress codes sprang up everywhere to enforce the view of the elders upon the young.

It all seemed obviously correct, and anyone who pointed out that Jesus Christ wore long hair, beard, and sandals simply met with a blank stare. There was only one way to dress and the elders knew what it was. And all these dress codes were uniformly enforced by supposedly well-educated teachers in a nation that was still telling itself that we valued freedom of choice and individuality and non-conformity, all the while demanding the greatest degree of conformity among our young and each other.

I can remember at the time the photographs coming out of mainland China showing millions of Chinese wearing the same grey "pajamas". We all thought at the time, "How horrible to see a government that forces such mindless conformity on its people." But that thought did nothing to change our demand that others conform to <u>our</u> image of what is "good." And all of us still wore our button-down collars and short haircuts and identical suits (we would never be hired for a job if we had not!).

I had a beard all through graduate school. When I graduated, before I ever applied for a job, I shaved off my beard. Because I knew that the older generation who did the hiring believed that anyone with a beard must be a hippie or a war protester, although I was not smart enough to be either back then.   I applied for a position as a psychologist working for the State of Texas. I showed up, clean-shaven, in suit and tie; even if you applied for a janitor's job, they expected you to show up in a suit and tie. When I was ushered into the suite of the Boss of Bosses, he had a private bathroom in his office so no one would know he peed, I did not know what to expect.

He did not ask me a thing about what my grades were, or if I knew how to do psychological testing, which the job required; you can get a degree in psychology without learning this. The only question he asked me was, "Now, if we hire you, you aren't going to stop shaving and start showing up in jeans and a t-shirt, are you"

"Who? Me?"

The first female psychologist we hired, the only thing he asked her was, "If we hire you, you aren't going to come to work wearing a mini skirt and makeup, are you?"

She never stopped talking about that.

Back then, supervisors were more worried about questions like, "Is this person going to get along, to "fit in"? Or are they going to "rock the boat", argue over issues, cause us trouble. Much like today.

To those reared in that generation, short hair, suits, and ties seemed so obviously correct, so clearly normal that any other perception of reality was quite impossible. It was all we were used to. Editorials appeared in newspapers assuring young people that if they had barbers in the time of Jesus, he too would have cut his hair, shaved, and probably bathed more often.

But the change had begun, a vague idea began smoldering in the minds of youth, a realization, however distant, had come into being: The youths had begun to learn that the adults did not know what it was all about. Of course, the young people didn't either, and they only barely glimpsed the magnitude of the changes that were upon us.

Some youth actually believed what we had taught them in school about freedom of choice, individuality, and individual rights. They did not see it was just an ideal to be spoken and ignored.

Today, we have "casual Friday" or even, in Steve Job's Silicon Valley, casual every day.

In the decade that followed, the sexual revolution was upon us. It overwhelmed shocked parents who did not know what was happening or why and whose only response was to wail and moan over "What's happening to the kids?" But it would not have come as any great surprise if we had been aware of how the mind really works and of the dramatic differences in sexual behavior in our own history.

And the young again discovered that the adults didn't know. It was not just that the adults did not know, it was far more; For the adults were not even aware that there was anything else to know.

THE SINGULARITY OF PSYCHOLOGY:
How Nothing Becomes Something

The human mind is far more like a "tabula rasa" than it is like the magical-mystical view of the inborn genetic identity we have been getting from many in the media. We start out with no view of what is good or bad, no idea of who our mother is, no understanding of what species we are, no idea who to have sex with, no idea about anything. It is the psychologist's version of the singularity in physics.

The singularity in physics is in the center of a black hole where light, matter, time, and the known laws of physics cease to be. Everything is reducible into nothing. Yet psychology knows far more than physics about how nothing becomes something.

We are not born knowing who we are. We do not know how to have sex, except for a few inborn moves and the existence of our hypothalamus. We do not even know what species to have sex with. We do not know that tiny feet are sexual. We do not know that big lips are sexual. We do not know that breasts are sexual. We are not born knowing that words can elicit a sexual response. Every tiny bit of information fed into our brain becomes our perception of reality.

We learn about food, sex, life from the ideas embedded in our mind by our experiences in society. We learn it the same way we learn the language we speak; in a way that is so subtle, so impossible for us to see, that we believe the ideas in our mind are reality.

6

ORIGIN OF THE INDIVIDUAL

"Never forget that each of you is a distinctly different individual, just like everyone else. " Margaret Mead

No area of psychology is more behind the times than personality theory. Ignore the theories, this is the hard evidence.

Not in innocence, and not by design is the child conceived. Biologist Amran Scheinfeld has calculated that a single spoonful of male sperm cells contains over 200 million sub-microscopic male sperm. If you doubt it, count them yourselves.

These half-cells are propelled into a long, dark journey. They are driven in every direction by blind, unconscious force. In a matter of hours, thousands of them will have made their way through the uterus to the fallopian tubes. Tens of millions of others will have dropped out of the race or will be lost in a fold of skin. For the survivors, this is the home stretch of a marathon race in which only one of the hundreds of millions of entrants may win. Only one will contribute its unique genetic material to the formation of an individual.

It takes an average of one-quarter of a billion sperm cells to fertilize one egg. The vast, vast masses of sperm cells get lost, wiggling their tails along the way. They are blind, deaf, and have no GPS locating device to direct their journey. That is why there must be so many to have any chance of succeeding. Only a few will get where they are going, by blind chance alone. That is why it takes hundreds of millions.

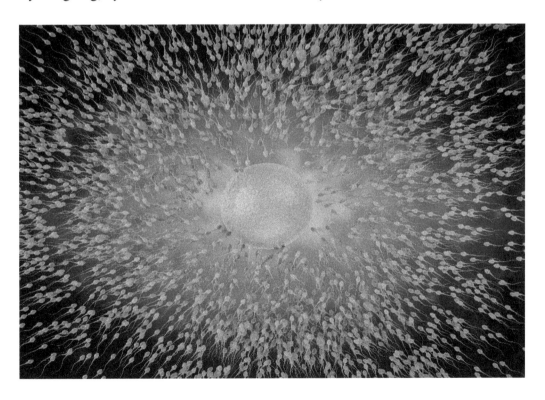

We all begin life as a product of blind chance.

If two parents were to live forever, reproducing consistently, what are the odds that some of their children would be identical? Each male sperm cell or female egg cell contains exactly half of the genetic material, 23 chromosomes, that is combined at conception to produce the individual. Yet each such cell is more unique than a human fingerprint. The 46 chromosomes may contain more than 20,000 genes that determine specific physical traits. Scheinfeld calculated that in any spoonful of sperm cells there could be 8,388,608 distinctly different individual combinations! The egg cell also has about 8,388,608 different possible genetic combinations, even though only one or two eggs are released per month. The number of different combinations of the two sets of 23 chromosomes is virtually infinite.

Although the female supplies only one or two eggs per month, on the average, Scheinfeld has calculated that the chance of the recombination of the same male and female chromosomes in the same parents would be less than once in 64 trillion times or about as unlikely as the odds of winning the Lottery. We are all very unique accidents.

In simpler language, no matter how prolific a couple might be it is probable that every one of their children would be unique. Except for identical (same egg and sperm that divide and separate) twins, all would have had brothers and sisters that were in some ways uniquely different from each other. They would have differed in the shape of the nose, chin, the color of the eyes, their height, weight, and bodily proportions, and perhaps, their temperament.

Yet we share more than 98% of our DNA with chimpanzees. And every individual human is 99.9% identical to each other. We differ only a tiny percent from each other in our genes.

Everyone who has seen the rows of newborn infants at a hospital has noted the individual differences they display--not only physical differences, but differences in temperament or in how they react to the environment. Some cry readily while others sleep oblivious of any holocaust that might occur around them. As the weeks pass into months, the differences in temperament become increasingly apparent. While one baby responds with giggling and cooing to the sound of mother's voice, another may react with wide-eyed interest to everything they hear or see. The responsiveness that is basic to personality is beginning to gel.

Are the differences we observe in temperament in the nursery caused by our DNA or is something more involved. Are these differences a product of an accident

from the gene pool? Or are they an end product of different mothers' own experiences from the very first? How do we find out?

The nature-nurture controversy is again revisited. Now the questions change. What is the evidence that temperament or responsiveness is inherited? What is the evidence that it is produced by the environment? The most convincing observation of innate emotional differences comes from observing breed differences in dogs. Across the centuries we have been breeding dogs for individual differences in physical characteristics.

Intentionally or accidentally, we have also bred dogs for marked differences in temperament. The Chihuahua is a feisty, emotional little terror that barks ferociously at any and every newcomer and runs and hides behind its master at the slightest move a stranger makes in its direction. The Cocker Spaniel is a calm, even-tempered family dog whose reaction to strangers is more muted and calmer. The German Shepherd, a one-man or one-family dog, is fiercely loyal and will defend its home and family from strangers. In contrast, the well-known "hound dog" is so affable and outgoing that it easily makes friends with all comers, including unwanted late-night intruders.

Human personalities seem to be mirrored in the breeds of dogs. The Chihuahua is a model of the nervous excitable person who snaps at others or reacts with suspicion to their attempts at friendship. The calm, easygoing, imperturbable family man could be symbolized by the spaniel. The ambitious, aggressive, business person may be symbolic of the worldly behavior of the reserved shepherd. While the gregarious, outgoing "extrovert," who could sell refrigerators to Eskimos, or be taken advantage of by everyone, is the soul of the hound. With only a little imagination, each of these classifications could be expanded into many types and subtypes.

But are choleric Chihuahuas and phlegmatic hounds really inborn personality types? And if they are, do they apply to people?

In a classic study, C.S. Hall reasoned that if emotional reactivity is influenced by heredity, it should be possible to breed for increasingly more "fearful" or less "fearful" animals in the same way that we breed for physical traits. If we want only shepherds with black and tan coats, we allow only black and tans to mate. Shepherds with tinges of white, grey, or red are excluded from breeding; hence we have *artificial* selection. Eventually, we can breed a group of dogs, with only black and tan coats.

So, we should be able to select the most fearful or least fearful animals out of a liter and allow only these to mate. Then take the most fearful or least fearful pups from their liter and allow only these to mate, and so on. If fearful temperament is genetically based, we should end up with animals that produce offspring that are nearly always fearful or fearless.

But how do you tell if an animal is fearful or fearless? Subjective judgments have proven too unreliable. Before Hall could begin his study, he needed an objective measure of emotionality. He decided on an "open field" test. Normally, when you place an animal in a new, unfamiliar environment its first reaction is to freeze, to try to orient itself before it moves out into the strange new world. Human babies may cry, puppies may whine, rat pups typically freeze in place.

Slowly, they may begin to gain confidence and gradually move around to explore the environment. Such reactions are characteristic of all animals in strange places. A human child's first day at school or a puppy's first walk in the woods is met with the same initial fearfulness. Some animals lose their fear of strangeness quite readily. Others take a long while before exploring. Those who explore quickly are classified as "fearless" or "nonreactive".

Hall divided a room into a series of grids. Hall measured how long it took before they would "unfreeze" and begin to explore, and how many grids in the novel environment they would cross. Animals classified as fearful took a long time to begin to explore and venturing over fewer grids.

Hall proceeded to mate the most "fearful" rats with the other most "fearful" rats. And he mated the least "fearful" with other least "fearful" rats.

Q					

Within seven generations he had bred two different strains of rats that could be identified as fearful and non-fearful. Fearful strains were approximately three times as fearful as non-fearful strains on Hall's measures.

Of course, one should be careful of the value judgment we place on such emotions. It might seem better to be fearless than to be fearful, but fearless rats in the real world would quickly be eaten by fearless cats. Fear has survival value, it produces caution.

Hall's pioneering studies were later expanded by P.L. Broadhurst who carefully controlled for environmental influences. Two separate personality "types" had been bred; they seem to reach their maximum differences after about seven generations. Further breeding did not noticeably affect their fearfulness.

Soon, other investigators found genetic links to aggressive traits. The role of genetic differences in human temperament was still unclear, but none could deny that individual differences in temperament were linked to the genetic throw of dice.

Evidence of genetic influence on temperament is strong, but it may be misleading. Unlike dogs, humans have never been bred for temperament. Genetic studies show that genes can affect temperament, but they are extreme examples. Humans have never been bred like dogs or rats.

Thus, the difference between one human and the next is more likely to be like the difference between one German Shepherd and another German Shepherd, not like the difference between a Shepherd and a Chihuahua.

LEARNING TEMPERAMENT

The success of breeding studies should have been enough to put the nurture sympathizers on the defensive. But environmental psychologists had not been napping. Psychologist David Spelt had already investigated the role of learning in the prenatal environment. He found that the unborn fetus in a human mother could learn.

He touched a vibrator to the mother's stomach. The vibrator produced no response from the fetus. He followed this immediately with a loud noise. The noise produced a startle reaction from the fetus. The fetus would jerk or twitch. He continued to pair the two; first the vibrator, then the loud noise. After several pairings, the fetus would startle in response to the vibrator alone, showing that it had learned to anticipate the loud noise that would follow the vibrator. This is classical learning at its most basic.

Clearly, an unborn fetus of seven months of age could learn. The question then becomes, *what* might it learn?

Part of the answer came from a study by W. R. Thompson at Wesleyan University. Thompson subjected two groups of virgin female rats to a fear-producing situation. One group of rats learned that the sound of a buzzer would be followed by a fear-producing stimulus (Buzzer-Shock) as in Bell-Meat. For these mothers, the buzzer by itself would produce an anticipatory response of anxiety.

The second group of rats was also exposed to the fear-producing stimulus, but the buzzer did not sound beforehand (Shock--------Buzzer); So that the buzzer would never come to elicit anxiety.

After the rats had learned to fear the buzzer, Thompson allowed them to become pregnant. During their pregnancy, the buzzer was sounded three times per day. *No shocks were given.* The first group of rats responded by becoming fearful. The other group did not.

When they gave birth, Thompson tested the offspring of both groups after they reached thirty days of age. One by one the rat pups were given the open field test. As the data came in, it was apparent that the rat pups of the frightened mothers covered only about two thirds as much ground as the rat pups born to the mothers who were not frightened during pregnancy.

The rat pups of frightened mothers took an average of 15 minutes before they would leave their home base to explore the rest of their world. That contrasts to only 5.2 minutes for rat pups born to mothers who were not frightened during the pregnancy. Roughly, the pups in the group whose mothers were fearful during their pregnancy were 3X more fearful than the group whose mothers were not anxious during pregnancy. The effect seems to have persisted.

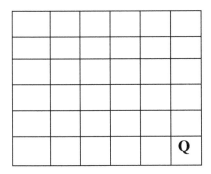

That does not mean that this experience persists into adult life. As adults, the rats born to fearful moms took 4.8 minutes before leaving their cage compared to 2.1 minutes for the pups born to mothers who were not frightened during pregnancy. So, it may dissipate as experience makes the fear of novelty less.

However, it would suggest that the idea that human infants in a nursery, one crying, one anxious, one laid back, are not due to any innate biological basis of personality. They may have just had a difficult birth, or were subject to more stress, or their mothers were anxious during pregnancy.

Here at last was clear-cut evidence that environment influences temperament. The results were as impressive as anything produced by the genetic studies, yet largely ignored by the press. More recently, two studies in psychology journals have found that babies born to human mothers who were anxious during pregnancy, had babies that were more anxious after they were born.

No, they did not shock the human mothers, they asked them to rate the degree of anxiety they felt at different stages of their pregnancy. The more anxious the mothers, the more anxious the babies were, even to the point of the babies failing to gain as much weight. When you are scared, you are not as hungry.

We know that the differences between the two groups of rats were produced by the differences in the environment of their mothers, not in their genes. We also know that the fear in the rat pups was not produced by either the original fear stimulus or the buzzer itself, but by the mother's anxiety alone, since the mothers were never shocked during pregnancy and second, the buzzer did not affect the fear of the offspring born to rat mothers who had never learned to fear the buzzer.

The only apparent cause of the fear in the rat pups was the fact that their mothers had been fearful during pregnancy.   However, if a mother were anxious during pregnancy, what if she were also anxious when the child is one-year-old? 16 years old? We have no hard evidence.

PROGRAMMING THE MIND:
TEMPERAMENT IN PLAIN SIGHT

But the best evidence is not from psychologist's studies, the best evidence is all around us in plain sight.

Take two pups from the same litter. They could be either male or both female, or one male and one female. Send one to the Army guard dog training school. Send the second to the Seeing Eye School for the Blind. In a brief time, you would produce two dramatically different temperaments.

The effect of experience on temperament can be dramatic. The army and police have conditioned dogs to become so fearless that they will attack a group of men armed with guns or knives with no thought of their own safety and no regard for the consequences. Sentry dogs and police dogs are fearless because they are conditioned to be fearless, not because of their genes.

Their training begins at about one year of age. They are first habituated to one man, the man who will be their master throughout the training. When attack training begins, a second person will play the role of the aggressor. Dressed in a padded suit, the aggressor will tease the dog, first by flailing at the dog in a feigned attack, and then by quickly retreating and allowing the dog to chase after him.

A golden retriever being trained as an attack dog. This series of attack-retreat, attack-retreat interactions has two purposes. The dog is first aroused by being teased in the attack phase.

The trainer knows that the dog must never be beaten. The dog must consistently and repeatedly win. Each time the feigned attack by the trainer ends with the aggressor retreating and eventually fleeing in mock terror and being subdued by the dog. This training begins with a very mild attack, and gradually, as the dog gains confidence, the attack becomes increasingly hostile; yet every time the dog wins.

TWO PERSONALITIES CAN RESULT FROM A SMALL CHANGE:
If the dog were teased or attacked with too much gusto, it could become frightened and end up as an animal who cowed in the face of the aggressor; a very different personality type; a dog who is a "fear biter" or a "fear barker", but not a good guard dog. A good trainer never lets this happen.

What seems to be the same "training" can produce dramatically different personality types, with an apparently minor change in how it is done.

More than any other factor, it is this sense of successful encounters that gives the dog the confidence it needs to succeed in future "real life" situations. The dog always wins. Every encounter is a success. So far. That is what gives him the "courage" to attack a man with a gun or knife with no thought to his own safety.

Of course, one has to note that there is such a thing as "false confidence". In "real life" the dog has very little chance against a man with a real gun. He might, quite unknowingly, save the life of his master while sacrificing his own.

Such training takes advantage of the tendency that all predatory animals have to attack anything that runs away from them. The initial conditioning seems to involve associating the neutral stimulus, the aggressor, with the natural stimulus (the natural response to being teased or to running away from the dog). The dog learns that by being aggressive, he will always win. The sight or scent of any strange person may then be enough to send the dog into an attack. The dog might then be said to have an aggressive "personality". Another training occurs, however, to teach the dog to discriminate between who to attack and who to consider friendly.

Just as important, is the fact that if the trainer kept backing the dog up instead of retreating, if the dog were teased, or lost more encounters than it won, it would have been conditioned to have a fearful or timid "personality". It might become a "fear biter" or a "fear barker" but it would not be useful as a guard dog or a seeing-eye dog.

Even a small amount of training early in life can produce a change that may last far into adulthood.

SEEING-EYE DOGS WITH A VERY DIFFERENT PERSONALITY

For a seeing-eye dog, you want just the opposite personality type as for an attack dog. Starting when one is very young, the puppy must be habituated to young children, other dogs, even cats. You want to be sure that if a child sticks his fingers in the eye of a grown seeing-eye dog you do not want the dog to bite his finger off. If the dog is helping his blind master across the street, and a cat runs in front of him, you do not want the dog dragging his master down the street after the cat.

Above: Young retriever becoming accustomed to children, dogs, and cats must be absolutely tame and calm. Just the opposite of a guard dog. Such training must begin early as a puppy.

Next, the older dog receives training on avoiding obstacles while leading the blind.

Now the point of all of this is not to teach you how to teach your children to become aggressive. Not hardly. But the element of success in early experiences is essential to any task, not just teaching a dog that he will succeed every time he encounters an aggressor. The experience of success in childhood can influence other areas of self-confidence as well.

The difference in the psychological experiments in a laboratory and the observations made in real life dramatically shows the advantage of psychologists using Observation along with Experimentation, something our textbooks have been reluctant to do.

TRAINING PARENTS:

Further, and equally importantly, the "personality" of the child can be powerfully influenced by early exposure to emotional experiences.

Having raised dogs all my life, there is one experiment I have always thought everyone who is going to be a parent should have to do themselves before they are allowed to become parents. After all, you cannot get a license to drive a car without passing a written test and a driving test.   But all you need to become a parent is a set of gonads.

To prepare for being a parent, simply take three puppies from the same litter, male or female, it does not matter. The first puppy you rough house with every time y5you interact with him. It is not being cruel, puppies love to rough house, and they do it with each other. Take the second puppy and never rough house with him or her if they want to play just hold them and pet them every time you interact. The third puppy, you do not interact with, you leave him or her with the litter mates, but you do not interact with the puppy. In a very short time, months, weeks, even just days, you will have produced three puppies with quite different temperaments.

The first will want to rough house every time he sees you, whether you want to or not. I do not recommend you do this; my puppy grew up into a 60-pound adult and I could not take the trash out to the garbage can without him grabbing me by my trouser leg, shaking his head back and forth, sometimes tripping me or my having to drag him along, attached to my trouser. It does not make them mean, not at all, it just makes them want to rough house all the time.

I have seen fathers' rough house with their boys, then later punish them when they wanted to rough house and he did not. Surprise; we are often unaware of how what we do affects our children (or our dogs).

The second puppy will never want to rough house with you. He or she will come up to you, expect to be petted and be quite tame; a different "personality".

The third puppy, the one you had no interaction with, will have little interest in interacting with you. You are just the pizza delivery boy, the one who brings him his food.

Keep in mind that a puppy's biological curiosity response, and its equally biological tendence to chew on everything, often win over training them the way you want them to be. That is why much of training occurs only after they have gone through their puppy stage.

In the real world, suppose puppies from the same genetic mold, the same litter, were each exposed to a slightly different environment. Suppose that one pup was frightened by strangers, (kids throwing rocks, etc.), a second pup had only positive petting experiences with other people, a third was roughhoused with--not enough to be scared, just enough to get a reaction--and a fourth was teased by strangers. What you might well find is that from the same litter one dog would grow up timid and fearful, the second would grow up comparatively playful, the third would love to roughhouse, even with strangers when too big to handle, and the fourth would have an exaggeratedly hostile reaction to strangers, perhaps even a fear barker.

Most children are going to meet a bully in the schoolyard, be teased by older children, be put down by others. Many will experience this from their own family. Each encounter tends to produce a lack of confidence, a feeling of helplessness, or fear to some degree. Yet each time we can help them succeed, give them emotional security, make them feel needed, make them feel their opinion is important, we help contribute to their wellbeing. We help make them a success.

The child who is allowed to win, to tackle jobs that allow success, to encounter academic and social experiences that are positive, will develop self-confidence. The child who is browbeaten by parents or peers, who rarely succeeds in academic or social encounters, may become fearful of trying. An attitude of success or failure can be conditioned by the early experiences of childhood.

That bully on the playground is no accident either. They are often a product of the same type of behavior at home. They may imitate the bullying shown by their father or an older brother or sister. It is no accident too, that of those men who physically abuse their wife or children some 70% of them report growing up in a home where their father physically abused them and their mother. That does not mean that all children who are abused will abuse their children, but patterns set early in life tend to determine how we are as adults.

There was one bully I remember from junior high school, I always wondered why he was so mean to everybody. One day I happened to end up over at his house. All the time I was there his father put him down, made fun of him and bullied him. He never spoke back to his father; he would not dare. But when he got to school, he imitated his father's behavior toward smaller kids who would not fight back. Studies have shown that the kids who were bullies in school, 25% will have a felony arrest conviction on their record within five years of getting out of high school. There are other reasons why kids become bullies, it does not require training, but this was a lesson I never forgot.

That is no longer the only cause of bullying. Today, it is often the "popular" kids who bully. If they make fun of another, they get a laugh from the kids. It is the laughter of others that ensures bullying will happen.

FAMILIARITY BREEDS FAMILARITY

Dogs and cats are considered to be natural enemies. Yet if you raise a cat and dog together from six weeks of age, they will grow up to be playmates, or at least tolerant of each other. Much of the behavior of animals that is considered "normal" may depend on the early experiences of the animal.

Most of us think of jealously as inborn, in our DNA. It is partly true, based on the biology of the amygdala; the fight-or-flight response; on the principle of two dogs with one bone. But it does not occur without experience.

Take a puppy who has never had a bone before and give him a bone. He will quickly lay down with the bone and begin to gnaw on the bone. While he is gnawing on the bone, right in front of him, you can reach down and take the bone away from him. He will not react until he sees the bone leaving, then he will try to grab it. The second time he is gnawing on the bone you can still reach down, while he is watching you, and he may even growl at you and bite down on the bone, but you can still take the bone away from him easily. The third time you start to reach for the bone, he will grab the bone and try to run away with it; a learned response in action.

Psychologist Zin Kuo reared young kittens with mouse pups. Normally, an adult cat will kill and eat a mouse if their mother did this early in their life. But when these kittens grew up, they not only did not kill other mice, but they were friendly with them. The former "enemies" now played together. The cats would roll the mice around with their paws like a ball.

Kuo found that if he shaved the hair off of the mouse, then all social amenities vanished. Hairless mice were not in the memory banks of the cat. The cat killed and ate the naked mouse.

Kuo found a remarkable degree of imitation in the killing behavior of kittens. If kittens were raised by mother cats that, for whatever reason, would kill but not eat a rat, these kittens would also learn to kill but not eat their prey.

If psychologists were asked to observe adult cats from each of these different backgrounds without knowing their background, what conclusions would they reach? If one cat kills and eats a mouse, would the cat have a "normal" cat personality? If a second cat sees a mouse and plays with it as if it were another kitten, would this be an abnormal cat... an incompetent cat... an affection seeking mouse maniac trying to make up for an early failure to fulfill its need for affection? And if a third cat kills the mouse but does not eat it... is this a sadistic personality that kills for pleasure?

SYSTEMATIC OBSERVATION AND PERSONALITY

A psychologist who observed these behaviors without knowing their origin might begin to analyze them into personality types or traits. He might even wonder at the thoughts or feelings that go through the mind of the animal when it is acting. A biologist, seeing the same patterns of behavior, might suspect that inborn genetic differences in the cat's neural wiring have led to differences in how they respond to the environment.   He might wonder if it is due to some obscure difference in biochemical makeup... too much serotonin here, too little neurotransmitter there...

"Personality type" theories and biochemical theories have come and gone. Yet none has ever produced as compelling a piece of evidence as that provided by scientists who simply change the environment of an animal and report what they observe.

CULTURE: Personality on a Grand Scale

The effect of experience on the temperament of animals is apparent. It is more difficult to determine the effect of experience on human temperament. One way is to observe the differences between different human cultures.

Anthropologists such as Ruth Benedict have studied different American Indian tribes. Others, such as Margaret Mead have studied neighboring tribes in New Guinea. In such cases, the neighboring groups of natives are very close biologically. Any differences between tribes of American Indians or tribes of New Guinea natives must be due to the experiences of the child growing up in the culture, and not a result of biological differences. A study of cultural differences is, therefore, a study of personality on a grand scale.

In *Patterns of Culture* Ruth Benedict provides an extensive evaluation of the personality differences of several major tribes. Benedict reports that the Zuni Indians of the American Southwest are relatively calm and even-tempered. For example, while adultery by a woman in a neighboring tribe may result in her being beaten or even having her nose cut off, among the Zuni, her behavior causes no great stir, and she may leave her husband at will. All she has to do is to leave his belongings outside the wikiup, he comes home, knows it is over, picks up his belongings and goes on to build another wikiup; which is probably cheaper than building another 3-2 brick. Not a word of anger may be exchanged, no divorce lawyer, no alimony.

Zuni women are also moderate in their reactions to an adulterous husband. In one case, Benedict writes: ...

> *The season before one of Dr. Bunzel's visits in Zuni, one of the young husbands of the household in which she lived had been carrying on an extramarital affair that became bruited about all over the pueblo. The family ignored the matter completely. At last the white trader, a guardian of morals, expostulated with the wife... The trader set forth with great earnestness the need of making a show of authority and putting an end to her husband's outrageous character. So, his wife said, "I didn't wash his clothes. Then he knew that I knew that everybody knew, and he stopped going with that girl." It was effective, but not a word was passed. There were no outbursts, no recriminations, not even an open recognition of the crisis.*

In contrast, the Dobuan society studied by Benedict valued aggression and hostility. Benedict notes:

> *The Dobuan, therefore, is dour, prudish, and passionate, consumed with jealousy and suspicion, and resentment. Every moment of prosperity he conceives himself to have wrung from a malicious world by a conflict in which he has worsted his opponent. The good man is the one who has many such*

conflicts to his credit, as anyone can see from the fact that he has survived with a measure of prosperity. It is taken for granted that he has thieved, killed children and his close associates by sorcery, cheated whenever he dared. As we have seen, theft and adultery are the object of the valued charms of the valued men of the community...

One of Ruth Benedict's students was Margaret Mead. In *Sex and Temperament in Three Primitive Societies*, Mead challenged even the belief that the temperamental differences between males and females are inborn. Mead studied the Arapesh culture in which males and females both develop traits that are considered feminine in western culture. The males often did the same work as the females. By contrast, many tribes have such a sharp distinction between male and female work that either would be ashamed to be seen doing the work of the other. Neither sex was expected to be aggressive, and the ideal was one of mutual cooperation and nonaggressive behavior.

In a second tribe, the Mundungumor, both males and females were physically and sexually aggressive. Tenderness was looked upon as of no value. Both sexes were ruthless in pursuing their goals. In yet another tribe, the Tchambuli, the women took on a role of being dominant in sexual and business matters. The males tended to be vain about their looks, emotionally dependent, passive, and they stayed at home to gossip and care for the children and maybe watch Oprah reruns, while their wives went to work in the fields.

In America we often see the results of our cultural conditioning in producing aggression. Following one example or another, boys may hear other males say, *"I wouldn't put up with that from her/him. Would you?"* That simple statement can determine how aggression is directed and toward whom. It is the basis of prejudice, and many other opinions.

CULTURE AS A LEARNED PHENOMENA;
"You people never stop talking"

There is a story, possibly apocryphal, of two Japanese professors who had written a brilliant paper who were invited to a conference in America. The conference was attended by other professors across the world to present their ideas. As they sat around a conference table loudly discussing their ideas and their theories, the director of the conference noticed that the two professors from Japan had said nothing all morning. In the afternoon he approached the two and asked them why they had not spoken out about their great paper. "We were taught," said one Japanese professor politely, "…that it is not polite to interrupt another when they are talking. And you people never stop talking."

We learn our manners and our culture from our mothers, from the stories told by the elders, from the fabric of our culture.

Can temperament be controlled by the expectations of the culture? History seems to bear out the conclusions of Benedict that it can. For one example, at one time the most feared nation of warriors in Europe was the Swiss pikemen. They were the most capable and fearless warriors in the mercenary armies of Italy and France until the advent of guns ended the advantage of their weapons. Today, Switzerland is a symbol of neutrality and peace.

Can temperament be conditioned in males and females by the expectations of culture? Mead's findings seem supported by work by Money, Hampson, and Hampson at Johns Hopkins University, who studied the sexual behavior of nearly one hundred children born as hermaphrodites, with the sexual apparatus of both males and females. The researchers found that twenty-three of their patients had been reared in a sexual role that was opposite of what their biological sex type would indicate, and all but one continued in the sex role in which they had been reared.

The pink and blue blanket syndrome that greets the newborn infant in our culture influences much more than the female and male preference for color; it influences their behavior, their sex desires, and their temperament. But how can our culture have such a pronounced effect on our likes and dislikes?

How does culture mold the individual to prefer one pattern of behavior over another or one temperament over another? For one thing, we reward males for "masculine" traits such as bravery, we encourage them to play rough-and-tumble games, and we shame them as "sissies" when they cry or play with "sissy" toys. At the same time, females are encouraged to take an interest in "little Suzie Homemaker" type toys, they are discouraged or actively shamed for playing rough or dirty games, and they are held and allowed to cry. Our culture encourages such differences from the very moment that we select the pink or blue blanket for the infant's bed.

A study of American society found that when females have problems they are encouraged to talk about the problem. Yet when males try to talk about a problem, they are likely to be ignored or brushed off by another male or female. Strikingly, this even held to be true of children. When little girls had a problem, they were likely to be listened to and helped. When little boys had a problem, they were likely to be told to "work it out yourself" or to "be a big boy".

Both males and females in our society tend to react this way. It is hardly surprising that, as adults, males are less willing to talk about their problems. They have learned from vivid experience that other people will think less of them if they do. It should also not be too surprising that males occasionally commit suicide and leave behind others who say "he never said a word about having a problem".

Such subtle conditioning seems to play a crucial role in the molding of the child's life goals. For the most part, this conditioning goes on all the time in an unplanned and unintended way. It may depend on nothing more than a series of random experiences in the peer group of a child during a critical time in life. But the direction a child's interests take may set the course of the rest of his life.

THE STUDY of INDIVIDUAL DIFFERENCES

The study of personality is a study of individual differences. Each of us is an individual because each varies somewhat from every other person. These variations are not just physical variations of height, weight, and shape, they are also variations in individual reactions. Some of us are either slow or quick to anger, some are shy or fearful, while others go "where angels fear..." some are adept at physical sports while others are quick of mind. Yet if these variations are so random, so unpredictable, so capricious, how is it possible to study them?

The answer is that even capricious disorder conforms to a certain order: in this case, the "law of chance"; the normal probability curve. All genetic traits may vary. But the variation is distributed in much the same manner as the roll of dice. We cannot predict the outcome of a single shot in the dark that leads to conception. We cannot predict an individual unborn child's height, weight, or I.Q. Yet for great numbers of such rolls of the dice, we can predict the result with admirable accuracy.

Some genetic variation is a heads or tails affair. Sex is one such trait. Flip a coin. Heads or tails? Either the child is a boy or a girl. Occasionally the coin lands on its edge, and we get a hermaphrodite, which has physical traits of both sexes, but even this permutation may be statistically predicted from our past knowledge of its frequency of occurrence. We know how often it happens in any large group.

Most traits are more complex than sex. Height results from a combination of genes regulating growth hormones and bone length. Height even depends on the nutrition available in the environment. Yet a predictable few of us will be very tall, a few will be very short, and most of us will fall at points in between. If genetic factors influence the temperament of a child, then we would expect this to follow the same pattern. Thus, a few of us may inherit genes that make us tend to be very fearful, a few may be genetically disposed to be "fearless," and most of us would fall somewhere between the two extremes.

In summary, biological individuality is assured: No two individuals, except identical twins that came when the same egg divides into two separate individual cells with the same genes, can have exactly the same genetic structure any more than they can have the same fingerprints. Further, order exists among the disorder: All individuals vary, and they vary predictably. This variation is predictable because it is distributed according to the law of chance; the Normal Distribution Curve.

Psychologists believe that any psychological trait with a genetic base would also be distributed in the same manner. Second, and just as important, order exists because there is a tendency for parents to pass on similar genetic traits to their children. Thus, tall parents tend to have tall children, and presumably, shy parents would tend to have shy children, bold parents to have bold children, and so on.

The problem now becomes one of finding and studying the genetic factors that influence personality. The geneticist had to measure and control the trait (sex, height, smooth or wrinkled peas) before he could find order among the disorder. The psychologist must measure and control a far greater number of variables before he can find order in human personality.

7

THE GREAT MYSTERY
OF BIOLOGICAL
PROGRAMS IN OUR DNA

If you want to solve the oldest mystery in psychology, of how much of our mind is due to our biology (nature) and how much is due to learning (nurture), the famous *Nature vs. Nurture* controversy, the first place you would look for the biological basis of the mind is with what is essential for survival. What is essential for the survival of the individual is (1) maternal "instincts", how to care for our young and how to find food. (2) Sex; which is essential for the survival of the species. How much is written into our DNA and how much is learned?

The mystery was posed by philosopher John Locke, who is perhaps most famous because Thomas Jefferson wrote much of his ideas into the Declaration of Independence. He posed the famous question of the origin of knowledge; does it spring from within awaiting only experience to bring it out? Or is it learned by experience in the environment?

Suppose that a man was born blind were suddenly given his sight. Would he know the difference between a circle and a square? Would he know the difference between his sweetheart and a lamp post? Where does knowledge come from?

Locke answered that the mind at birth is like a "tabula rasa", a blank slate, devoid of knowledge or understanding: Much like Einstein who said, *"All knowledge is from experience."* Yet it is common to hear in psychology textbooks that "we know now that the brain is more than a tabula rasa". And the brain indeed contains biological programs that make speech possible; Brocca's area and Wernicke's area. But we have known that since the 1800s.

Sometimes psychologists look aghast at anyone who says the mind is a tabula rasa today, yet it all depends on what you think "knowledge" is. It is important to remind ourselves that Locke and Einstein were both talking about knowledge. What do we *know*? What do we *understand*? They were not talking about programmed behavior as in instincts. What is it we will see when we look inside the brain at the "instincts" for survival we see in all species?

INSTINCT: WHAT
DNA WRITES INTO OUR BRAIN

What is the origin of the abilities that make up the biological basis of our behavior? One of the first scientists to begin to crack the code that DNA writes into our brain was Konrad Lorenz. Lorenz started to go into the medical profession but found he liked studying animals more than people. He went on to win the Nobel Prize for his work.

Lorenz started out studying the behavior of Graylag Geese. In watching their behavior, he was struck by the fact that the goslings begin following their mother around shortly after birth. He wondered what would happen if the first thing these goslings saw after birth was not their mother, but instead Konrad Lorenz? It was dirt simple science; the best kind.

Collecting some of the eggs in the wild, he became the first thing the babies saw after they hatched. They saw Lorenz walking around. They fell in line behind him like goslings in the wild following their real mother. They followed him everywhere he went, even going into the river and swimming around with him.

Lorenz found that there seemed to be a Critical period when these goslings would imprint to their mother or any figure, they saw walking around. He thought this period was zero to two days after birth. By that, he meant that, after two days of following Lorenz around, if their real mother came along, they would run away from their real mother and continue to follow Lorenz.

We know today that this critical period is not quite as critical as Lorenz thought. Eckhard Hess found the most critical period for ducklings was about one to three weeks after birth. In fact, you could take them away from their first "mother" and imprint them to someone or something else, even their real mother. Even more, you could imprint them to two different mothers, human and duck "mothers".

The point at which they can no longer imprint to just anyone seems to come at the point where the fear of novel stimuli, or stranger anxiety in human children develops. This is 2-3 months for cats, dogs, and monkeys, about 9 months for human children. Once they become afraid of new stimuli, they will not easily imprint to new stimuli.

WHAT IS LEFT OUT OF THE TEXTBOOKS:
Blind Instinct and Beer

At the University of Chicago, Eckhard Hess and his students found something even more remarkable. His graduate students, possibly after getting bored with their success, hit upon a bizarre idea. What would happen, they wondered, if the first thing the ducklings saw when they hatched was not their real mother or even a human "mother" but instead, a moving beer bottle?

They took a long-necked beer bottle, apparently after having emptied several, tied a string around the neck of the bottle, and when the ducklings hatched, they moved it around by the string. The ducklings quickly began following the moving beer bottle all around the room quacking, in effect, "mama, mama".

These ducklings are not born "knowing "anything at all about who their mother is or even what their mother looks like. Instead, they have an inborn biological program in the brain that tells them to follow anything that moves. That was a profound revelation. Just as clearly, they are not born "knowing" even what *species* they are. None of this is in their DNA, it is recorded in their mind code, S-S associations, the images in their mind, the stimulus imprint on their brain.

The instinct hunters such as Konrad Lorenz used terms such as "releasing mechanism" to describe what triggers the behavior and "Fixed Action Pattern" or FAP to describe what today we would call an inborn biological program in the brain. Instead, we are going to call them by simpler terms, common to both biology and psychology; that is "Stimulus" for the trigger and "Response" for the inborn biological program in the brain that determines the behavior.

In effect, you have a Stimulus, "motion", which triggers an inborn biological response, "following."

STIMULUS   RESPONSE

Motion ------------------- Following

This is a critically important survival mechanism in most species. If the ducklings or goslings had not had a program for following their mother, if they had just scattered in all directions on their own, predators would quickly have eaten them. Staying close to their mothers, who have learned where to go and what to avoid, is important for their survival.

Nor is it limited to birds. I was walking down the street in front of my house one day while there were two kids across the street playing games. They had about a four-month-old puppy in the yard, which they were largely ignoring. When the puppy saw me walking, he quickly ran over and fell in right behind me. After walking about fifty feet I turned to look at the puppy. He looked up at me and I guess he did not like what he saw, because he yelped, and ran back where he came from. You see imprinting in a wide variety of species.

In Australia, widely known for their sheep herding, they tell the story of a family that adopted an orphaned baby sheep. He lived with people for the first several months. They decided that they must put him back out into the pasture with the other sheep, thinking he would join the other sheep. But in the sheep pen, the little sheep avoided the other sheep and they avoided him. He would stay as close as possible to the house and bleat pitifully whenever a person came out of the house. He was not a sheep; he was a people.

Long before Lorenz, our ancestors used the imprinting mechanism to domesticate animals. Sheepherders would wait until a Ewe gave birth to her kids. Then they would take a puppy, not long after birth, and put it in with the Ewe's kids. This has to be done within the first four hours after the Ewe gives birth, or it will not take. The Ewe will learn the scents of all of her kids, and then reject any other mother's kid or puppy.

The sheepherders would then double imprint the puppy, both to sheep and humans. As the puppy grew up with the sheep, they would accept him as a sheep. Because the puppy grew up with sheep, it would never consider them prey as a normal dog would. As an adult dog, the dogs have a more forceful personality than sheep, so the dog would become the leader of the pack. The humans would now train the dog to come when he was called, and all the other sheep would follow his lead.

More than this, because the dog now considered himself a sheep-person, when a wolf, coyote, or another dog came around looking for a meal, the sheepdog would bark and chase them away.

When cats and dogs grow up together, they do not consider each other as enemies, but more like brother and sister. Other psychologists have raised mice and kittens together. One even raised a chick with a kitten. The kitten would play roughly with the chick, rolling him around with his paw, but never attempted to harm the chick. The two were separated shortly after and years later the chick had grown up to be a rooster.

The psychologist wanted to see if the rooster still remembered his early experience with a cat. He brought in another cat, one who had not been raised with a chick. The cat looked at the rooster. The rooster looked at the cat. The rooster began clucking and went directly toward the cat. The cat began to freak out and started running away from the rooster, with the rooster in pursuit.

The profound implication of all of this is that these animals did not know what their mother looked like. They did not even know what species they were. All of this depended on learning on top of the biological program for imprinting already in the brain.

FEEDING INSTINCTS:

Why Chicks Choose a

Red and White Stripped Pencil over their Mother

Why would chicks ignore a realistic-looking mother and instead, spend most of their time with a pencil painted with red and white stripes?

Niko Tinbergen, a Dutch naturalist who along with Konrad Lorenz won the Nobel Prize for his work, was studying how instincts develop in Herring Gulls. He noticed that baby chicks, shortly after birth, would peck at the red spot on their mother's beak. The mother would then regurgitate half-digested food for her chicks. Much like Lorenz, with his dirt simple science, Tinbergen wondered if the red spot on the mother's beak had anything to do with the chick's behavior.

After capturing several baby chicks, he developed cardboard cutouts similar to the mother's head and beak. Some were very realistically drawn, and some bore little resemblance to a bird, except for a red spot on the end. Amazingly, the chicks treated the cardboard models as if they were their real mother, pecking at the red spot enthusiastically and repeatedly. When he tried the same models without the red spot, he got little response from the chicks.

Extensive studies found that the color red, or contrast (a gray beak with a white spot was almost as effective) were the stimuli that triggered the chick's begging response. But this was a symbiotic relationship. There is also a maternal instinct that triggers the regurgitating of half-digested food by the mother.

In effect, neither "know" what they are doing; these are automatic responses, not much different from the automatic responses by the figures in a computer game. If you shoot the "bad guy" five times, he explodes. He does not explode because he "knows" he has been shot five times; he explodes because the computer is programmed to respond this way.

	STIMULUS	**RESPONSE**
In chicks	Red Spot ---------------------	Pecking at the red spot
In mom	Pecking at her beak----------	Regurgitating food

The ultimate proof of what was happening comes with another bit of information that is left out of the textbooks.   Tinbergen took a pencil and painted it with red and white stripes. He then gave the chicks a choice between pecking at a realistic-looking gull head with a red spot or pecking at the pencil with red and white stripes. The chicks ignored the realistic-looking head and spent twice as much of their time enthusiastically pecking at the pencil with the red and white stripes.   The chicks had no awareness of what they were doing; they were only responding to red and contrast.

Tinbergen showed convincingly that there are biological programs in the brain of both chicks and mothers that control feeding behavior. Birds do not live for more than a few years in the wild. They have no time to learn these behaviors. The only way they could survive is if these mechanisms were biologically programmed into the brain.

He also showed convincingly that they have absolutely no conscious awareness of what they are doing. They are simply responding to the stimuli their genes have written into the biological programs in their brain.

Primatologist Jane Goodall has a remarkable movie on The Wild Dogs of Africa. Although I have never seen this behavior in domestic dogs, the wild dogs behave much like Tinbergen's Herring Gulls. She digs a den into the earth and has her pups in the den. After they get a bit older, she has to go hunting and cannot take the pups along. She makes a kill far away from the den and eats all she can. She has no hands to carry it back. When she gets back to the den, the pups nip repeatedly at the muzzle of the mother, causing her to regurgitate food.

INSTINCTS:

MONKEYS, APES, AND HUMAN

In the higher animals, monkeys, apes, and humans do we have biological programs in our brains? Of course. Some of the most important work ever done that applies to humans was done by psychologist Harry Harlow at Wisconsin. Harlow was trying to raise baby Rhesus monkeys in a laboratory setting. He gave them all the food and water they could have needed to survive. Yet he found that when they grew up, they were fearful and incompetent as mothers.

The one thing Harlow found that is every bit as important as food and water for normal development was the one thing the monkeys did not get;" contact comfort". Harlow studied how profound an effect contact comfort has on the mind's normal development.

He started by raising baby Rhesus monkeys with a choice of mothers; a wire cylinder that had a bottle of milk, and a wire cylinder, wrapped in a terry cloth towel, with no milk. He quickly found that, unlike previous theories, the monkeys spent eighty percent of their time clinging to the soft terry cloth mother that had no milk, and only went to the wire mother when they were hungry.

But that is not the most important finding Harlow made. Even textbooks rarely include the most significant discovery he made. What is critically important is what he did next. He took the monkeys, after several months with their cloth mother, and put them, one at a time, into a fear stimulus room. In his films, the fear stimulus room looks like someone's dirty basement.

The room contained many stimuli that the monkey had never seen before, novel stimuli. We know from decades of experience, that all mammals are afraid of novel, or new, stimuli they have never seen before. In human children, this is called "stranger anxiety" and begins about nine months of age. But it has to do with the inborn fear of novel stimuli, not just strangers.

When put into this fear stimuli room, filled with common objects like pieces of paper, a coat hanger, toy blocks, the monkeys were struck with terror. They huddled in a corner at the edge of the room, clutching themselves. They were so fear-stricken that they would not explore the room, but remained huddled and clutching themselves.

Then Harlow put the terrycloth "mother" they had been raised with, into the room with the frightened monkey. His response was electric. He ran to his terrycloth mother, grabbed tightly to her, rubbed his body up and down on her. Shortly after getting his contact comfort, the monkey relaxed, slid down the mother, and started to explore the fearful stimuli. He grabbed a piece of paper. When the paper moved, he ran back and touched base with his mother. But now he began to explore the fearful stimuli. As long as his terrycloth "mother" was there, he became more and more fearless.

The truly important discovery of Harlow was that contact comfort, grabbing hold of his mother, reduced his fear. This is a clear survival reflex. In the wilds of Africa, baby monkeys stay safely close to their mother. The farther they travel away from their mother, the more novel fear stimuli they encounter. If the lookout of the troop spots a leopard or hyena, the lookout will let out a whoop. This scares the monkey, and he runs to his mother, and grabs hold of her fur. The mother cannot save her infant if he wanders off. But now, with the baby grabbing hold of the fur on the underneath of her stomach, she can escape to the trees using her hands and feet.

Without this survival reflex, the species would have disappeared long ago. What is happening is a simple stimulus-response reaction:

<u>STIMULUS</u>   **<u>RESPONSE</u>**

Contact Comfort ------------------------------ **Fear Reduction**

Have you ever brought a new puppy or new kitten home for the first time? What do they do when left by themselves at night? They cry. This is also a survival mechanism. If they wander away from the nest, they encounter fearful, novel stimuli. This triggers a fear response, along with crying. When the mother hears them cry, she goes to find them, picks them up by the scruff of the neck, and brings them back to the nest.

What happens then is most important. After they are returned to the nest, the mother licks them vigorously, analogous to contact comfort in monkeys. This causes them to relax, and the fear goes away. In extensive studies by Saul Shandberg, they found that if rat pups are removed from the mother, they display marked anxiety and even a deterioration of their biological hormones regulating growth.

The only way to correct this behavior, other than returning them to the mother, is to stroke them vigorously with a one-inch paintbrush, in the same manner as the mother would. This calms them down and reduces their fear the way a mother would do by vigorously licking them. So now you know. If you ever bring a newborn puppy or kitten home, and it starts to cry during the night, be sure and lick it vigorously.

Many studies have since been done with human infants who were born prematurely. In similar studies by Tiffany Fields, she found that if you give a premature baby fifteen minutes of massage, three times a day, while in the hospital, they will gain forty-seven percent more weight than premature infants who do not get such a massage. The contact comfort of the massage seems to reduce the anxiety that they otherwise might feel. And if you are frightened, you lose any feelings of hunger as the brain focuses on the most salient emotion.

Identical behavior has been seen in human children reared in orphanages. In separate studies by John Bowlby and Rene Spitz, they found babies with no mothers would waste away, showing a medical condition called "failure to thrive". A few of them even died for no apparent cause. In Bowlby's study, he demonstrates that these babies would at first engage in crying, the type of behavior most likely to lead to their mother's picking them up and reducing their fear. But in the orphanage, they received little care from the caretakers except to feed and change them. In his documentary of their behavior, those babies who have been there for some time no longer even could be comforted by contact comfort, they would continue to cry even if someone tried to hold and comfort them.

Why did they waste away? If you are scared, all of the brain's attention is focused on the fear, not on the hunger. It was a tragic reminder when recently our government took hundreds of babies and young children away from their mothers and put their mothers in prison for "illegally" coming to America, even though it is quite legal to seek asylum. The children, some 3,000 of all ages, were kept in cages, some given up for adoption.

Only following outrage at the Trump administration's callous disregard for the children, and a court order, was there any attempt by the government to reunite the children with their parents. When the parents were finally reunited with their own children months later, these children often failed to recognize their own mothers. In one video the mother is crying and hugging her son, as her son stares vacantly off into space, showing no reaction. Many of these sad stories were captured on video by the press. More than 600, were never returned to their mothers or relatives.

In real life, if a mother were to treat her child the way our government treated these children, she would be arrested and charged with child abuse. But if the government does it…

I was in a supermarket once where there was a mother and her older son, about four years old. The boy was playing with something on the shelf and not paying attention to his mother. The mother walked around to the next aisle, still not far away. When the boy looked up and did not see his mother, he panicked. He started to cry, "Mama, mama" and was running up and down the aisles in the wrong direction, looking for his mother becoming even more frightened when he could not find her. It ended happily of course, but it is a vivid reminder of just how powerful this Stimulus-Response behavior is, even in humans.

One of Harlow's studies, usually left out of textbooks, tells us something important about abusive parents. He took a monkey, already imprinted to a terry cloth mother, and temporarily removed him from his mother. While the monkey was out of the room, Harlow arranged for a hose to be run from a compressed air machine to the front of the terry cloth mother.   Then he put the monkey back into the room. When the monkey ran to his mother and tried to cling to her, he would get hit in the face with a blast of compressed air. It was not harmful, but it is intensely frightening to a monkey.

What would the monkey do when he got hit in the face with a blast of compressed air from his mother? Some might think he would run away from the now frightening stimuli. But no, he did the only thing he had learned to do to reduce his fear; he clung even more tightly to the punishing mother.

If you work in medicine or psychology or social work you may have occasion to see a child taken away from an abusive parent. You might expect the child would be glad to get away. No, like Harlow's monkey, they cling even more tightly; cry even more piteously, when taken away. Even abusive parents are not abusive all of the time and the learned behavior of reducing his fear by running to his mother is incredibly powerful.

There is a popular urban myth, especially among men, that you don't want your male child to grow up a "mamas-boy". You sometimes see fathers shaming their son's for running to their mothers crying when they are upset. "You don't wanna be a mamas-boy, do you?" but studies suggest that children who are allowed to reduce their fears, by running to their mother, or father, for contact comfort, develop independence sooner than those who are shamed or punished for doing so, just as the infant monkey in the fear stimulus room would be too afraid to explore when his mother was not there, but eagerly explored when she was. Common sense does not always turn out to be right.

I hasten to point out that there are multiple causes for similar behavior. Harlow's study does not mean that children who are afraid around others are being abused by their mother. If an only child is not raised around other children, he would be more afraid when starting school. Not because he was abused, but just because of the fear of novelty, the "stranger anxiety" that is common in all species.

COMPLEX BIOLOGICAL PROGRAMS:

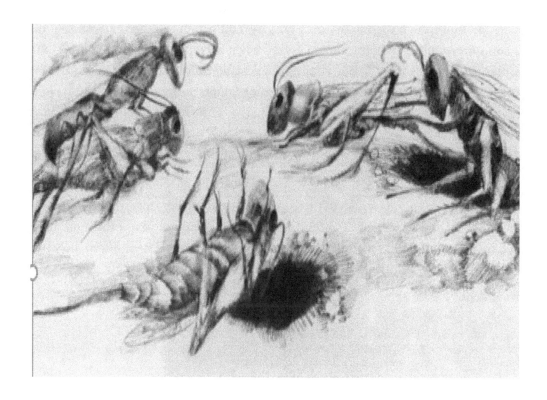

Jean Henri Fabre found that the female Sphex wasp has a very complex program for taking care of her young. When she is ready to lay eggs, she digs a hole in the ground, hollows out an area, and then lays her eggs. But before she seals the nest, she goes out to hunt for a cricket, which she seems to do by zeroing in on the scent given off by crickets.

She stings the cricket, which paralyzes, but does not kill the cricket. Then she takes the stunned cricket back to her nest, leaves it just outside the door of her hole, goes inside the hole, turns around three times, goes back for the cricket, takes it inside the hole for the young wasps to feast on when they hatch, seals up the hole and leaves forever.

Now that is incredibly complex behavior for a wasp. How does she "know" how to do all of this?

The secret becomes clear with a simple experiment from Fabre. When the wasp brings the cricket back, she first leaves it outside the hole. Then she goes into the hole and turns around three times (this seems to be to chase out any ants or spiders that might have fallen in the hole).

Wait until after she leaves the cricket outside the hole and then goes inside. While she is inside the hole turning around you move the cricket four inches away from the hole.   When she comes out of the hole and does not find the cricket there, she goes and retrieves the cricket again, brings it back to just outside the hole, goes inside the hole… now if you again move the cricket four inches away from where she left it, when she comes out of the hole, she once again retrieves the cricket, goes inside the hole, turns around three times, and…

At least up to a point, the wasp will, again and again, retrieve the cricket, bring it back to the hole, etc. If you are in computer programming, you will recognize this as what happens when you get caught in a DO LOOP, an IF-THEN statement, or a decision diamond. The only decision a computer can make is based on a decision diamond. The computer executes statement after statement in the program. In the decision diamond you will find a comparison statement such as; *if* X=Y *then* go to the *next* step in the program. If X does not equal Y, then return to a *previous* step in the program.

When the wasp cannot find the cricket outside the hole, even if it is only inches away from where the wasp left the cricket, the wasp has to return to a previous step of the program, retrieve the cricket and again go inside and turn around three times, before completing the program.

This wasp has no more cognitive understanding of what it is doing than the frog-eating BBs. It has not the slightest awareness of why it does what it does.   It blindly follows the program just as surely as the figures in the computer game DOOM shoot at the monsters five times and the monsters explode. They do not explode because they "want to", they do not explode because they "know" they have been shot five times, they do it because that is the sequence embedded in the computer software at a given statement.

Even in a computer game, they write some variability into the program, random variables, so that it does not always behave predictably. Nature itself also has some variability because the programs are never perfect.

Hypothetical computer flowchart of Fabre's wasp.

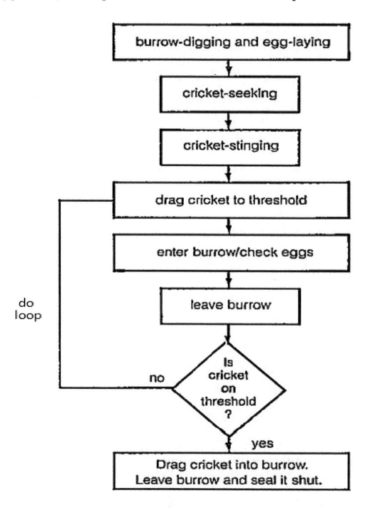

THE GREAT BEHAVIORIST
AS AN ETHOLOGIST:
Watson's Mystery at Bird Key

One of the most forgotten of all the contributions of the early psychologists is a remarkable puzzle discovered by John B. Watson. You never find this story in textbooks, although it has been reenacted by the BBC for their series on the great naturalists. Early in his career, Watson followed closely in the footsteps of the great naturalists like Lorenz and Tinbergen. He spent time on Bird Key, off the east coast of the United States observing the behavior of the sooty tern. His observations rival some of the observations of Lorenz and Tinbergen.

Bird Key has no humans, no dogs, and no predators. It is a small island inhabited almost solely by crabs and birds. With no natural predators, the birds nest out in the open very close to each other. They make a scrape in the sand and lay their eggs in the sand. Then they sit on them until the eggs hatch. Watson was amazed at how the birds came directly back to their own nest each time. Did they "know" they were coming back to hatch their own eggs?

Watson devised an ingenious technique to find out. It was dirt simple science. Watson simply waited until the terns left the nest. While they were away, he moved the egg in the nest four inches to the left. When the tern returned, would it go to the egg, or to the scrape in the ground, their nest?

The tern returned. She looked at the egg. She looked at the nest. She looked at the egg again. Then she settled on the empty nest. They showed her going through the motions to tuck the egg underneath her, even though the egg was in plain sight just four inches away. For about fifteen seconds the tern fussed over an imaginary egg underneath her, clearly ignoring the visible egg.

Finally, the tern retrieved the egg. Decades later, zoologists discovered that terns do have an egg retrieval program in their brain. If you put golf balls all around the nest of a tern it will eventually retrieve every one of those golf balls and sit on them until they hatch, or at least until they get very tired and the other terns have flown off.

A strange aside from this, a few years ago a bale of marijuana washed up on the shore of one of the keys. The terns got into the marijuana. The newsman who reported the event quipped that "the incident left no tern un-stoned."

In David Attenborough's new classic *Seven Worlds* he shows an identical example in Antarctica. Here, the Albatross tend to their chicks with great ability. But when high winds knocked a chick out of its nest, and its parent came back, the parent settled on its nest. It repeatedly ignored the chick, just outside its nest, despite repeatedly cheeping desperately for attention. The parent ignored the futile cheeping of its own chick in favor of the nest. Only after repeated attempts by the chick to climb into its nest, did it succeed. Then and only then, the parent reacted to it as its' own chick.

Left: Albatross parent with a chick. Sir David Attenborough found, similar to Watson, that if the chick fell out of this high nest, the parent would return to sitting on the nest and ignore the chick, pitifully crying and trying to get back in the nest. If it cannot get back into the high nest on its own, it will not survive.

Once again, we see nothing in animal "instincts" that indicates any "knowledge" of what they are doing or why. It is a matter of biological survival responses programmed into the brain. The terns or the albatross do not live long enough to learn how to care for their chicks, this has to be programmed into the brain by their genes or their species would not survive.

BIOLOGICAL MYSTERIES
OF THE HUMAN MIND:

Humans also have survival responses built into their brains. What is hidden in the deep levels of our brain?

The most basic feeding reflex is seen in a baby's sucking reflex. All you need to do is brush the lips lightly and the baby begins sucking automatically. It would be hard to teach such a reflex if it was not built-in. The Rooting reflex is incredibly important in most species. That is the behavior that triggers a newborn kitten or puppy to "root" around, even though it is born blind, until it finds a nipple and latches on. The only vestige of that reflex in human babies is to respond automatically to the sense of touch on a cheek. If you brush the left cheek the baby will turn its head to the left. If you brush the right cheek, the baby will turn its head to the left.

Fathers are often proud to show others that his baby boy is so strong that if you stroke his palms with your finger, the baby will grab hold of the fingers and the father can lift the baby completely off of the bed, just through the strength in his hands. Of course, girl babies can do this too, but strength is not as prized in daughters so it may go ignored. There is a classic photo of a nurse who has a newborn baby in the nursery that has grabbed hold of her thumbs as she lifts the baby completely off of her crib.

This palmar reflex for the hands and the planter reflex for the feet have little value in humans but it is a powerful survival mechanism for all of our ancestors. This is what a newborn baby monkey or ape uses to hold on to the fur on the underside or back of its mother. Their feet are also hands, and with this strength, the baby will hold on to the mother in times of danger, so the mother can escape through the trees, since they cannot carry the baby and move on too

The mothers use all fours, they cannot carry their babies. In humans, the grasping reflexes are only a vestige of a reflex that was once essential for survival.

The crying reflex is nature's way of telling the mother that something is wrong. It does not tell her what is wrong, just that something is wrong. Many mothers say they can tell what the problem is by the intensity of the cry. A shrill cry means pain. It may be colic or getting caught in the arms of a crib. A moderate cry may mean the baby is hungry. A low-level cry may mean the baby is wet and needs the diaper changed.

But the one extraordinary survival mechanism for human infants, a mechanism no other species has, is the social **smile** reflex. It may not be present for several days or weeks after birth, but it is powerful. When the mother makes faces at the baby or coos at the baby, the baby responds with giggling and cooing and the profound social smile.

A human baby has the most prolonged period of total dependency of any species. It is a grueling, prolonged period of infancy and childhood dependency. Some say the dependency does not end until they marry and leave home. Some say that even then they come back.

The social smile may be the only thing that has saved the human species, because it is the only thing that keeps us from throwing out the baby with the bath. No other animal has the same survival response as a baby's smile and their giggles and coos. This is seriously important because the social smile, along with the giggles and coos, help establish the relationship between the baby and parents. It is not just contact-comfort that establishes the connection. Otherwise, the incredibly long period of dependency on the parents might not end well. Studies suggest that those babies who do not smile as much, such as males, do not get as much attention from their mothers.

WHY WERE THE FACTS
OF LIFE CENSORED?

For over a hundred years when children asked where they came from they were told "the stork brought you" or "we found you under a cabbage leaf" hence, the "Cabbage Patch Kids"

We long believed that the truth about where babies come from was too indelicate to tell to our children, or even adults. No other species, and few other cultures, have ever had such an attitude toward sex and birth. Today, we still censor much from our children. A "real" newborn baby is commonly covered with blood and amniotic fluid and often, excrement. The nurse will clean this off before it is ever shown to the parent, and it is always censored from our television and our schools. New parents might be shocked.

SCIENTISTS ARE PRISONERS
OF THEIR PERCEPTIONS:
Is Behavior Innate or Learned or an Interaction?

Even scientists are captives of their perceptions. How much of human behavior is biological and innate? How much is learned? The answer to that question depends on what we are talking about. If you think in terms of the difference between an ape and a human, much of the difference seems totally biological, at first. Humans and parrots can speak, apes cannot. The *ability* to learn language is innate, biological, programmed into our brain by our genes. A scientist who only looks at this, will say nature rules. Without a brain, learning could not occur.

The understanding of language, the emotions attached to words, what we comprehend, our motivation, the ideas embedded in our brain, the associations of ideas, is a product of learning. If you think about the difference between one human being and another human, or one culture and another culture, the difference is overwhelmingly programmed by the environment. A scientist who looks only at this will say learning rules.

Whether you are thinking of a difference between an ape and a human or the difference between one individual and another, a scientist's perception determines what we look at, and how we would answer that question. The current bias is to dismiss this as "all an interaction between biology and learning". To dismiss it as "all an interaction" is just another bias that ignores what is important to understand.

We must understand what is *biological* and what is *learned* and what is an *interaction and how all this works*.

Not in our genes, but in our environment, lie the subtle forces that shape and determine our mind: our thoughts, our beliefs, our behavior, our very perception of reality. Experience shapes our personality, our politics, our sexual interests, our goals in life, our fantasies, even our success and failure in life.

8

THE ORGANIZATION
OF KNOWLEDGE
COGNITION AND CREATIVITY

"Knowledge is power." *It is nothing of the sort! Knowledge is only potential power. It becomes power only when and if it is organized into definite plans and directed to a definite end.*

Napoleon Hill

An Israeli anthropologist tells about interviewing children who immigrated from an iron curtain country at the end of WWII. These children could read... but they could only read upside down and backward!

Why? Was the wiring in their brain backward? Did they suffer from some unique form of dyslexia? Was it the final proof that our brains determine our ability?

These children grew up in a poor village where they had little opportunity to read and few books. Yet each week they went to be taught by the Rabbi. Their teacher would sit and read from the Torah, his finger moving along under each word he spoke. The children would sit directly across from him at the table, watching him move his finger under the words as he spoke them.

They were not formally taught, they learned simply from the *association* between the word he spoke, and the upside-down figures they saw on the book as he moved his finger under the words he read.

Words written on a piece of white paper have no inherent meaning. They acquire meaning only by what they have associated with.

Chinese writing looks like gibberish to Americans. It makes no sense. Yet any eight-year-old Chinese child can easily read it.

The association of ideas is basic to learning.

Educator Edward Thorndike showed decades ago that animals and people learn by one of the most basic of processes... by trial-and-error. When faced with a completely new problem, any animal or human will fumble around until he happens on to a solution. This is still learning by association, but it implies an active participation by the individual.

But what is the creative process? And what about our ability to think and reason and change our mind? The question now becomes "What is the origin of thought." What happens at the moment of a sudden change in perspective? What about insight? What about creative thinking? Are there forms of learning that are more important than trial-and-error and conditioning?

Psychologists have often expressed the idea that we are more than the sum of our separate experiences in the Gestalt statement that *"The whole is greater than the sum of its parts."* If you spread out all the separate components of a computer, this array of parts would not be the computer. The computer is the sum of its parts, *plus* the organization of those parts. When assembled, the computer can do a great deal: without this organization, it is nothing. Inadequately wired, it is still nothing. By analogy, we too are more than the separate, discrete bits of data that are fed into us. We are that, plus the organization of these data.

If we wanted to learn about the functioning of a computer, we would have to study more than its parts. We would have to study the computer as it was being programmed and as it was functioning as a whole. Similarly, if we wish to learn about human behavior, we must also study ourselves as we are "programmed", as we gain knowledge, and we must study behavior as a product of the organized whole.

Cognition, awareness, and thought all describe the process that allows us to "work" problems in our mind without having to go through the fumble and find of trial-and-error learning.

What is "thought"? What is this flexibility of behavior that allows us to solve problems "in our mind" without having to experience them? Do we have some innate power of reasoning that exists independent of experience?

We often present Human creativity and intelligence as magical and mystical abilities. We talk of them almost as if they existed as actual characteristics. But do they? To understand what creativity and intelligence are, we must start with the most basic, and least magical of discoveries, the discovery of how learning occurs in animals and children.

This is especially important too, because those who are unaware of what the mystical terms of intelligence and creativity mean, may expect too much of their children or themselves.

KOHLER: THE ISLAND OF CHIMPANZEES

In the Spanish-owned Canary Islands, where Columbus stopped for provisions before his epic voyage to the new world, is an undistinguished island known as Tenerife. At the outbreak of World War I, psychologist Wolfgang Kohler was studying the behavior of chimpanzees at the Berlin Anthropoid Station on this equatorial island. Kohler probably did not intend to stay on Tenerife for long, but war has a way of influencing the best-laid plans. Kohler stayed for seven years.

What did Kohler do during those seven years in paradise? Kohler wrote of the personalities, foibles, and idiosyncrasies of our first cousins, the chimpanzees. And when Kohler wrote, he wrote well. Kohler's book *The Mentality of Apes* is still one of the most readable works by a psychologist ever published. It was almost ten years after the initial publication of his work, however, before it was translated into English.

It seemed to many of his readers that if Kohler's observations were accurate, then Thorndike's meticulous studies of trial-and-error learning would have little application to apes and humans. Kohler believed that learning happened in sudden jumps, or "insight" rather than fumble and find. His studies suggested that learning by trial and error was mechanistic, superficial, and irrelevant to many learning situations.

Was Kohler correct? Or, as other psychologists were to argue, had he missed something? The issue was joined. Was learning by trial and error or by insight? Was one more important than the other? Not since the nature-nurture controversy began had psychology seen a debate of quite this importance and magnitude. And not until very recently have we come close to resolving the question.

TRIAL AND ERROR OR INSIGHT?

Is trial and error necessary for problem-solving? Kohler arranged a problem that would allow him to observe how the chimps solved a "new" problem. They led a young chimpanzee named Sultan down a corridor from the courtyard into a room. While the chimp watched, Kohler opened a window onto the courtyard and dropped a banana outside the window.

The chimp was familiar with both the room and the courtyard from prior experience. Would he know to retrace his steps back into the yard to get the banana, or would he stand at the window staring at the spot where he last saw the banana?

Sultan had never seen the problem before, but by the time Kohler had closed the window, Sultan was racing out of the door, and down the corridor to the playground. When Kohler got back to the window to observe his progress, Sultan was already enjoying the banana.

They repeated the observation using a dog with meat as a reward. The dog jumped on the window once and then raced out the door after the meat. Both the chimp and the dog had previous experience inside and outside the house. Yet even though they had never performed this task, no trial and error was necessary.

Kohler went on to more complex tasks involving the use of tools to solve problems. The problem was how to get a piece of food placed outside the animal's cage and just out of its reach. Attached to the food was a rope that the chimp could pull with his hands or the dog could pull with his teeth.

The task proved easy for the chimps. They quickly pulled the food into reach with the rope. But for the dog, this seemingly easy task proved to be impossibly difficult. Although showing the greatest interest in the meat, the animal would have starved to death before hitting on a solution (moviegoers take note, in the movies, they train the dogs in advance).

Now Kohler's problems were becoming increasingly difficult. They were reaching a point at which even the chimpanzees could not immediately solve the problem. But this is exactly the point where Kohler observed the very moment of problem-solving—the point at which a seemingly insoluble problem gave way to the animal's "power of reasoning."

Kohler suspended a banana high off of the ceiling of the testing room. In a corner of the room were some packing cases. Then he introduced a hungry chimp. The chimp immediately spied the fruit, jumped at it repeatedly, threw sticks at it, and finally beat his hands angrily against the wall. Eventually, he sat down and gazed blankly about the room. After a while, he noticed the boxes. He began moving the boxes. Then in an instant, he pushed the boxes under the bananas, stacked them hurriedly, climbed up onto the shaky structure, and retrieved his prize.

The sequence of discovery was similar for most chimps; first, a period of single-minded and futile attempts to jump high enough to get the banana; then a period of rest or exploration; and finally, a glance at the banana, the boxes, or both, and the rush to the prize. Still, great variation existed in their behavior. One required five minutes to recognize that it could use the boxes as a ladder, another took fifteen minutes, a third took an hour, and a fourth took over a week's worth of trial before solving the problem.

To Kohler, what was significant was the behavior of the animals at the moment before it solved the problem. The chimps did not pull the box under the fruit by accident, climb on it by accident, and get the reward by accident. No trial and error seemed to be needed. A chimp is playing nonchalantly with the boxes one moment, and the next moment he suddenly rushes to a successful completion of the task.

The solution was (1) without trial and error, and (2) frequently quite sudden. The moment of solution was much like our human reaction on reading an idea in a book and hours or days later suddenly finding oneself thinking "Aha, so that's what it meant." Kohler called this "aha" phenomenon, *insight*.

In a later version of the same experiment, Kohler was trying to get the chimpanzee Sultan to use a ladder to reach the fruit. Sultan had already mastered the

fine art of stacking boxes, but this time no boxes were available to him. Try as he would, he could not grasp the idea of using a ladder to reach the fruit.

Discouraged, Sultan shot a disdainful glance at the banana and gave up. Kohler may have lost his patience too, for he records that he walked into the testing room, and went over and pointed at the banana as if to say, "Come on, now. Don't you know what ladders are for?"

Suddenly, as if a lightbulb appeared above his head, Sultan grabbed Kohler's assistant by the arm and pulled, tugged, and jerked him into position underneath the banana. Using the assistant's belt, shoulder, and head as handholds, Sultan scampered up this substitute for a stack of boxes, squatted briefly on his head, triumphantly snatched the banana, vaulted to the floor, and consumed his reward.

FIXATION ON ONE IDEA

Once Sultan had perfected this simple technique, he was reluctant to give it up merely to further Kohler's scientific curiosity. When Kohler and his assistant refused to be led under the fruit, Sultan would throw a tantrum. Later, when he was with a group of chimps working on another suspended banana problem, Sultan attempted to try the same technique using another chimp in place of a human. But the other chimps were not impressed by his technique. Unable to explain his purpose, Sultan tried to force the other chimps into position. But when Sultan tried to stand on their heads, they were not having any of this. Some of them panicked at this peculiar behavior. Others, too terrified to run, crouched flat on the ground while Sultan vainly tried to reach the fruit by leaping up and down on their back.

By the second day, Sultan's idea had caught on with the group, and the other chimps began to *imitate* Sultan. Kohler records with amused desperation how each chimp struggled to grip another, lifting their feet to climb, all wanting the reward but all refusing adamantly to sit still long enough to be a footstool while the other fellow got the banana. Preoccupied with this method, they ignored new implements in the room that might have been used successfully.

Are humans likely to be more adaptable than Kohler's chimps in similar tasks? The psychologist N.R.R. Maier provided an interesting comment on this question. Using adult humans as problem solvers, Maier suspended two strings from the ceiling of a room.

The task for Homo sapiens ("wise men") was simple. All they had to do to earn the distinction of being "smarter than a monkey" was to tie the loose ends of the string together. But there was a catch. The strings were too far apart for a man to hold on to one string while grabbing the other at the same time.

What solutions did the humans come up with? Some reasoned that they had to make one string longer, so they could reach the second string. Others reasoned that if they could stand on boxes, they would be taller and the first string would pull farther toward the second.

Nothing wrong with this logic at all. Except for one minor detail: there was nothing in the room that could lengthen the string and nothing in the room they could stand on! The only object in the room was a pair of pliers, but the pliers were not long enough to help in lengthening the string.

The solution seemed clear. lengthen the string or stand on boxes. But the obvious solutions did not work.

The only possible solution was an ingenious one. If you tie the pliers to the end of one of one string, and start the pliers swinging back and forth like the pendulum on an old clock, then while holding on to one string it was possible to catch the one with the pliers when it swung closest to you.

Simple? Perhaps. But only a few of the sapiens could solve it. Most spent their time attempting the "obvious" solutions. Creativity was stifled. Of those who caught on, many did so only after brushing against the string and accidentally setting it in motion.

In part, the problem was hard because it was novel. We are not accustomed to this type of problem. In part too, it was difficult because we already have a fixed idea of how pliers may be used. This stereotype of the use of pliers may be so strong that we cannot see other uses for them. If we replace the pliers with a pendulum bob, the problem becomes easier to solve, because that would suggest the idea... it would tie it to other knowledge (about how a pendulum works).

Kohler found many similarities in the behavior of humans and apes. Two examples are of importance here. First, Kohler noted animals learn not just by doing, but by imitating the behavior of others. They observed many instances of such imitation. Chimps learned to climb poles, vault poles, knock fruit down, and do other tasks more rapidly if they had observed another chimp doing the same thing.

Not only did chimps imitate other chimps, they clearly empathized with each other's efforts to get the fruit offered as bait. Kohler describes how one chimp in a cage watched another trying to lift fruit off a hook with a pole. The caged animal went through all the motions with its hands while intently watching the progress of the worker. We may observe similar behavior in people watching an all-important football game on television and physically react to seeing the quarterback hit on the two-yard line while struggling vainly for the goal line.

Second, Kohler noted that once the animals had formed a leaned method-, once they had learned one way to work a problem—they had great difficulty putting that concept aside and adopting a new, easier method of problem-solving. Even when the old method no longer worked, as in the chimp's attempts to use each other as ladders, they continued to ignore sticks, ladders, and other implements they might have used until they had thoroughly exhausted their preoccupation with the old method. In short, they displayed stereotyped behavior, not unlike that of humans.

Kohler noted that problem-solving is at its best when both the problem and the solution are in view at the same time; in Kohler's terms, "closure" (putting ideas together) was more likely.

Kohler found the chimpanzees were much less successful at solving the box-stacking problem if they left the boxes outside the room. In one such test, animals that had formerly been successful at box stacking were led past the boxes in the hall and into the testing room. Would they "remember" the boxes in the hall while trying to reach the suspended banana in the room? Even the resident genius, Sultan, had difficulty in such a test, and only after repeatedly trying to get the fruit in other ways, did he remember the boxes in the hall and race out to get the boxes?

Anthropologist Jane Goodall surprised some of her colleagues with the important discovery that chimpanzees in the wild not only use tools but "manufacture" them as well. Goodall observed and recorded on film that chimpanzees will break off twigs from bushes, strip them of their foliage, and use them to draw termites out of the holes in their nests. They insert the stick, wait until it is covered with termites, and withdraw the stick. Then, like a child licking the milkshake off of a straw, they draw the stick over their tongue, licking off the termites.

Other anthropologists have noted that baboons will use rocks to kill scorpions. How many more brain cells or mutations in their wiring diagrams would be necessary before they began making arrowheads or war clubs? Chimpanzees can make and use implements in the wild. But psychologists are not so interested in that fact as they are in the *process* by which learning to use tools develops. And no one, not even the intrepid anthropologists, has been a more careful observer of this process than psychologist Wolfgang Kohler.

Kohler's apes had already mastered the art of using a pole to rake in a banana from beyond their reach outside their cage. This time, Kohler placed the reward farther than one pole's length outside of the cage. They gave two hollow bamboo poles of equal length to the chimp. The poles could be fitted together, much like a short version of a cane fishing pole. Only by fitting them together could the chimp make it long enough to rake in the banana.

Sultan began the task. Straining through the bars, he groped with a single stick in the direction of the banana. When one stick did not work, he tried the other. Neither worked. Frustrated, Sultan made a futile gesture at adaptation. In an apparent retreat to a once successful learning set, he pulled a box toward the bars as if the box could somehow be useful in getting the banana. Quickly recognizing its uselessness, he pushed it to one side. Next, in a close try, he took one stick and pushed it out as close to the fruit as he could. With the second stick, he pushed on the end of the first until he actually moved the fruit. Kohler notes some satisfaction in Sultan's behavior after just being able to move the objective, even though he could not get it.

The first stick they gave to Sultan and a little coaxing. As the animal watched, the observer put one finger into the opening of the stick. But Sultan was not ready for imitation. He quickly tried the previous method of pushing one stick out with the other to touch the fruit.

An hour passed. Kohler tired, remarking that it seemed hopeless. They left Sultan with the sticks and they left the keeper to watch him. Within five minutes after Kohler's remark, things happened. First, Sultan connected the sticks while playing with them, with no apparent consideration of their value in getting the bananas. Shortly thereafter, the keeper reports the moment of triumph:

> *Sultan first of all squats indifferently on the box, which has been left standing a little back from the railings; then he gets up, picks up the two sticks, sits down again on the box and plays carelessly with them. While doing this, it happens that he finds himself holding one rod in either hand in such a way that they lay in a straight line; he pushes the thinner one a little way into the opening of the thicker, jumps up and is already on the run towards the railings to which he has, up to now, half-turned his back, and begins to draw a banana toward him with the double-stick...*

Kohler found chimpanzees are not just users of tools, they are also makers of tools. He describes vividly the inventive process in Sultan:

> *In another experiment, further manufacture of implements is demanded of Sultan. Besides a tube with a large opening, he has at his disposal a narrow wooden board, just too broad to fit into the opening. Sultan takes the board and tries to fit it into the tube. this is not a mistake; the different shapes of the board and the tube would tempt even a human to try it, because the difference in thickness of both these objects is not obvious at first sight.*

> *When he is not successful, he bites the end of the tube and breaks off a long splinter from its side, obviously because the side of the tube was in the way of the wood ("good error"). But as soon as he has his splinter he tries to introduce it into the still intact end of the tube, a surprising turn, which should lead to the solution, were not the splinter a little too big. Sultan seizes the board once more, but now works at it with his teeth, and correctly too, from both edges at one end toward the middle, so that the board becomes narrower. When he has chewed off some of the (very hard) wood, he tests whether the board now fits into the round opening of the tube, and continues working thus (here one must speak of real "work") until the wood goes about two centimeters deep into the tube. Now*

he wishes to fetch the objective with his implement, but two centimeters is not deep enough and the tube falls off the top of the wood over and over again. By this time Sultan is plainly tired of biting at the wood; he prefers to sharpen the wooden splinter at one end and actually succeeds so far as to get it to stick firmly in the sound end of the tube, thus making the double stick ready for use. In connection with this treatment of the wood it must be remarked that contrary to my expectation, Sultan bit away wood almost exclusively from one end of the board, and even if he took the other end between his teeth for a moment, he never gnawed blindly first at one, and then at the other. His way of dealing with the tube was also satisfactory. The one opening of the tube that had been spoiled by breading its side is thereafter left unheeded. I had some anxiety for the other opening during the further experiment, but although Sultan, when the wood and splinter did not fit in, put his teeth into it several times, he never really bit into the side of the tube so that the opening could still be used. I could not guarantee that each repetition of the experiment would turn out so well. Sultan evidently had a specially bright day.

Kohler noted that the sharpening of sticks with the teeth as Sultan had done seemed to be well within the capabilities of chimps—even when unnecessary to solve a problem. One chimp named Grande was fond of sharpening sticks in such a manner and using them to  poke at anyone who passed by her cage. Apparently, it required only one extra step ("insight"?) to make this practice useful. But what about this 'one extra step'? What is the origin of thinking?

The sudden, insightful problem solving of Kohler's chimps seemed markedly different than the fumble-and-find problem solving described in the trial-and-error studies of educator Thorndike. Why? Do chimpanzees learn through insight rather than trial and error? Or did Kohler's chimps have some advantage from experience that Thorndike's cats did not?

Although Kohler's chimps did not seem to engage in trial-and-error behavior, their problem solving was often erratic, fumbling, and inept. Kohler accurately recorded their inconsistencies, which would take on meaning many years later when Herbert Birch of the Yerkes Primate Laboratory, tried to repeat Kohler's studies using chimpanzees that had spent most of their life in a cage rather than in the jungle.

In the wild, Kohler's chimps had climbed trees, swung from vines, and used sticks. Yet the cage-reared animals had great difficulty with the same problems as Kohler's wild chimps. After many trials, they solved the problems. There was little of the sudden initial insight described by Kohler. Only after experience were the chimps able to show "insight" in using the sticks and boxes as tools.

Does thinking arise spontaneously from within the mind? Does it already exist, awaiting only the raw materials? Or does thinking develop from prior learning?

Even though Kohler spoke of "insight", that sudden connection of ideas in the mind, it was clear that much trial and learning was involved before they got to that point. From Kohler's detailed description we can see that insight was not magic. It required effort and Trial-and-Error learning along the way. Only when the association was made in the mind was the sudden "aha" moment of insight reached.

There is a danger of expecting too much from our children... or from ourselves. Is there such a thing as innate "genius", or is all learning determined by experience?

To determine what is happening, it becomes even more important to control the entire learning history of the animal. Only by being observing the learning process from the very beginning is it possible to see the process in action.

THE LEARNING SET:
The Program for Learning to Learn

Although cognitive psychologists have often talked of "schema" or "information processing" or "brain imaging" these are largely words that have little ability to explain what these words relate to the brain. Harry Harlows's Learning Sets and Edward Toman's Cognitive Maps have the clearest experimental evidence of what they mean by these terms. Yet Harlow's experiment has been ignored even though it has perhaps the potential to operationally define the bridge between Behavioral and Cognitive psychology.

One of the least known, but most important, findings in learning came from an almost unknown work began by Harry Harlow at the University of Wisconsin on "learning sets", or "learning to learn". Harlow discovered what he considered one of

the most basic concepts in the thought process: the *learning set*. Others might call it a concept, or cognition, or insight.

Harlow began by controlling the entire learning history of the monkeys he studied. If the experiences in the wild of Kohler's chimps had aided their learning, there would be no way of knowing which experiences had been important. Such control could only be possible by using rhesus monkeys reared in captivity—when their entire learning history could be studied.

Second, Harlow had to have problems for the monkeys to learn to solve. He devised problems basic to learning itself--problems involving discrimination, transfer of training, and operant conditioning. He began with a discrimination test.

They presented a monkey with a tray on which they had placed two objects. The objects were different in shape, size, and color. One object always had a peanut or raisin as a reward under it. If the monkey picked up the correct object, it got the reward. If the monkey picked the wrong object it got no reward, and the tray was withdrawn, rearranged, and presented again. The objects were switched from left to right, from trial to trial, to be certain that the animal was learning the object rather than the position.

The initial learning began with a slow fumble-and-find process. The monkey's behavior was closer to that of trial and error than to insight. Over a series of trials with the same object, they learned that the reward was always under the square object and not under the round object. They learned this well enough they eventually chose the correct object virtually every time.

It took 30 trials before they stopped picking at random and always picked the symbol that had always had the peanut under it.

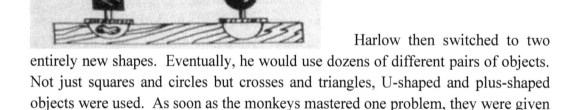 Harlow then switched to two entirely new shapes. Eventually, he would use dozens of different pairs of objects. Not just squares and circles but crosses and triangles, U-shaped and plus-shaped objects were used. As soon as the monkeys mastered one problem, they were given a second problem.

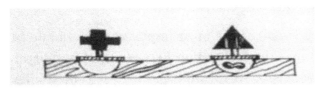

Now the question is posed. After having learned to work the first discrimination problem perfectly every time, would the monkeys be able to transfer the knowledge they gained from the first task to the second task? Would they learn the second task more easily than the first? Had "insight" developed? Or would it require as many trials to learn the new problem as it took to learn the first problem?

Two new stimuli were presented--objects the monkeys had never seen before. The second task began. Trial followed trial; failure, success, failure, success... On the second problem, as many trial-and-error failures were made as on the first! Out of two choices, the monkeys started out making as many wrong responses as correct ones. It again took another 30 trials to learn the concept; that the peanut would always be under the same stimulus. Again, they finally mastered the problem to the extent that they were correct on every trial. Then they were presented with a third problem, a fourth, a fifth...

Problem followed problem. As they mastered each one; the new problems were being solved more and more easily. After fifty such problems, and many trials on each problem, the monkeys could pick the correct solution to the problem (after the first trial) on 90% of the trials. After 300 trials, the monkeys could be given two new stimuli, never seen before, and learn which one was correct after only one trial.

If they picked the correct stimulus the first time, they continued to do so. If they picked the wrong one the first time, then ever after they would pick the other one. Harlow called this "learning to learn". The monkeys could now show "insight" when working with new stimuli. They had learned how to learn. They had learned a "learning set", a set way of learning how to work a problem.

The results of Harlow's study were quite striking. And they suggested to Harlow that trial-and-error learning and "insight" are but two aspects of the same learning process.   Insight does not exist without experience.   Only through experience can "insightful" learning (a learning set?) develop.

This little-known discovery is one of the most important ever made in the field of learning. It clearly shows the interaction between trial-and-error learning and the development of concepts. It fills the void between the studies of S-R psychology and that of cognitive psychologists and actually agrees with the discoveries of Piaget that showed, for example, that a concept like "object permanence" developed only gradually from 6 to 9 to 12 months, instead of a sudden realization that popped out of nowhere.

Yet this study is nowhere to be found in the textbooks that imply that Developmental and Cognitive learning are somehow different from any other kind of learning.

It is most unlikely that we are talking about different realities of learning but, like the story of the blind men who grab hold of an elephant at different parts, and each describe the tail, leg, trunk, belly of the elephant differently, they are seeing the same phenomenon from different viewpoints.

COMPARING HUMAN CHILDREN TO APES

So how do human children do on such a test? In a variation of this, they presented three objects to human children. Two of the objects were identical, the third was different. The task was to pick which object was different. They gave both monkeys and nursery school children the same series of tests. Harlow allowed 24 tests on each problem before presenting each new problem.

ARE MONKEYS SMARTER THAN HUMAN CHILDREN?

At first, the process of trial and error was common. Not just for monkeys, but for children as well. Gradually their performance improved as they mastered problem after problem. Finally, they were all able to solve a new problem in only one trial.

Remarkably, Harlow notes the monkeys did better than the human children. The difference may have been because of the difference in the reward's value however; hungry monkeys may work harder than curious children. But learning was identical in both.

Harlow's concept of the "learning set" is an organizing principle that explains much of learning and thinking. From repeated trial-and-error experience, an organized response set develops. It can apply this learning set to similar problems never before experienced. The individual can now solve problems similar to those it has solved in the past without going through the laborious fumble and find process. We may now combine simple learning sets into more complex ones, which may then be applied to more complex problems.

This step-by-step process can be seen in the chimps studied by Kohler or in human children. In learning to use the sticks to reach bananas outside of their cage, they relied on countless experiences of reaching for distant objects with their arms. Usually, they were successful. Thus a "reaching to pick up an object" learning set already existed.

Harlow's concept of "learning sets" provides a much-needed hard-evidence bridge between the observations of Piaget and hard science, much as associations (S-S or S-R) provides a bridge between sensation and perception.

Second, Kohler noted they had often used sticks in play to touch distant objects and occasionally to poke at the observers as they passed. Combining these and other such elements of experience led to the use of sticks to reach the banana.

Later, on more complex tasks, Sultan joined two sticks together in play, apparently by trial and error. He did not immediately use the joined sticks to reach the food, but it was only shortly thereafter that he "joined" the learning sets together to solve the problem.

HUMAN PROBLEM SOLVING

What about humans? We have seen that nursery and preschool children go through a trial-and-error process in learning. Do human children display more "insight" than the chimps? Do they show evidence of a different, distinctly human type of learning? Of course, language gives humans a substantial advantage over the ape, but for now, let us stick to the type of problem-solving that both apes and humans can do before examining our unfair advantage.

Child psychologists Kendler and Kendler devised a simple but unique test of a child's ability to combine two ideas (learning sets?) An apparatus was built and training began.

First, they taught the child that pressing the button on the left would deliver a steel ball into the cup.

Second, they taught the child that pressing the button on the right would deliver a marble.

The experimenters then closed off both side sections and opened the center section. The child now learned that if they put if a steel ball into the hole in the center, a charm would drop into the cup.

Finally, all sections of the machine were uncovered, and they asked the child to get the machine to deliver a charm.

Will the child be able to combine the first and third learning sets? Will the child push the button on the left, get a steel ball, and put the ball into the hole to get the charm?

It seems so simple to an adult. You would think a child could understand. They do not.

Preschool children have great difficulty in solving this problem. They do not seem to associate the steel ball they get by pressing the button with the steel ball that will get them the charm!

The second learning set with the marble serves to interfere with the connection. Regardless, little insight is shown by preschool children.

If they allowed the children to play around (trial and error) with the puzzle, would they eventually catch on? Probably. **But only 6 percent of the kindergarten children and 50 percent of the third-grade children solved this problem on the first trial!**

Not that preschool children do not show "insightful" learning. They do. But given a problem they have never experienced; they resort to trial and error, just like adults.

CAN ADULTS DO BETTER?

Nursery school children and rhesus monkeys learn by trial and error and pyramiding learning sets, but what about adults? Surely adults have reached an intuitive stage where reason takes over and such steps are no longer necessary.

Perhaps, but have we? Now let you try a problem very similar to the one Harlow's monkeys had to master by fumble and find. This will be slightly more complex, since humans have the benefit of far more experience than Harlow's monkeys. But it is sufficiently unfamiliar that it will offer somewhat the same challenge to our thought processes without having to be tricky.

Harlow used two stimulus objects with his monkeys. Your problem has four. Harlow had a peanut under one object as a reward. Your only reward will be the challenge of doing better than a monkey if you succeed. The peanut-cross problem is stated verbally so you can rely on experience. See what you have to do to solve the problem.

This problem is especially important because it shows to adults just how very difficult it is for children to solve a completely new problem. Try it yourself because only by trying it can you understand.

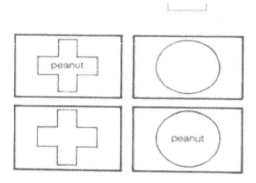

THE PEANUT-CROSS PROBLEM°

Here are four cards. Each card has a Cross on one side and a Circle on the other side. Each card has a cross (*with* or *without* the word "peanut") on one side and a circle (*with* or *without* the word "peanut") on the other side. Which cards are the only cards that you will you have to turn over to determine if this statement is true? Based on similar problems by P.C. Wason.

"Every card that has a "peanut" cross on one side has a circle without "peanut" on the other side."

Read the instructions carefully. When you are certain of your answer, but only when you are certain, then check note number 1 below. Pay attention to this problem because it illustrates two crucial points of learning.

Note 1: Did you figure that the cards that must be turned over are the "peanut" cross and the circle without "peanut"? Most people pick these cards. If you did, however, then like most people you are incorrect. Try again, then read note 2.

Note 2: Do you not think the answer should be both of the crosses? Or should it be both of the circles? Either answer is incorrect. If you are following the standard course of logic, you must now think that the answer is all four cards. Right? But you are still wrong. You have just about run out of possibilities (fumble and find?), but go back and try again. There is no trick to the logic of the problem, so do not blame it on that. Then see note 3.

Note 3: Usually by the third try, two or three students out of a class of thirty understand the problem well enough to explain it. Do you? The answer is that the "peanut" cross and the "peanut" circle must both be turned over. Can you explain why? Or did you get it right, as most of us do, by trial and error (mostly error)?

By the time you continue reading here, you will have already been through three notes and should be moderately exasperated. Why is the problem so difficult? Do you think it was that much harder for a human than Harlow's problem was for a naïve monkey? What happened to all those years of public education, not to mention any innate insight we credit ourselves with having?

Although this is a simple problem, it is not one we have ever seen before. That makes it very hard to follow. Perhaps after 300 different trials... Of course, if we could pick up the cards and turn each one over, we would figure it out very quickly, but having to follow the words and only imagine in our mind what is on the other side, is not so easy.

If you want to understand the logic, read on. If your brain is already going into apoplexy, skip the next section.

Analysis of the Peanut Cross Problem

Almost everyone says that the "peanut" cross must be turned over because if it has a circle without a peanut then the statement is correct and if it has a circle with a "peanut" then the statement is false. Therefore, to find out if the statement is true, we must turn this card over. So, most people are half right. But so was Harlow's monkey.

What people do not note is that the "peanut" circle is every bit as crucial to our "proof" as the first card. If the "peanut" circle has a cross without a peanut, then it matters little. We have made no predictions about either card in the statement. But if the "peanut" circle has a "peanut" cross on the other side, then our statement is flatly false! After we have pointed this out, almost everyone sees the logic in this. We must turn this card over. So why is it so difficult to see this before we point it out?

Students invariably want an explanation of why the other two cards do not have to be turned over, so bear with me. First, the circle without "peanut" could have either a cross with "peanut" or a cross without "peanut" on the other side. These are the only two possibilities. If it has a cross with "peanut" then fine, the problem statement is correct, but not proven. If it has a cross without "peanut," who cares? We have made no predictions about crosses without "peanut".

It does not matter which is on the other side of the circle without "peanut" because it cannot *disprove* your statement. Interestingly, most of us have difficulty grasping the fact that finding a "peanut" cross on the other side is of no importance— it merely supports the statement. What is important in this problem is which cards can *disprove* the statement (another learning set?).

For the same reason, the cross without "peanut" is of no importance. We have simply made no predictions about crosses without peanuts. Even if it has a circle with "peanut" on the other side, it in no way affects the prediction.

There seem to be two reasons this simple problem is so very difficult for the average adult human. First, as with Harlow's monkeys on their first trial, it is a *new* problem to us. Most of us have simply never had experience with this type of problem. After 300 trials, more or less, we might learn it well. Even after it is explained to us in detail, most people would have difficulty working a second such problem, with different stimuli than a cross and circle and peanut!

But more than this, we are usually so certain that our first answer is correct. Why? The answer seems to be that we have already formed a certain way of dealing with problems, a learning set. When we try to apply our "logic" (the learning set) to this problem, however, we fail because our standard learning cannot work the problem set. As with many such problems encountered (as with Copernicus and Darwin), we go blissfully on our way, confident that our logic is correct.

Like Kohler's apes trying to use each other as a ladder, we ignore other ways of looking at the problem.

MENTAL TRIAL AND ERROR:

What did you do when you tried to solve the problem? A monkey might have physically turned the cards over. Humans do not have to. We can turn the cards over in our minds. We can imagine what could be on the other side. By turning the cards over in our mind—by imagining all possibilities—we are free to work problems, by trial and error, in our mind. It gives us a tremendous advantage over the apes, maybe.

Thought is no more free from error than physical trial and error. Psychologists could make a good case that this form of logic is far more prone to error. But if thought is based on enough physical experiences, as were the learning sets developed by Harlow's monkeys, then the thought process gives us a tremendous tool—a shortcut for working new problems. Harlow called that concept, or algorithm, a Learning Set.

In our daily life, we are continually turning over cards to anticipate the effect. In social situations, we may think about how another would react if we said or did something. We learn from experience to anticipate their reactions. Often, we are wrong. But by thinking out all possible reactions in advance, we may avoid many mistakes and perhaps learn to produce the effect we hope for.

A similar form of thinking may involve the use of visual models within the mind. If we can visualize a problem by using our experience, the problem becomes easier to solve. Try answering this question, for example; "How many doors (including closet doors) are there in your house?" Think about the question before reading further.

How did you solve this problem? Usually, we have to picture in our mind each room in our house and count each door. We reconstruct a visual model of our home in our mind.

Isaac Newton once said that he could imagine nothing of which he could not make a model. Newton was speaking of models made on paper and in the mind. Copernicus constructed a new physical model of the solar system and compared it with the model that was popular. This is how he gained his insight. Thinking often involves imagining things within our mind.

For example, try the following. Think up a two-digit number, say 17. Then multiply that number by a second two-digit number in your mind, say 19. Stop for a moment and see what you must do to come up with an answer.

Albert Einstein, in describing how ideas came to him, said that ideas came as images to his mind. Only later, did he take on the laborious task of translating the ideas into words that described the ideas.

Most of us have to visualize the problem in our mind before working it, almost like chalking it on a blackboard. Yet many of us have learned to multiply single digits by rote memory, so that the answer comes instantly.

Not all thinking is visual. Most are so quick, even instantaneous, that we are not even aware of the thought process. We come up with an answer by simple association. Yet ideas and thoughts are connected in the brain so rapidly that we do not think about how we think. This thinking is not visual, or in models, it is simply the matter of associating ideas or thoughts within the mind. Only when we force ourselves to think, in slow motion, do we observe some of what is happening.

Thought with words may follow similar steps. We first need to visualize a new idea or problem in concrete terms. Then, after experiences with this or similar ideas, the thought, if it has become well learned, may become as reflexive as that of a mathematics wizard.

THE CREATIVE PROCESS

Prior learning is essential before any kind of creative thinking can occur. Insight does not just happen. But the moment of creative insight may be sudden, with no apparent thought at all. How does this happen?

Consider an analogy of how this sudden change of perspective may operate. Consider the Necker cube illusion. Look at the Necker cube and ask yourself if the shaded area represents the front of a box or the back of a box. After you decide, stare at the cube again for a few moments.

If you move your eyes up and down while looking at the cube long enough, the perspective will change suddenly and dramatically. The front will become the back or the back will become the front. If at first you do not see it, try again; the perspective seems to change more readily after a little experience.

But why does it work at all? Why does the mind perceive the shaded area as obviously the front one moment, and obviously the back the next moment?

It is almost as if one were listening to two arguments about a controversial subject and being convinced first by one, then by the other. It seems as if the mind were trying out all possible perceptual fits on this simple figure, as if trying to find the "correct" interpretation.

Note that no "conscious" activity is necessary at all. The figure may move from one interpretation to the next without effort on our part. Could it be that the moment of insight requires no more conscious effort than this? If we conceive of the mind as composed of video-taped memory traces, stimulus-response associations, or learning sets, is it difficult to imagine how these may trip in and out of sequence in much the same way as the Necker cube? Indeed, this seems to be basic to the creative process in apes and humans.

DEVELOPMENTAL DIFFERENCES:

Sensori-Motor: 0 to 2 years

Piaget believed that the first two years of life are consumed with developing sensori-motor coordination such as visual-muscular tasks. One of the concepts he saw as not developed in very young children before six months of age is the concept of *object-permanence; The idea that objects can still exist even if we cannot see the object.*

If you move a toy the baby likes across his field of vision the baby will follow the toy with his eye movements. But, if you move the toy behind a barrier, where the baby cannot see it, the baby will turn away as if the toy no longer exists.

A baby who is shaking a rattle may lose the rattle and it may fall out of sight. A five-month-old will not look for the rattle if it is not visible.

By nine months of age if the baby watches you move a rattle across the baby's field of vision the baby will follow the object with their eyes. If you move the rattle behind a barrier, the baby will then crawl over and look behind the barrier. They are beginning to form an idea or concept, or schema or learning set, that objects to not cease to exist just because they cannot see the object.

Yet the concept of object-permanence is still not complete. If you show an 11-month-old a rattle, then let the baby watch you put it into a cigar box, the baby will crawl to the box and get the rattle. However, if you let the baby watch you put the rattle in a box, then put the box behind a barrier, and remove the rattle and leave it behind the barrier, then put the empty box out for the baby to open, after the baby opens the box and finds it empty, the baby will not crawl over to the barrier to look for the rattle until it is about 12 months old.

Trial and Error is still an important method for discovering reality.

The concept of object permanence does not suddenly snap into being at a certain age. It evolves from 6 to 9 to 12 months in a manner not too unlike what Harlow observed in his study of Learning Sets.

Pre-Operational-Stage
Ages 2-7

What we have learned at any age also affects what we know. Swiss psychologist Jean Piaget showed this convincingly in his classic water glass experiment. He showed children two identical glasses filled with the same amount of water. He asked children which glass had the most water. The children said that they were both the same.

Immediately, while they were watching, he then poured one glass into a tall, thin glass. The water in the tall glass came up to a higher level than in the short glass.

Piaget then asked children, "Now, which glass has the most water?"

Five-year-old children, the same ones who had previously said that the water  was the same, now said that the tall, thin glass had more water in it, even though the only difference was that the tall slender glass would have the water go higher.

He asked children to count out fifteen marbles and put them in the short glasses. Each glass contained fifteen marbles carefully counted out by the child. They then asked the children to put the marbles into a tall, thin glass.

Now, when the children were asked which glass had the most marbles, they again said the tall glass had more marbles.

Not until the age of seven do children in our culture learn that "taller" does not mean the same as "more". But why do they make this mistake in the first place? Think about it. When a child asks for "more" milk, what happens? Mom pours more milk into his glass, which raises the level higher than before. Thus, they come to a learning set, by association, that says that "higher" is "more".

Piaget originally believed that children did not develop the idea of "conservation" of matter until the age of eight. It seems far more likely, however, that their development of one learning set (for taller or higher) had interfered with the development of another learning set (for amount). By the age of seven, children in our society learn that "tall" and "amount" are two different concepts. But they have to "unlearn" the previously learned concept (for taller or higher) before they can learn the new one.

This illustrates a very important point. Children may verbally express a concept; they may say which glass has the most water in it. They may even use a word correctly most times. Often, however, a child may parrot the verbal ideas of his elders without fully understanding what he is saying.

Parents and teachers may not recognize that the child's grasp of reality is limited by his experiences. Parents may fail to understand how their child could express an understanding of an idea so beautifully in one situation and fail so badly in another. The child may simply have a different concept—an idea shaped and limited by his or her experiences.

Concrete-Operations: Ages 7-12

By the age of seven, the child has mastered the set of conservation of quantity with liquid and with numbers. Why? What happens between the ages of 5 and 7 that might account for that?

School. Today, our schools actually teach the same concepts studied by Piaget; more than, less than, over, under, amount, etc.

A five-year-old simply has not learned these concepts yet. Contrary to what Piaget though, learning was the key, not development. Yet that does not diminish the brilliance of Piaget's experiments. They provide us with an understanding of the limits of a child's understanding that we could not easily see before.

But does the child understand abstract ideas related to space? Inhelder and Piaget arranged a task in which they present glasses of colored water to seven-year-olds. Try this one on paper by yourself. It is easy to work, but see if you do not experience at least a temporary intellectual pause before the moment of insight.

They show the child two glasses. They fill one with water and one is empty. The child is asked to predict what the surface of the water will look like if they tilt the glass to the left, as if someone were drinking out of it.

Did you find you could not work the problem without stopping to construct a mental image of what the glass would look like if tilted to the left? It seems to be far more difficult for us to draw a hypothetical water surface level in a tilted glass when the glass we are looking at is still vertical. Children are ordinarily not capable of doing this problem until they reach the age of nine.

Formal-Operations 12+

By the age of twelve, a child can do a great deal more than the concrete and imaginative problems discussed above. Now they can deal with hypothetical "what if" problems they have never experienced. They can imagine ideas within their mind and manipulate these ideas in their thoughts. Algebra, computer science, the fundamentals of physics are all within their ability. As far as we can tell, by the time children are twelve, they have reached all the physical development of intelligence they are likely to have. If you give a problem in nuclear physics to an adult and to a twelve-year-old, who would solve it first? If this were a completely new problem, and neither had the benefit of prior learning experiences with this type of problem, then both should do equally well. Of course, no twelve-year-old has ever had the wide background of experience of an adult, but a twelve-year-old can learn anything an adult can.

Even though Piaget's concepts have not turned out to be as absolute as developmental psychologists believed, their experiments are a milestone in understanding. The richness of Piaget's experiments was a great addition to our understanding. One of the most important discoveries of the developmental psychologists is the critical understanding that children do not see reality quite the same way as adults. That is important to know for anyone who works with children.

Jerome Bruner, Harvard educator, found he could teach algebra, what Piaget said had to wait for 12 years old, to 10-year-olds, just by using concrete operations and going step-by-step into algebra.

"We began with the hypothesis that any subject can be taught in some intellectually honest form to any child at any stage of development."

Jerome Bruner

The brilliant work of Piaget and the Developmental psychologists have left a legacy of useful studies. They clearly show the gradual development of cognition over time. This is very useful to show that children and adults think differently. Yet they have failed to prove that these stages are due to maturation (development) or if they are learned.

Piaget's concepts of Schema, Assimilation, and Accommodation are vague and untethered to hard evidence. If Developmental psychology had used Harlow's concept of Learning Sets as a bridge between more basic learning and the concepts of Piaget, they might have had a far more useful basis to explain their otherwise brilliant studies.

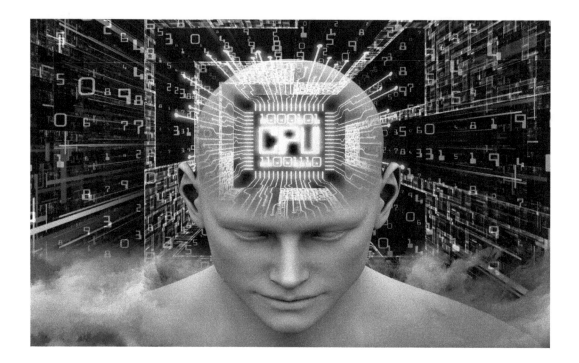

COGNITIVE PSYCHOLOGY

Cognitive Psychologists often see themselves as having replaced Behavioral Psychology, yet it is more accurate to say that they added an important new dimension to psychology. Cognitive psychology could never explain what Behavioral Psychology could explain, and Behavioral Psychology could not explain what Cognitive Psychology demonstrated.

By selecting a few studies that only cognitive psychology could explain, it gave a mistaken impression that the advantage always went to their position. Perhaps more likely, both saw a portion of how the mind works, but not the whole picture.

- Wolfgang Kohler's extensive study of "insight" in chimpanzees was a major step toward recognizing that something was going on at a higher level inside the brain, although trial an error learning was clearly a part of the puzzle.

- Selective Attention, demonstrated by Donald Broadbent having students wear headphones, playing different stories into each ear, were told to pay attention to only one story. When asked questions about what was happening in both ears, they were able to effectively answer those questions that were about the story only happening in the ear they were attending to.

- Tolman's studies of latent learning and "cognitive maps" strongly suggested that we learn far more than just a simple stimulus-response association. This presaged the realization that we may learn all sensory input, not just an S-R relationship.

- Piaget's experiments with human children provided a rich source of understanding of how children understand reality differently than adults; from their own experiences, and how this understanding changes throughout life.

- Studies of memory and the fallibility of memory by Elizabeth Loftus and others have found our memory is vague and easily re-written. Eyewitness testimony, often considered the best evidence, is a serious problem which has led to the jailing of innocent people. The number one cause of innocent people being convicted of crimes they did not commit, is eyewitness testimony.

https://www.oxfordbibliographies.com/view/document/obo-9780199828340/obo-9780199828340-0026.xml

The major contributions of cognitive psychology are important, but not paradigm changing. They add to the paradigm.

WHERE COGNITIVE PSYCHOLOGY FAILS

The failure of cognitive psychology to provide a bridge between simple learning, such as trial and error, conditioning, and cognitive processes, left their theories without substance.

- **Piaget's concepts of Schema, Accommodation, and Assimilation are subject to the problem of the Nominal Fallacy: the belief that, by having named something, we have somehow explained it.**

- **Without a basis in hard evidence, these words have no substance.**

- **Studies that rely solely on how long an infant spends looking at one picture, rather than another, are not well grounded. Guessing at what the infant is "thinking" is not scientific.**

- **Harlow's study of "learning sets" provided a hard evidence ground for going from simple association to cognitive psychology, but has been largely ignored by cognitive psychologists.**

- **More important, they ignore the most recent discoveries of cataract studies in babies that show the brain itself is profoundly molded by experience. Without visual experience, the brain itself will never develop the ability to see. Experience itself changes the biology of the brain and our perceptions.**

In addition, the brain is molded by experience in a manner so profound, that we can only "see" (understand) what experience allows us to see.

One of the problems of Developmental and Cognitive psychology is the lack of any clear evidence for what a "schema" is, or how "information processing" develops. Some have even proposed that there is a "schema" for every action. They say children have a "carrying schema" for carrying things, an "object schema" for recognizing things, a "turning schema" for turning things over... They have lists of schemas to supposedly explain everything.

It is too reminiscent of early "instinct" theory which made lists of instincts to explain every aspect of human behavior. Early psychologists said we have an "instinct" for hunger, sex, maternal instinct, laughter, sleep, and curiosity instincts. It explained nothing. Neither does the word magic of "schema" or "assimilation" or "accommodation".

The studies of Piaget have contributed greatly to psychology, but they have failed to explain the most basic understanding of how our mind works. Instead, we are left with vague terms such as schema, assimilation, or accommodation, that fail to provide a hard-science explanation for reality. Where is the beef?

"SCHEMA", "INFORMATION PROCESSING" AND THE NOMINAL FALLACY

The word "schema" has fallen victim to what psychologist Frank Beach called "the Nominal Fallacy", the belief that, by having named something, we have somehow explained it.

By the same token, merely describing something, does not provide any understanding of what is happening.

Harlow's study of learning sets, provides the most important link between all of our vague concepts, including concepts, ideas, schema, information processing, cognitive maps and more. If we add one more addition to the mix, that is, the perception of reality that experience embeds in our brain, we have a far greater understanding of how our mind works.

Harlow's work provides a much-needed hard-evidence bridge between the observations of Piaget and hard science, much as associations (S-S or S-R) provides a bridge between sensation and perception.

AND ADULTS?

Yet new ideas still need to be presented in measured, concrete examples. Adults do not grasp a new symbolic idea unless they can visualize it or experience it in concrete terms first.   No amount of neural development can be useful without prior experience as a basis.

Child psychologists Stone and Church provide a simple demonstration in which adults were asked to draw a picture of an island. Not just the part above the water, but the part below the water. What does an island look like underwater? Most of the adults, from the island of Hawaii, did not know. Many drew the island's underside as round!

Not knowing what the underside of an island looked like, they generalized from their experience. They saw it as round, like the underside of a canoe. They used their "intuition." They used their common sense. We base all intuition and common sense on generalizations from past experiences; in this case, experiences with boats. It was a good idea, but it was not correct.

We have exposed children to geography courses in school. Most knew that islands are the tips of mountain ranges, often volcanic, that project above the floor of the sea.

But if you do not learn it, you do not know it.

Of all the theories of what cognition is, from Tolman's "Cognitive Maps", to Piaget's "Schema" to Behaviorist's ideas of "stimulus generalization" or concepts of "Concepts" no one has ever shown more clearly than Harry Harlow how concepts develop. His idea of "Learning to Learn" describes beautifully, in step-by-step detail, how concepts develop. It seems unlikely that his Learning Sets are different from the many other ideas of concepts, except that Harlow showed how they form.

If psychologists had been able to combine the experiments of Harlow that showed how "learning sets" can develop out of trial-and-error learning, with the experiments of Piaget that showed how children perform at different ages, with the insight of Jerome Bruner, we could have had a far better view of how learning leads to different stages of ability than the fragmented puzzle we present to students today.

One piece of the puzzle that is missing from our textbooks is the brain's ability to *generalize* from past experience to build a new biological program in the brain that allows the brain to *anticipate* what will come next; to Learn to Learn.

One point worth noting, it seems no different from the ideas of generalization in psychology. The brain itself seems to automatically generalize from past exposure with reality, even in our visual experience. The best example may simply be the study of psychologists who showed students pictures of 10 males and 10 females, and asked them to pick the most attractive face in each series. Most students picked the 10th picture, which turned out to be a computer-generated composite (generalization) of all of the 9 others.

Stimulus generalization in action, somehow an ability of the biology of the brain itself.

Both psycholinguistics and neuropsychology have benefited from the shock and awe of fMRIs and PET scans, yet neither has come close to providing the wealth of simple explanations for the mind that originated from the most basic elements of stimulus-stimulus associations. Their explanations are the Facebook of psychology, full of image grabbing excitement, but, like living on ramen noodles, we come away unsatisfied with the lack of relevance to how the mind works.

They have overwhelmed today's psychology. Yet they have no ability to predict, to explain, to allow an understanding of how the mind works at the level of human behavior. Behavioral and perceptual psychology have been largely ignored in the race for the new Picasso, the pretty pictures of an fMRI scan, an obscure idea of schemas, a turgid description of cognitive behavior.

How can they explain the behavior of a Kamikaze pilot, the value of a Picasso painting, the beauty of tiny feet for 1,000 years in China, the emotional effect of the witch hunts, the roar of the crowd on the mind of football players, when "their" team scores?

By this analysis of perceptual psychology, the brain is not the linear computer imagined by Turing, although the function is similar. Instead, it is closer to being a holographic computer, more accurately a perceptual computer, ruled by emotion, steeped in the prime experiences that are now hardwired into the brain by experience. We come to "know" our reality from the images embedded in our brain, the scanning of perceptions. We come to perceive our reality from the anticipatory ability of our mind, not unlike Pavlov's dogs salivating in anticipation of what comes next.

Yet no analogy is entirely adequate to describe what the brain does. Just as the chapter on the senses noted that we still cannot explain how the brain gives us color, sound, taste, smell, out of simple neural responses, we are not at a point where any analogy seems adequate. Perhaps a future neuropsychologist will enlighten us.

We cannot understand the human mind without borrowing from the greatest ideas in every area of psychology; Behavioral, Brain, Cognitive, Computer analogy, neuropsychology, perception.

9

PERSONALITY

The term *personality* comes from the Latin word *persona*. A persona referred to the theatrical masks used by the players to create a mood. The masks—one laughing, one crying, one frightened, one angry—are classic symbols of drama. By switching from one mask to another, an actor could play many parts.

People differ from animals in part because we can represent to others what we wish ourselves to be. We can take on whatever role-playing behavior that we think is called for. Psychologist William James, the "Father" of American psychology, put it well:

...a man has as many social selves as there are individuals who recognize him and carry an image of him in their mind. To wound any one of these is to wound him... He generally shows a different side of himself to each of these different groups. Many a youth who is demure with his parents and teacher,

swears and swaggers like a pirate among his 'tough' young friends. We do not show ourselves to our children as to our club companions, to our customers as to the laborers we employ, to our own masters and employers as to our intimate friends. From this there results what practically is a division of the man into several selves; and this may be a discordant splitting, as where one is afraid to let one set of his acquaintances know him as he is elsewhere; or it may be a perfectly harmonious division of labor, as where one, tender to his children is stern to the soldiers or prisoners under his command.

We behave in accord with how we have learned others expect us to behave. We conform to our image of our role.

... Thus a layman may abandon a city infected with cholera, but a priest or a doctor would think such an act incompatible with his honor. A soldier's honor requires him to fight or die under circumstances where another man can apologize or run away with no stain upon his social self. A judge, a statesman, are in like manner debarred by the honor of their cloth from entering into pecuniary relations perfectly honorable to persons in private life. Nothing is commoner to hear people discriminate between their different selves of this sort: "As a man I pity you, but as an official, I must show you no mercy"; "As a politician, I regard him as an ally, but as a moralist I loathe him," etc., etc. What may be called "club-opinions" is one of the very strongest forces in life. The thief must not steal from other thieves, the gambler must pay his gambling-debts, though he pay no other debts in the world. ... You must not lie in general, but you may lie as much as you please if asked about your relations with a lady; you must accept a challenge from an equal, but if challenged by an inferior you may laugh him to scorn...

George Herbert Mead noted Three Stages of role-playing. Beginning at about the age of two, the first stage is simply "monkey see, monkey do" behavior. The young child puts on Daddy's or Mommy's clothes and parades in front of a mirror or in front of others. The child may seem an incorrigible copycat. Children may imitate the mannerisms of their parents by praising or scolding other children, real or imaginary, in the same tone as their parents have used on them.

Other common forms of imitation include "telephonitis," or play-acting at answering the telephone, an infectious case of the giggles, and the "all-fall-down" game in which one child suddenly pretends to collapse unconscious to the ground and is followed by all the other children in imitation. All these may spread like the plague through a group of children. The highly contagious nature of such behavior is simply imitation in its most intense form. There is little evidence that imitative behavior is ever "cured," although as we grow older the dictates of culture make it more orderly (and take all the fun out of it).

If you want to see the greatest example of the natural human ability to imitate, yes, it seems to be a biological program in our brain, go to:

https://www.youtube.com/watch?v=c5BXdDdsPL4

In this simple video we see a 1 ½ year-old child rocking to the beat of "All the Single Ladies", trying to imitate the dance moves of Beyonce' on TV.

Biologists who study the brain have found what they call "mirror neurons" in the brain that cause the brain to imitate what we see. These are actually groups of neurons, not single neurons.

Using an fMRI, they can see that if a person is just watching a video of another person moving his hands, the brain of the person watching, will "light up" in about 20% of the same brain areas as the person actually moving his hand.

How much of these mirror neurons depend on learning and how much is built into the biology of the brain is unclear. Yet the above video is convening evidence that this quite primate like behavior may be inborn.

Children at this stage display comparatively little insight into the minds of others. When playing with other children their age, they play side by side with them, usually in separate activities, but they do not need to interact with them. When they talk, they may talk at each other simultaneously, neither caring if the other answers the babbling. But out of their developing symbolic ability, they carry on an active conversation with themselves and with others. Self-awareness and other-awareness develop. Out of this gradually increasing sense of awareness comes the second stage in role-playing—the play stage.

Between three and six years of age, the child takes on increasingly more sophisticated levels of symbolic interaction. In the play stage, a boy may take on the role of cowboy or Indian, cop or robber, etc. usually he always wants to be the "good guy" or the guy that wins. He shoots a thousand bullets through his six-shooter, and when he shoots, he expects his opponent to play the role of the "bad guy" and "die." If his opponent does not play his role and "die", the other boy's failure to play his expected role may outrage him. This sense of moral outrage when the other boy does not properly play his role and "die" is significant evidence of a developing concept of role-playing. As the boy gets older, he will learn that he too must play a role— that he too must "die" when he is shot or others will be morally outraged at his failure to play his role.

In the "play stage" children begin "taking the role of the other" rather than simply imitating others. They begin to act toward themselves as others do. They begin to see themselves through the eyes of others. Through the give-and-take of social interaction as simple as that of cowboys and outlaws, they learn the concept of roles. And they learn they must live up to the expectations of others. Still, they are egocentric. They think in terms of their own perception of a situation. They are only taking on a concept of the roles of others.

By seven to eight years of age, the child enters what Mead called the "game" stage. Mead likened this third phase to a "micro-society", as, for example, in Little League baseball. Here, for the first time, the child uses "the group" as the reference for his role. He must visualize the roles of others before he can perform his own. Before he can play the game, he must visualize the roles of the pitcher, who will try to make him strikeout, the infielders, who will try to catch his ball; and the umpire who must call the play. He must abide by the rules of the game, or be thrown out.

The game stage involves learning a complex set of rules to govern his role. He is no longer allowed the free, uncontrolled behavior of the play stage: Now he must cooperate with others or his team will lose. And if he cannot learn his role, he must suffer the taunts and outrage of his peers.

This is the generation of the "corporation man" of our industrial society. Here we learn to play the game according to the rules, to expect certain behavior of others according to their roles, to behave according to the expectation of others, and to change our role as conditions change--as we come to bat, are sent to the outfield, or play first base. Here we learn the lessons of our society, and the lessons mold our society. The spontaneous, unproductive play of youth gives way to cooperative, productive, social interaction (which may give way to worry and ulcers, stagnation, and boredom.).

SELF IDENTITY

William James described the concept of self-identity as the sum total of all a person can call theirs. The "me" with which we identify ourselves is...

... the sum total of all that he can call his, not only his body and his psychic powers, but his clothes and his house, his wife and children, his ancestors and friends, his reputation and works, his land and horses, and yacht and bank account. All these things give him the same emotions. If they wax and prosper, he feels triumphant; if they dwindle and die away, he feels cast down--not necessarily in the same degree for each thing, but in much the same way for all.

In part, we are what we own. If we have money, a conditioned stimulus, we feel secure. If our money is lost or stolen, or our stock investments crash or our house and possessions burn, we feel downcast, depressed, and a great sense of personal loss. We react as if the loss is a physical blow. We may moan and cry or react in anger or despair, as did many who committed suicide during the stock market crash of 1929 that led to the great depression. Even in the more modest stock market crash in 1988, one man who lost everything took a gun and went to Merrill Lynch and killed his stockbroker and himself.

We may even attribute our "self" to our inanimate possessions, as pointed out by Charles Horton Cooley. If we hit a golf ball, we may say "I'm on the green" or "I'm in the rough." The position of the ball is a comment on our standing in the game. And we identify with that position with ourselves.

One man who won a blue ribbon for his prize hogs was so proud of his ribbon that he framed it and hung it on the wall. His pride of achievement was so clear that when the house caught on fire, that ribbon was the first thing he thought to save. His wife and kids were next.

Not just our prize-winning ribbons, but our merit badges, our good conduct medals, our purple hearts, our autographs... all of these become a part of our self, at least for a time, symbolic of our accomplishments, and thus our very self-confidence.

When we identify with someone or something, that object or person becomes a stimulus of great value to us. As James put it:

Our father and mother, our wife and babies, are bone of our bone and flesh of our flesh. When they die, a part of our very selves is gone. If they are insulted, our anger flashes forth as readily as if we stood in their place. Our home comes next. Its scenes are part of our life; its aspects awaken the tenderest feelings of affection; and we do not easily forgive the stranger who, in visiting it, finds fault with its arrangements or treats it with contempt...

James is vividly describing the power of experience over our behavior. Each nation's flag is repeatedly paired with stimuli signifying all things great and noble. We react with hostility toward those who desecrate the flag. When I was teaching at a university in Dallas in the early 1970s two students were arrested for flying the American flag upside down from the balcony of their apartment in protest of the killing in Viet Nam (flying the flag upside is an international signal of distress, ships at sea commonly used it). It outraged the people of Dallas. They were tried and convicted and sent to prison. The conviction was later overturned on a technicality, but the outrage was real. We have fought wars between nations for less.

The incident again occurred in 1988, when the Supreme Court ruled that a man in Dallas who was arrested for setting fire to the American flag in a protest against the Vietnam war, had a constitutional right to this expression. People were again outraged. President Bush called for new laws, congressional representatives led a movement to get an amendment to the constitution to prohibit the desecration of "our" flag. The news media whipped up a massive amount of public opinion, all of them saying the same thing.

Yet in all that the news media said about the incident, the only position they presented was "Should people be allowed to burn the American flag?"

That was never the issue. The issue was that the good citizens of Dallas had sentenced a human being to two years in prison for his act of protest by burning a piece of cloth? Should we be allowed to give a human being a prison record that will follow him for life, in every job application, merely because he protested what he saw a lack of justice in America?"

But emotions ruled. Human values of freedom were eagerly trampled by a herd of politicians and press alike in favor of pushing the drug that was currently popular... the adrenalin surged through the veins, the endorphins coursed through the brain... a thrill went up the spine when the anthem played... hairs stood on end...

Now if the flag that was burned had been a Russian flag...

What we respond to depends on our history of experience, and little more. Words signifying "all things good", paired with a piece of cloth, possess enormous power. The same words have started every war in human history... every call to defend the nation, fight for justice, stand up for the principles. And justice and principles are the first to die.

And we have never taught generations of children to understand the emotions that have killed so many human beings in so many wars.

So, we root for "our" football team. We boo the referee if he calls against us, we boo their fumble recoveries, we boo anything that smacks of injustice toward "our" team. Yet we do not cheer when "their" team makes a good play. We do not demand a replay when our team gets a break that should have gone to their team. We feel a sense of triumph if our side wins a point, and a sting of injustice if we lose.

We do not limit it to our feelings about the flag, or "our" football team. The same emotions apply to all areas of our identity. It may be a political issue or a religious belief; or a court decision about abortion, censorship, or prayer in public schools.

We do not carefully weigh the issues, determine what is fair, and act with justice for all. We react with whatever triggers our adrenalin... and shoots those endorphins into the brain. All logic fails before the power of America's most powerful legal drugs.

THE SOCIAL YARDSTICK:

When I was very young, I occasionally would visit my grandparent's house. As a ritual part of every visit, they would stand me up against the wall and make a mark with a pencil on the wall to show how tall I was. With every visit, I could compare my new mark with the mark of my last visit. From repeated experiences with these changing marks, I formed one of my first learning sets, the meaning of a yardstick. I was only five years old, but the experience is so vivid in my mind that I think I can remember the moment I came to realize the meaning of those marks.

Each of us grows up amid a continued barrage of appraisals by others. Our physical appearance and behavior as infants are approved or disapproved by parents, grandparents, and total strangers. Fortunately for infants, the meanings of these positive and negative appraisals have little impact on their physical well-being. But infants mature, language develops, and gradually the benchmarks take on meaning. We judge ourselves by the appraisal of others; not of just any others, of course, but of the *significant others* in our limited environment.

We take on the values of others; the concepts of beauty, goodness, and behavior that are projected as ideals on the wall of our cultural cave. Once conditioned, these standards become the measure by which we judge ourselves and others. They become the standards of what is attractive or unattractive, moral or evil, skilled or incompetent.

All self-appraisals are based on contrast. We compare our skills in sports, mechanics, cookery, and mate-attracting with those of others we know. We contrast our physical image in a mirror with our friends or our competition in the dating game. Do we come off better or worse? We compare our skill at sports with the others in our gym class. We compare our dress, our manners, and our status to others around us.

Every time we make a positive or negative comment about someone to a friend, we employ a conditioned yardstick, however unjust our judgment might be. And we often ignore the fact that the yardstick we use to judge others is never so strict as the yardstick we use to judge ourselves or those we like.

We also base our self-esteem on some high-water mark of our past accomplishment—the number of points we can score in a game compared to our last game, the number of pounds we lose compared to last week, the amount of money we make this year over last year. When we come out favorably in our comparison with others, we briefly congratulate ourselves—not enough to seem conceited, just enough to make us feel good. The endorphins flow. We call it pride. We self-reinforce. When we top a previous high mark, we pat ourselves on the back... when we do not measure up to those standards, a moment of depression may set in.

Imagine two students who both get a grade of "C." One may feel a sense of elation. Another, with the same grade, may feel depressed. For a student who has a self-ideal of making the best grades, such a grade may produce a great feeling of depression. Indeed, I have had students who argue with passion and anguish over the difference between an 88 and a 90 on a test. Yet a student who was afraid he had failed the test would be happy to find he made a "C."

SELF-ESTEEM: Success/Pretensions

Our self-esteem is related to our pretensions. We may fancy ourselves as the best in some area among our friends or in comparison with the entire world.

Psychologists William James noted that we can increase our self-esteem either by increasing our successes or by reducing our pretensions. This led to his simi-mathematical formula for self-esteem; SE=Successes/Pretentions.

10

WHAT INTELLIGENCE REALLY IS

"If people knew how hard I had to work to obtain my mastery, it would not seem so wonderful after all."
Michelangelo

HOW TO RAISE YOUR I.Q. 15 POINTS WITHOUT STUDYING: The Flynn Effect

If you want to go from Average (100) to Above Average (115) or from Above Average to Seriously Smart (130), all you have to do is raise your I.Q. by 15 points. That is something you can easily do, without the boredom of having to study. Just take the WAIS I.Q. test used in the 1970s and you will automatically score 15 points higher than if you took the WAIS I.Q. test used today.

If you want to raise your I.Q. 20 points, all you have to do is take the Stanford-Binet I.Q. test used by Lewis Terman in the 1920s for his *Genetic Studies of Genius.*

https://www.youtube.com/watch?v=9vpqilhW9uI

James Flynn has convincingly described the relativity of intelligence. Flynn has written and spoken about his own experiences of being fired repeatedly because of his support for "controversial" ideas that would no longer be considered controversial. He left America and became Chair of Political Studies at Otego, New Zealand.

https://www.youtube.com/watch?v=khWxYlO5w-M

Nothing in the biology of the brain has changed in the last 100 years. The biology of humans cannot change that fast. Only the environment has changed. That made it necessary to revise our I.Q. tests to keep every I.Q. score "*relative*" to each other. We had to once again force the test questions to produce a normal curve, the Bell-Curve.

Today, we have vastly greater sources of information. More television news (they had no television in the 1920s), Sesame Street, Speak and Say toys, books that teach math and reading to preschoolers. In the 1950s almost no children ever went to kindergarten, much less to Early Reading or Math courses. Now we have even greater information on the internet with Google and Bing. More of our population goes to college than ever before.

Yet compared to the rest of the world, the U.S. is falling farther and farther behind in relative knowledge of science, math, and ideas.

THE GREAT I.Q. CONTROVERSY

Everything that exists in nature seems to exist in some degree. Some people are very tall, some are very short: Some are very heavy, some very light; some have very dark hair and some very light. In between the two extremes is where the vast majority fall.

Consider any physical trait; height, weight, varying sizes of biceps or busts. If you take one thousand American men and arrange them in order from tallest to shortest, you find a few are very tall, a few very short, but most bunch up in a smooth curve rising toward the middle. The curve looks like a mound of sand, with a large lump of people in the center trailing off to increasingly smaller amounts of people out at either end.

Belgian astronomer Adolphe Quetelet found that this same curve applies not just to physical measurements such as height or weight, but also to the same "laws of chance" that govern the roll of dice or the flip of a coin. If you flip a coin one hundred times, what are the chances that it will land heads and what are the chances it will land tails? It should land heads fifty percent of the time and tails 50% of the time.

It doesn't happen that way. Out of any straight run of one hundred flips, you may find that sometimes it comes out more often heads than tails or vice versa. But if you flip that coin 1,000 times you will discover that for each run of one hundred, some runs will sometimes come up sixty percent heads and forty percent tails. Some series will have 70% heads and 30% tails. A few will have 80% heads and 20% tails. And fewer still will have mostly all heads or tails.

Yet of 1,000 flips of a coin, about half will be heads and half will be tails.

If you arrange these sequences in the same way that you might arrange the number of men by height, you will find that only in a few cases do you come up mostly heads, and only a few cases do you come up mostly tails. The vast majority of all series will come up somewhere in between. Most of them will lump up around 50% heads and 50% tails.

When you plot this out in a graph, you see what psychologists call the *normal distribution curve*. Most physical traits such as height, weight, and chance measurements, all fit in fairly remarkably, to this standard curve, A cousin of Charles Darwin, Sir Francis Galton, later extended Quetelet's discovery of the law of chance curve to include not just physical traits such as height and weight but also what he believed to be genetic intelligence.

The assumption was obvious. If genetic traits such as height and weight would fit into such a bell-shaped curve, then intelligence must surely fit in as well. Yet there is no way to directly measure genetic intelligence as we can measure height and weight. So how do you measure something you cannot directly see?

Intelligence tests are _artificially fit_ into the same bell-shaped curve that height and weight presumably fit. This is done by selecting a few test questions that are so difficult that only a very few people can get them right... just as only a few people are very tall. But they select a few test questions that are so easy that virtually everyone, except a bare few, can get those right (just as there are a few very short people).

Then the rest of the test questions are gradually built up to make a test whose scores fit into that bell-shaped curve. Where most will end up in the middle and the rest of the scores will taper off on either side. Thus, we have an average, a mean, which is artificially set at 100. We consider anything which is markedly above that superior. We consider anything markedly below it inferior in intelligence.

But the important point is that this test is constructed artificially... to *force* it to fit into our assumption of what genetic intelligence should be.

Psychologists will argue that there is more to it than this. That all tests are cross-validated. But all that means is that we correlate them with other I.Q. tests or measures of success to see if they come up with a similar curve. But having made a test that fits into our theoretical model of how individual variations should look tells us nothing at all about the value of the I.Q. test.

The fact that when large numbers of people are tested, they all fall into Adolphe Quetlet's curve does not prove that intelligence fits the same genetic curve as height. It only proves that we constructed our tests to make the scores fit into the same curve.

I suggest that we have been using the wrong model for intelligence. Intelligence is not a continuously variable thing like height or weight. To the contrary. Intelligence is an either-or thing, like sex. You are born a male or a female. Only a tiny percentage of people are born hermaphrodites.

The variations that we measure are superficial. For example, do you have eyes? Yes or no. Of course, some people are born color blind, some have become nearsighted, yet all eyes function the same way. Variations in eyes are nowhere nearly as important as the fact that we all have eyes. The same is true of legs. You either have them or you do not. A few have very long legs, which only gives them an advantage in an artificial game like basketball, where being tall gives you an artificial advantage. Yet all people have legs, and they all work the same way. The differences are superficial.

The story is told of how Abraham Lincoln was once kidded by the press for his long legs. The question was asked; *"How long should a man's legs be?"*

To which Lincoln replied, *"Long enough to reach the ground."*

It is not "how tall are you" that is the important question. All of us are born with basically the same legs, eyes, hands, etc. That is important.

Only when we artificially make the relatively tiny differences into something artificially important, do the differences seem to mean a great deal. The differences are misleading. They are not that important.

What is important is the acquisition of knowledge and skills, the organization of that knowledge, and the strategies we adopt for learning and dealing with life.

We are all born with the same make and style of the brain, just as we are all born with eyes and legs. A few may suffer from brain damage, caused by genetic defects or physical trauma, yet the functioning of the brain itself is virtually identical from one person to the next. It simply does not vary in the same biological way as height or weight vary.

"I am not smarter than most, just more persistent." Albert Einstein

It does, however, differ in the information fed into it, the organization of that information, and the way in which the brain interprets reality (for example; the scientific methods or the idea that anything is possible, etc.).

WHAT WE KNOW ABOUT THE BOTTOM 2-3%

We *know* what causes people to be in the bottom 2-3% of the I.Q. test scores. There is no doubt whatever causes this... brain damage. It is a clear-cut biological cause. A car accident that harms the brain, or by a stroke or hemorrhage that kills brain cells, may cause the brain damage. Or the brain damage may result from oxygen deprivation at birth, when the umbilical cord is pinched, or from a failure to breathe properly. Or, brain damage may result from some of the 6,000 known genetic defects that prevent the brain from developing normally (as in microcephaly, hydrocephaly, Down's syndrome, etc.).

Until about sixty years ago, one preventable cause of mental retardation was the use of metal forceps during delivery. When the doctor had a difficult delivery, he would grip the baby's head with tongs and pull. The baby's skull was soft and pliable. Brain damage resulted. Today, we know better.

The crucial point is this: We know what causes people to be at the bottom 2-3%, *yet we do not know of any biological cause that would put people at the top 2% of an I.Q. test.* We do have a great deal of evidence that experience and knowledge put people in the top 2% of an intelligence test.

Biologists are often enamored over the fact that the I.Q. test fits so beautifully into a Normal Distribution Curve, which is used in all biological measures, even blood tests. That makes them think I. Q. must also be biological. No, it looks so good in a Bell Curve only because it has been artificially designed to fit the curve.

I have to add that I am not saying that I.Q. tests are useless. I have given many hundreds of these tests and I consider the test to be very useful. *All I am saying is that we cannot assume that an I.Q. test measures biological intelligence.* The whole purpose of the test that Alfred Binet developed was to distinguish between which school children needed more help and which needed less help.

Even though the I.Q. test is not considered diagnostic, it is still very useful. It can distinguish between Alzheimer's disease and Korsakov's syndrome. Both show a deterioration of short-term memory. But Alzheimer's disease affects the entire of the brain, Korsakov's syndrome affects the areas such as the hippocampus, that relate to short-term memory but not other abilities. I could go on and on about the value of I.Q. tests, but this is only about "intelligence".

For a better understanding of intelligence, we need to look at the discoveries of Harry Harlow about how Learning to Learn forms, at Piaget's and Kendler's brilliant studies of ability in children and even at how Rat's learn to run in a maze.

THE SMARTEST RAT IN THE MAZE

There is a BBC film about rats running in a maze that is a classic. First, they put a rat in the maze. He runs it lickedy split. He never stops or dawdles; he puts all his energy into his single goal of getting to the food in the center. At every choice point he never makes the wrong turn; he gets to the goal in the center with ease. He looks like a genius rat.

Then they put a second rat in the maze. He has run the maze before. He knows there is a reward in the center. Yet he dawdles along the way. He sniffs at every turn. He often makes mistakes, turning down a dead end in the maze and having to retrace his steps, over and over. And over... He looks like a retarded rat.

The first rat looks like a genius. The second rat looks like a slacker. Both have run the maze before. Both know there is food in the center. The only difference between the two rats is that the second rat has run the maze only about a dozen times. He has only a confused memory of the choice points where he should turn left or right. The genius rat has run the maze close to a hundred times. He has it down pat.

If other people seem smarter than you, it rarely has anything to do with your brain. It typically has to do only with the amount of experience the two have had. *"I am not smarter than others, just more persistent."* Einstein.

Breeding Animals for Intelligence

Some studies have indeed bred animals for "intelligence". Dogs or rats bred for their ability to work puzzles, run mazes, and work discrimination problems show a slight improvement compared to the average, and they reach the maximum of "intelligence" after only 4 generations. Further, an animal bred for the ability to run a maze (as a test of intelligence) may not work a discrimination problem better than average, and vice versa. When we breed for intelligence, we may be breeding for selective attention instead. Doggy ADHD?

The question must be asked, are we breeding for intelligence, or for freedom from distractibility? Any learning study involves slamming doors, strange odors, inconsistent sights, and sounds, all of which distract an animal from the task we want to teach. Animals who are nervous or anxious or have less ability to concentrate on the task at hand and will score less well. An animal that is calm, not anxious, or is better able to pay attention to the task will learn faster. So, is it intelligence we are looking at in animal breeding studies? Or is it freedom from distractibility or calm temperament? The answer is not clear, but there is no evidence that we are breeding for intelligence.

We should not leave another point unsaid. Even if it is possible to find differences in intelligence by breeding dogs to become more intelligent, this cannot explain human differences in intelligence. Humans have never been bred for differences in intelligence. All it would show is that intelligence can be genetically determined to some degree.

PREJUDICE AND PERCEPTION

In one study, psychologists gave students two groups of rats. Half of the students were told they were being given rats that had been bred for generations for their "genius" ability to run a maze. The other half of the students were told they were being given rats that were noted for their inability to run a maze, in effect, "retarded" rats.

The students were then allowed to run the rats in the maze and record the results.

Exactly as predicted, the "genius" rats way outperformed the "retarded" rats.

Then the students were told that all of the rats were exactly the same. They had not been bred for any differences.

What? How could this be? It seems the students who were told they had been given a "genius" rat treated them like princes. In effect, they cuddled the rats, spoke nicely to them, petted them up. The students who had been given the "retarded" rats picked them up by the tails, dropped them into the maze, and generally treated the rats with at least some contempt, and probably resented having to run a known "retarded" rat.

When rats are treated this way, it is very disturbing for them. They are somewhat frightened, slow to respond due to fear, and disturbed enough to interfere with their performance.

That is a hugely important as a lesson for humanity. How we treat individuals by ignoring them due to prejudice based on race or religion or what we think intelligence is, leaves an imprint. The way people treat us, parents or teachers, may have a profound effect on our emotions, and our performance. Yet the effect is so subtle, we rarely notice.

We are all trying our best to run our best in the rat race of life. We should not be inhibited by the idea that other people have a better brain than we do.

PREDICTING ANYTHING?

Now that the I.Q. test has been fit into that bell-shaped curve, you have to find some way to validate it, to prove it means something. So how do you find out if it means anything when you cannot even measure the biological basis (as you could measure height)? The answer is that you correlate the best scores with some measure that is considered to show intelligence. You might correlate the score to see if people

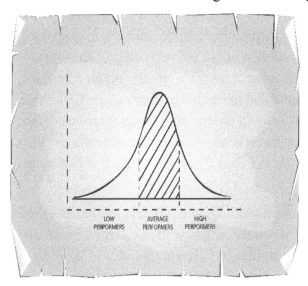

who score high do well on grades at school. You might want to see people who score high do better in terms of the income they bring in. Or you might want to find out if people who score high on these tests are more likely to graduate from college.

I.Q. tests do not do very well at predicting any of these things. The best test psychologists have in their arsenal are the academic achievement tests. Yet the best correlation I have ever seen between an academic test and the college grades or success in college that it is supposed to predict is a correlation of .42. Most such tests and most I.Q tests have correlations of no higher than .40 between the test score and any variable you want to choose. Our best personality tests such as the Minnesota Multiphasic Personality Inventory (MMPI) do not correlate with the observations of personality and behavior any better than .24.

THE HERESY OF CORRELATIONS

Suppose students were to file by my desk and I flipped a coin for each one, heads you pass, tails you fail. The flip of a coin is nothing but chance. It has nothing to do with what you can accomplish. Yet, and this is critical to understand, *sometimes it will be right, just by chance alone.* The same is true of correlations. Sometimes they are right, or wrong, by chance alone.

To be able to predict anything, we must subtract that chance from the actual result of a study.

But here lies a terrible problem. Most journalists, doctors, even, gasp, most psychologists, seem to believe that a correlation of .42 is a percentage. That perhaps 42% of the people with high scores do better than the normal. A. N. Flanzbleu, whose specialty is statistics, has calculated that to be able to predict 25% better than chance the correlation would have to be .66. To predict 50% better than chance, the correlation would have to be .86. Even our best academic achievement tests can only predict success in college at barely 20% better than flipping a coin. It is better than going to a fortune teller at a circus.

The studies on which the arguments that I.Q. is biological are based on the difference between the I.Q. scores of identical twins (with identical genes), and fraternal twins (whose genes are no more similar or different than that of brothers or sisters}. In one such study, it has been shown that identical twins reared apart have I.Q. scores that differ by perhaps 6 or 7 points on the average compared to fraternal twins reared apart whose I.Q.'s may differ 15 points and more. This would suggest that identical twins have more similar biological intelligence and that environment does not much affect it. But there is difficulty with this type of study is the amount of similar experience that these twins had before they were separated to go into separate environments. And this is on top of the more serious question of what the I.Q. measures.

There is another way to look at this same question. One can compare the correlations of the test scores of identical twins and those of fraternal twins, reared in the same environment. A massive study of 850 sets of twins has been completed by John Loehlin and Robert Nichols at the University of Texas. They correlated the test scores of one identical twins with the other twin's test scores and the test scores of one fraternal twin with the next. In theory, any difference between fraternal twins and identical twins would have to be due to genetics, not environment. What they found was this:

Trait	Identical Twins	Fraternal Twins
General Ability I.Q	.86	.62
Special Ability I.Q.	.74	.52
Personality Inventory Scales	.50	.28

Now that looks like very impressive evidence. Identical twins are more alike than fraternal twins. Yet in virtually every trait measured, whether I.Q. or personality, the difference between fraternal twins and identical twins is a correlation of only .24 at most! Presumably, that difference reflects the difference between twins because of heredity alone, since both sets of twins grew up in the "same" environment. One has to first ask; just how much is a correctional difference of .24 worth? And secondly, one must still ask what the test is measuring in the first place.

The substantially larger correlations of .62, .52, and .28 are what both identical and fraternal twins have in common. In short, the similarities far outweigh the differences.

There is more to it than this. Identical and fraternal twins do not grow up in the "same" environment. Loehlin and Nichols found that parents were more likely to treat identical twins the same than to treat fraternal twins the same.

And there is still more. Identical twins can be only male-male or female-female. Yet fraternal twins can be a male and a female. Since males and females are treated dramatically different by our society, in terms of what they are expected to do in school, and even in terms of physical discipline (which is more likely to be used on males), they cannot be said to grow up in the same environment. Studies of identical and fraternal twins (including those for schizophrenia) cannot be unbiased unless they exclude all male-female fraternal twins.

The results suggest that environment may contribute a much greater part of the *similarity* between identical and fraternal twins... compared to the *difference* of only .24 between the two groups.

The current debate dates from the beginning of World War I when the army frantically searched for a screening device for draftees to separate those who had too little intellectual ability to make good soldiers from those who presumably had just enough. Stanford's Lewis Terman was one of several outstanding psychologists whose work led to the development of the Army Alpha Intelligence Test. What the test found was that white American's scored some fifteen points higher than black Americans. How could this be? Some said it was a matter of genes. Others said it was a matter of the environment.

But the tests showed more than this. They showed that northern whites were more "intelligent" than southern whites.

More striking still, it showed that northern *blacks* were more "intelligent" than southern *whites*!

There could not possibly be any difference in the genetics of northerners compared to southerners. Here was evidence that environment shaped I.Q. scores. And what in the environment could account for the reason why people in the north scored some 15 points higher than those in the south?   The answer seemed obvious. Northern schools must be superior to southern schools. They put more into their schools. They had better textbooks, nicer classrooms, and they paid their teachers more.

It was this belief that stuck in the minds of educators and psychologists for half a century. It fired the Supreme Court decision on Brown versus the Board of Education, Topeka that led the way to desegregation of our schools.

Psychologists Kenneth and Mamie Clark showed the Supreme Court that, given a choice between a black doll and a white doll, black children would typically pick the white doll to play with. This underscored the problem of self-concept that helped lead to desegregation in the public schools.

And that led to the head start program of the 1960s. But it was not until the Coleman Report and the reviews of the head start programs by the Congressional Commission on Civil rights that these ideas seemed to be called into question.

James Coleman is a sociologist of outstanding credentials who chaired the report that bears his name. In dramatic contrast to what people had always believed, his report found no evidence that the best schools had any advantage whatever over schools that had been considered average.

Studies done in Britain also found that the top name prep schools seemed to have no advantage over other schools. All this came on top of the failure of the head start program. More recent studies have not found major differences in accomplishments between the wealthy students who come out of Harvard and Yale and Ivy League schools, compared to those who come out of state schools.

So, if superior schools did not cause the 15-point advantage in I.Q. that northerners had over southerners, then what did?

We may never have hard evidence for what caused the difference. But it is difficult to avoid speculating on one probable cause. Southern schools were, in fact, worse off than northern schools. But that may not have been the cause of the poorer education, but an artifact of a more basic problem.

The fact that southern schools were poor was a reflection of the attitude that the south had toward education. Education was not valued as highly in the south as it was in the north. And the fact that southerners tended to disparage education and hold it in less esteem may well have contributed toward their own children having less interest and enthusiasm toward knowledge and education.

As one Texan put it, *"Texas is all about football."* That is what we learn to value in our pep rallies in high school.

Attitude, interest, enthusiasm, all seem more important than the amount of money spent on education. Giving children a "chance" to learn in a superior school does not guarantee that they will. Only the emotional attitudes, the enthusiasm, the interest, stimulate the development of knowledge. And that is something they get from their parents and their society; if they get it at all.

"Experience shows that success is due less to ability than to zeal."
Charles Buxton

Education only prospers when knowledge is valued for its own sake by the parents and the society. When you have a society where personal beliefs are valued more than science, you have a failure of the educational system.

"Ummmphhh"

25 Points

TOWARD A UNIFIED FIELD THEORY

Psychologists have made a name for themselves by criticizing another point of view and establishing their own as superior (behavioral, developmental, cognitive, perceptual, neuropsychology, etc. etc.). All have found some important pieces. What we need is to put the known pieces together.

We cannot call ourselves a science if we are only a gaggle of conflicting opinions.

Yet psychology has gone more toward a philosophy of differing opinions, instead of a unity of understanding. We need a Unified Field Theory that combines our knowledge of brain, behavior, perception, cognition, sociology, cultural anthropology and more.

The most basic sensory impressions can combine with the S-S associations to become sensory *perceptions*.

The more basic perceptions can combine to become *concepts* (or schema, or cognitive maps, or reason, or concepts, etc.).

The brain itself seems to have the biological ability to produce a form of stimulus *generalization*, that makes this possible.

S-S associations can combine with trial-and-error learning to become ideas or concepts or perceptions, as Harlow demonstrated.

It is more likely that all areas are similar to simply changing the frequency of electromagnetic radiation can produce everything from radio and radar to visible colors, to infrared and ultraviolet radiation. Or how changing the atomic structure can change the very nature of matter. Or, like the four base pairs of DNA can produce every cell, in every type, in the body.

Both cognitive psychology and neuropsychology have benefited from the fun of working with children and the shock and awe of fMRIs and PET scans, yet neither has come close to providing the wealth of simple explanations for the mind that originated from the most basic elements of stimulus-stimulus associations. Their explanations are the Facebook of psychology, full of image grabbing excitement, but, like living on ramen noodles, we come away unsatisfied with the lack of relevance to how the mind works.

They have overwhelmed today's psychology. Yet they have no ability to predict, to explain, to allow an understanding of how the mind works at the level of human behavior. Behavioral and perceptual psychology have been largely ignored in the race for the new psychology, the pretty pictures of an fMRI scan, an obscure idea of schemas, a turgid description of cognitive behavior.

How can they explain the behavior of a Kamikaze pilot, the value of a Picasso painting, the beauty of tiny feet for 1,000 years in China, the emotional effect of the witch hunts, the roar of the crowd on the mind of football players and fans, when "their" team scores?

By this analysis of perceptual psychology, the brain is not the linear computer imagined by Turing, although the function is similar. Instead, it is closer to being a holographic computer, more accurately a perceptual computer, ruled by emotion, steeped in the prime experiences that are now "hardwired" into the brain by experience.

We come to "know" our reality from the images embedded in our brain, the scanning of perceptions, the potshards in our brain. We come to perceive our reality from the anticipatory ability of our mind, not unlike Pavlov's dogs salivating in anticipation of what comes next. The relatively high speed of scanning creates the process of the conscious mind.

Yet no analogy is entirely adequate to describe what the brain does. Just as a chapter on the senses notes that we still cannot explain how the brain gives us color, sound, taste, smell, out of simple neural responses, we are not at a point where any analogy seems adequate. Perhaps a future neuropsychologist will enlighten us.

We cannot understand the human mind without borrowing from the greatest ideas in every area of psychology; Brain, Behavioral, Perception, Cognitive, Computer analogy, Neuropsychology, and the MORE that makes up an almost infinite number of *permutations* (selective attention, primacy effects, stimulus generalization, approach-avoidance, order, sequence, learning sets, emotions, and more, and more, and...).

COGNITIVE PSYCHOLOGY

Cognitive Psychologists often see themselves as having replaced Behavioral Psychology, yet it is more accurate to say that they added an important new dimension to psychology. Cognitive psychology could never explain what Behavioral Psychology could explain, and Behavioral Psychology could not explain what Cognitive Psychology demonstrated.

By selecting a few studies that only cognitive psychology could explain, it gave a mistaken impression that the advantage always went to their position. Perhaps more likely, both saw a portion of how the mind works, but not the whole picture.

- Wolfgang Kohler's extensive study of "insight" in chimpanzees was a major step toward recognizing that something was going on at a higher level inside the brain, although trial an error learning was clearly a part of the puzzle.

- Selective Attention, demonstrated by Donald Broadbent having students wear headphones, playing different stories into each ear, were told to pay attention to only one story. When asked questions about what was happening in both ears, they were able to effectively answer those questions that were about the story only happening in the ear they were attending to.

- Tolman's studies of latent learning and "cognitive maps" strongly suggested that we learn far more than just a simple stimulus-response association. This presaged the realization that we may learn all sensory input, not just an S-R relationship.

- Piaget's experiments with human children provided a rich source of understanding of how children understand reality differently than adults; from their own experiences, and how this understanding changes throughout life.

- Studies of memory and the fallibility of memory by Elizabeth Loftus and others have found our memory is vague and easily re-written. Eyewitness testimony, often considered the best evidence, is a serious problem which has led to the jailing of innocent people. The number one cause of innocent people being convicted of crimes they did not commit, is eyewitness testimony.

https://www.oxfordbibliographies.com/view/document/obo-9780199828340/obo-9780199828340-0026.xml

The major contributions of cognitive psychology are important, but not paradigm changing. They add to the paradigm.

WHERE COGNITIVE PSYCHOLOGY FAILS

The failure of cognitive psychology to provide a bridge between simple learning, such as trial and error, and cognitive processes, left their theories without substance.

- Piaget's concepts of Schema, Accommodation, and Assimilation are subject to the problem of the Nominal Fallacy: the belief that, by having named something, we have somehow explained it.

- Without a basis in hard evidence, these words have no substance.

- Studies that rely solely on how long an infant spends looking at one picture, rather than another, are not well grounded. Guessing at what the infant is "thinking" is not scientific.

- Harlow's study of "learning sets" provided a hard evidence ground for going from simple association to cognitive psychology, but has been largely ignored by cognitive psychologists.

- More important, they ignore the most recent discoveries of cataract studies in babies that show the brain itself is profoundly molded by experience. Without visual experience, the brain itself will never develop the ability to see. Experience itself changes the biology of the brain and our perceptions. The human brain, like a computer, has the functions in place, but without programming, both are a vast tabula rasa, without knowledge or understanding.

- In addition, the brain is molded by experience in a manner so profound, that we can only "see" (or understand) what experience allows us to see.

- The excitement of working with children, instead of rats and pigeons, has led many psychologists to accept the idea that this is more important, which helped extend cognitive psychology to a point where they have ignored more basic processes.

COGNITIVE NEUROSCIENCE
OR NEUROPSYCHOLOGY

The relatively new area of Neuropsychology has provided us with the shock and awe of beautiful multicolored pictures (artificially colored) to show the inner firing of groups of nerve cell. The use of fMRI and PET scans provide a dramatic view of the interaction of parts of the brain we could never otherwise have known. It is now being used to map the human brain.

- These studies have shown, for one example, that there are nerve tracts going from the temporal cortex and Wernike's area, to the Motor cortex and Brocca's area. These areas "light up" (the neurons absorb more oxygen or use more energy) when we engage in speaking.

- Professor Nancy Kanwisher of MIT has a remarkable series of lectures describing how this has been used to tease out how we know there are many specialized areas of the brain that respond to faces, language, and music. These are a series well worth watching if you are fascinated with the function of the brain itself. Not since the initial discoveries of Brocca and Wernike have we had such a complete view of how the brain works. Professor Kanwisher has used her own brain to demonstrate how the brain functions.

- https://www.youtube.com/watch?v=5Yj3nGv0kn8

- https://www.youtube.com/watch?v=ZueXhzQS1k4

- One perhaps surprising discovery at MIT is the relationship between language and thought. Different areas "light up" when we are thinking than when we are using language.

- Her associate, Rebecca Saxe found that there are specific parts of the brain that "light up" when we *think about what other people are thinking about us*. It does not light up for any other task. This area is above and behind your right ear. It takes many years to develop this ability. How much of this is biological or learned?

https://www.youtube.com/watch?v=IAiB6kmnxeM

https://www.youtube.com/watch?v=GOCUH7TxHRI

WHAT NEUROPSYCHOLOGY CANNOT TELL US

No matter how complete our map of the human brain becomes, it will never tell us about the origin of our knowledge, beliefs, or emotions. It cannot explain the behavior of a Kamikaze pilot or a suicide bomber, it cannot tell us why we speak English or Swahili, or where our prejudices or interests come from.

- Neuropsychology gives us no insight into personality differences, what makes for genius, why we love or hate or feel the emotions of shame or guilt.

- Only the low-tech methods of basic psychology, sociology, and cultural anthropology can provide us with an understanding of the uniquely human thoughts that control our mind.

- Even if we know everything possible about the functioning of the neurons in our brain, about every part of the brain and how they interconnect, it will tell us nothing about basic human behavior. In every final analysis we have to go on to the simple associations that are encoded in our minds.

COMPUTER SCIENCE AND ITS CONTRIBUTION

Although the brain is not like a hardwired computer, it shares remarkable similarities to a computer.

- SWITCHING: The Neurons that power the brain work in a simple ON or OFF function, much like a computer, with the addition of graded potentials. However, the neurons give us changes in the rate of firing, pattern of firing, and sequence of firing. Neurons allow a "decision" of whether or not to fire based on the excitatory or inhibitory (as in GABA) neurotransmitters firing.

- DECISION MAKING: Perhaps the most dramatic semi-similarity is the way in which both computers and the brain make decisions.

Computers use an IF-THEN decision diamond or DO LOOP to make a decision. In a flow chart, in the Decision Diamond, the computer compares two numbers (IF X = Y, THEN go on to the next step. IF X does not equal Y, THEN go back to a previous step in the program.)

- CONTRAST and COMPARISON: In a similar way, the human mind compares and contrasts two variables. This allows the brain to make a "choice" as to whether the two variables (or stimulus patterns) are similar or not. This is most evident in Approach-Avoidance conflict or seeing a solution to a problem.

- PREPROGRAMMED PROCESSING: Like a computer, the brain is biologically structured to process information. Just as a computer must have DOS or a Disk Operating System loaded into itself before new programs or information can be fed into it, so does the human mind. The early experiences described by Harlow and Piaget show how these operating systems are gradually loaded into the brain.

DESPITE THE SIMILAR FUNCTIONS OF THE COMPUTER AND THE BRAIN, THERE ARE ALSO DRAMATIC DIFFERENCES.

- EMOTION: Is the primary force that controls human motivation. There is no comparable method in the computer. Curiosity, Pleasure, Fear, Anger, and all of the various combination of these that produce excitement, shame, guilt, etc. are a unique product of the brain and experience.

- Although it is possible to simulate emotion in a computer, this tells us absolutely nothing about the programs and emotions that life and society feed into the human mind.

- Only the low-tech methods of learning in *psychology, sociology and cultural anthropology* can tell us how the brain uses emotion and comparison to make the brain into a useful, programmed, mind.

- PSYCHOLOGY (Learning) picks up, where biology leaves off. Sociology and cultural anthropology come in to provide the next step of information.

- The mind itself is structured by its experiences in a way that is quite unlike a computer. The information and perception, structure the brain itself (as in our unique perceptions), and determine what the brain is capable of "seeing" or experiencing.

25 PRINCIPLES OF PSYCHOLOGY

IMPORTANT GENERAL PRINCIPLES THAT APPLY TO A WIDE VARIETY OF PSYCHOLOGICAL EXPERIENCES:

1.   We are Each at the Center Of Our Own Perception of Reality: Each of us grow up as the center or our own background of experiences. No two are exactly alike, yet we have similar underlying principles of behavior.

2.   The studies of cataracts in babies, and the studies by Blakemore and Cooper of cats unable to see horizontal or vertical lines if they had not had experience with these lines, is a profound demonstration of the essential need for experience. The human brain is far more like a Tabula Rasa than we ever knew.

3.   *Learning does not just give the brain information to use in processing as a computer; it changes the brain itself so completely, that it creates a new reality in the brain. From this reality, our conscious mind "sees" what the brain's perceptions make it possible to see.*

4.   Insight: From the Necker Cube to the upside-down lady, our moment of insight comes from an automatic associating of perceptions in the brain.

5.   Our visual and verbal illusions (trapezoidal illusion and "take two apples from three apples, what do you have" illustrate our profound dependence on our previous experience for even the most basic cognitive processes.

6.   Emotion rules. In interpersonal interaction, politics, religion, and everyday experience. Even if we do not actually experience the emotion, the brain is quite capable of computing the association, based on the emotion.

7.   The WOW! Factor, that unique emotion we experience from the glorification of sports in our schools and entertainment in our media has hijacked the value of education. The public has little understanding of the value of science. The roar of the crowd has stripped education of any value in the minds of students.

8.   For most of reality, the mind does not "think", we *perceive* reality; based on our experiences.

9.   Our brain has the ability to process stimuli relatively rapidly, thus allowing us to "*consciously*" make our way through the stimuli in life by anticipating what we will encounter next, in much the same way that Pavlov's dog's brain could anticipate what would come next, after the bell rang.

10.   Anticipation and stimulus generalization are the basis of much of what we call the *conscious* mind. This much comes from the biology of the brain itself.

11.   **Our brains are hardwired and even rewired by our experiences.**

12.   PAVLOV'S SPECIAL THEORY OF RELATIVITY

1.   Pavlov conditioning a dog to salivate and wag his tail to pain. Even as important a biologically based reaction in our brain, our DNA, such as the *fight-or-flight* response, can be rewired by learning.

2.   The woman whose heart rate went from 76 to 143 beats per minute at sight of a feather, shows how this works explains how a learned fear reaction controls the biology of our body.

3.   The ability of S-R to control the pupillary response of the eye, or a knee jerk, and more, equal the power to control the biology of the body.

4.   The emotion we feel when we almost have a traffic accident, as adrenalin and cortisol shoot into the blood, and our heart jumps, is a dramatic indication of how our learning controls the biochemistry of our body.

Learning is subtle. It is not "free will"
1.   We are not aware of learning the language we speak, yet it is clearly learned, not innate.
2.   Why do you speak English instead of Swahili? Or Spanish instead of Quechua?
3.   How old were you when you decided (free will?) to speak English instead of Swahili?
4.   Why do we sit in the same seat in school we were sitting in by the second day of class?

5. Autonomic nervous system reactions from saliva, to dilation of the pupil of the eye, to lactation, to the immune system responses.

6. The movie JAWS conditioned people to have a fear reaction to the music that happened just before someone got eaten by a shark, and politicians use emotionally charged words to attempt to destroy their competition.

13. THE GENERAL THEORY OF RELATIVITY

Conditioned Emotional Reactions determine what we like or dislike, love or hate, what we seek, what we avoid, what we die for. Everywhere in advertising, politics, dating, interpersonal relations, others strive to tickle our amygdala with words that have been *associated* with positive or negative emotions or anger.

1. The Law of Effect and Approach-Avoidance Conflict: *"No matter how high or lowly the beast we all do what pleasures most or pains least."* Unknown Sage

2. Words can elicit emotional reactions in our brain. Politicians, the press, preachers and ourselves all use words to elicit an emotional reaction from others: "You Moron!" or emitting stimuli in dating to impress our date (dressing up, makeup, being polite, taking someone to a nice place to eat, etc.)

3. ***Thoughts*** can elicit an emotional reaction in the brain. Psychologist Neal Miller found students who were shown a T or a 4 and give a mild electric shock associated with the T, then asked to think T or think 4, showed a GSR reaction to the thought of T that lasted for 25 trials after the shock was stopped.

4. Our own thoughts, stimuli inside the brain, associated with something negative or positive can produce feelings of elation or depression or anger. Even if we do not have an emotional reaction to a word, thought or idea, the fact that they have been *associated* with an emotion in

the past, leads us to perceive them as positive or negative or anger producing (as in "politically incorrect" words, ideas, etc. resulting in censure by the media.

5. Conditional fear responses can control the body's release of adrenaline, epinephrine, cortisol, and more.

6. A learned (conditional) emotion can trigger a rush of adrenalin into our blood. Our heart may jump. From the Salem witch trials ("witch! witch!") to Hollywood horror stories, to Spielberg associating music with someone being eaten by a shark in JAWS,; to our politics and religions, emotion is profound...

EXAMPLES:

1. Conditional (Learned) emotional response in China to small feet as "sensual".

2. Conditional (Learned) emotional response in Surma society to big lips as valued.

3. Conditional emotional response to Surma boys who want to be a champion stick fighter.

4. Conditional positive emotions operate in sexual responses, pleasure responses, etc.

5. Approach-Avoidance Conflict results when the same thing is positive and negative as in whether or not to eat more pie or not, or whether or not to have sex.

14.   Patterns of thinking: Programs Embedded in the Brain

1. The automatic brain takes over after experience, even when we think we think. When we first learn to drive a car (or play a guitar or type on a computer keyboard) we have to consciously think before each action. After a while these actions are so well learned we no longer have to think. The automatic brain takes care of all the movements. We automatically brake when the car in front of us breaks, etc. We can daydream on

the way to work and be surprised when we get there.

2. These chains of conditioned responses become embedded in the cerebellum of the guitarist, typist or driver and become automatic.

3. We always sit in the same seat in class that we picked the first day of class. *WHY?*

4. Post-Traumatic Stress Disorder (PTSD) is most associated with the number of exposures to blood and death. *WHY?*

5. People who commit suicide have had 3 to 4 times more negative experiences than the average person.

6. Other patterns of thinking that can become embedded in the brain involve anxiety, anger, depression, etc. *HOW?*

7. We also develop automatic ways of responding to others often depending on what we have learned to anticipate from others (as in thinking "what will others think of me?") or in being afraid to give a speech in public for fear of "what will other people think".

8. If we have multiple experiences with anxiety producing events, especially early on, our brain may develop a pattern of anticipating that something bad will happen as in a feeling of impending Doom (Generalized Anxiety Disorder) in much the same way that Pavlov's dogs salivated in anticipation of food when the bell rang.

9. You see this same pattern of development in PTSD, Depression, Obsessive Compulsive behavior, anxiety disorders, even addiction.

10. Strategies of Thinking: If parents learn to think they have to watch out for every little mistake a child makes to insure they do not grow up spoiled or a brat or disobedient, they will react with more discipline and angst over everything the child does (as in the terrible twos, or teen-age independence thinking). Whereas a parent that thinks children grow up to be adults on their own may not be as involved in their upbringing. On the other hand, a parent that sees that their influence has some value, may provide a

somewhat in-between pattern of child rearing.

11. It is not the "type" of parenting that determines our behavior, but our "theory" or strategy of what parenting requires. Our learned ideas about discipline, knowledge, and life determine what parents do. That is learned, for better or worse.

15. Permutation Effects: anything that changes the very basic nature of physics (as in air, in which falls fastest--a book or piece of paper) or in learning.

Primacy Effects:

1. If Little Albert had many positive experiences playing with friendly white rats before Watson attempted to teach him to be afraid of furry animals, it would have been almost impossible to teach Albert to be afraid of furry animals. *WHY?*

2. "Take 2 apples from 3 apples. What do you have? 92% of student cannot answer that question. *WHY?*

3. America ranks 24th in the world in science. *WHY?*

a. the press and politicians rate *Opinions* as more important than the *Evidence.* This is evident in everything from global warming and climate change, where 97% of scientists agree and only 3% disagree, or to the dangers of smoking cigarettes in the 1960s (yet back then the press gives equal time to both), to the economy to political opinions on abortion to DNA to the cause of mental illness.

a. The hard evidence is ignored in favor of personal opinions because the hard evidence often does not support what people want to believe, so it gets censored so the press or politicians will not lose large numbers of viewers/supporters.

b. We do not teach WHY we need the scientific method in

schools, we only teach the bare bones of the formal scientific method.

c. People are accustomed to having their ideas served up in such a way that it allows them to ignore anything that does not agree with their personal ideas.

d. Our cultural heroes are athletes and entertainers. Every American knows who the fastest swimmer, the best golfer, the top football players, almost no one in America knows Jonas Salk, Philo T. Farnsworth, David Lloyd, Myra Kirshenbaum or Francis Crick.

e. Most Americans know the name of the first astronaut to land on the moon. Almost no American has even heard of the names of any of the scientists whose expertise put him there.

f. Our public schools glorify football. We have pep rallies every week for the football team, majorettes and cheer leaders cheer, the band plays for the team.

g. How many of you ladies would brag to your girlfriends in high school that you were dating the guy who just won the National Computer FreeCell Contest?

h. Text books cover thousands of studies, but do not relate them to any serious issue that might offend anyone (often called political correctness).

i. Psychologist David McClelland once noted that you can tell something about where a culture is headed by analyzing the books that children read (or maybe the movies they watch). Harry Potter? The Zombie Apocalypse? Transformers? X-Men? John Wick 6?

j. Are we all going to Hell in a Gucci bag?

THEORIES OF INTELLIGENCE?

1. Spearman's "G": General Intellectual Ability that applies to everything we do.

2. Gardiner's or Thurstone's Multiple Intelligences: Specific intellectual abilities such as Mathematical ability, Visual-Spatial ability, Memory, Verbal Comprehension, Reasoning, etc.

3. Biological Models: We are born with different types of Computers for brains. Some may have an 8088, or 486 or Pentium I-IV. They believe that Intelligence is in the biology of the brain.

4. Learning or Software Models of Intelligence: A computer is nothing but a very heavy doorstop. It only has value when computer programs (operating system, word processor, spreadsheets) *are* loaded into the computer. Likewise, the brain only has value if the knowledge that is loaded into our brain is accurate and adequate.

5. The accuracy of the information fed into a computer determines the output. As programmers put it, GI-GO (Garbage In-Garbage Out).

16. GENIUS OR SIMPLE ABILITY INVOLVES:

1. MOTIVATION: Einstein was a genius in physics, but an imbecile in geology. Why?

2. SELECTIVE ATTENTION: What we learn causes us to pay attention to some things but not others.

3. KNOWLEDGE: We learn what we are motivated to learn. If you don't learn it, you don't know it.

4. THINKING OUTSIDE THE BOX: Neither Copernicus nor Darwin nor Einstein nor Watson and Crick (DNA molecule) had any knowledge that was not readily available to everyone in their day. Their ability derived from being able to "Think Outside the Box", to doubt the ideas already embedded in their brain, to see new connections.

5. PUTTING IDEAS TOGETHER: Copernicus, Darwin, Freud, Einstein, Watson and Crick all put old ideas together to develop

a new concept that explained the known mysteries of life. This is like us doing the question; "Divide 30 by 'A and add 10. What do you get?" Even though we have all had fractions and we have all learned division, it is still almost impossible to put these two ideas together to answer this question. 96% of students get it wrong, even genius IQ students. Only the mathematics majors seem to get it right (experience tells).

6. Each of the above were able to go outside the Box only by questioning the ideas already embedded in their minds by the Primacy Effect (what they had learned before) and being able to put ideas together that no one else ever had.

7. Copernicus, Galileo, Darwin rarely had their ideas accepted in their day. The conditioned emotions attached to being different, the primacy effect, all worked to prevent their acceptance by the majority.

Never forget we are only a few hundred years away from a time when everybody on the face of the earth believed that the earth was flat and in the center of the universe, our grandmothers were witches, bleeding people made them well, Iraq had weapons of mass destruction, and All Men were Created Equal (except for slaves, Indians, women, gays, immigrants, people who don't believe what we believe, etc.). The human brain has not changed in tens of thousands of years, we are all still stupid.

Only the discovery of a new, learned strategy, a method of studying reality, the Scientific Method (Systematic Observation in Copernicus and Galileo, Experimental design as in Placebo control in Medicine) have made it possible to go beyond the powerful trap of personal opinions and cultural bias.

7. WORDS:

1.   Words, *associated* with an emotion, control most human behavior. Peer Group Pressure, the big lipped women of the Surma, foot binding in China.

2.   Why would we respond with hurt and anger if we were called a "Moron"? Why are people outraged if someone questions their political beliefs. Why is it so impossible to change an emotionally held belief? Why is it so hard to change the ideas first embedded in our brain?

3.   The media and politicians use words to tickle our amygdala, trigger emotions in our brain. Mostly fear or anger at witches, Indians, weapons of mass destruction, immigrants, etc., etc.

4.   In JAWS Spielberg used music, associated with the idea of being eaten by a shark, to trigger an emotional reaction in our brain to the music.

5.   In JOHN WICK the writers used anger, elicited by the bad guys beating up John Wick, stealing his car, KILLING HIS PUPPY! To justify Wick killing 36 men just to get to kill the man who KILLED HIS PUPPY!

> 1. Kids, and some politicians, use **words** as in name calling, nasty tweets, to control the limbic system of others. The man in the elevator who, faced with the fact that four others were facing the wrong way, turned to face the same way. What will people think?

2.   When little Billy was in first grade he tripped on the way to the board. Everybody laughed. Even if it does not happen to us, the idea is implanted in our mind that if we do or say something stupid, everyone will laugh at us. What will people think?

3.   When adults were asked what they were most afraid of, fear of death came in third (Book of Lists). Fear of having to give a presentation in public came in first. What will other people think?

4.   Why do we not sing out loud to ourselves when standing in the checkout line at an H.E.B. the way we might sing out loud to ourselves while driving alone in our car? What will other people think?

WHAT WILL OTHER PEOPLE THINK?
PEER GROUP PRESSURE:

"Peer group" refers to others of your same age level, employment or grade level. gradually the peer group comes to have more influence over most adolescents than parents (not in all cases).

Peer groups, Society, Psychological problems, psychosis

8. PSYCHOLOGICAL PROBLEMS OF THE INDIVIDUAL: EMOTIONAL WORDS, IDEAS,

- Beliefs: We react to what we believe is real, whether it is or not. Those with Anorexia believe they are fat even when everyone else sees them as too skinny.

- Those whose politics or religion are emotionally held, are likely to react with anger to anyone who seems to question those ideas. Copernicus made two models one of the earth in the center of the solar system and the second with the sun in the center. Only one model could explain what astronomers had been observing about the retrograde motion of Mars and the seemingly random brightening and dimming of the planets. These models enabled him to think outside the box. Now that you can explain how he explained the retrograde motion of Mars, you now know something that not one American in one million can explain. You are now a genius.

- Darwin had no knowledge that was not available to every biologist of his day, but putting two ideas together; Thomas Malthus's essay on exploding population growth) with individual variation, combined with what he already knew about how we have been breeding our horses and chickens, led to the concept of evolution. The biologist Huxley kicked himself for having seen the obvious so often, but missed its conclusion.

- Einstein learned early in life to distrust the ideas he was being told by others. In part this led him to be able to think outside the box and consider radical new ideas about how physics worked. He had no knowledge that was not readily available to every physicist of his day, but he organized that knowledge differently.

What psychological points are illustrated by the questions below?

- Take two apples from three apples. What do you have?
- Divide 30 by one half and add ten. What do you get?
- Why were our founding fathers so gay?

General Observations

1. In the example of excitement (the "WOW!" effect) was noted as...

2. In the case of the cows "humping" other cows, this was presented as an example of ...

3. In the case of the frogs their instinctual sexual response led them to....

4. In the case of dogs, the fact that a male dog that reaches puberty will attempt to mate with a human leg, a cat, even a dachshund attempting to have sex with a lion, all suggests that....

5. All of the above incidents regarding sex suggest that much of sexual behavior is ....

6. What problems are created by the fact that nature has biologically programmed young people to begin to engage in sex at puberty, yet society has changed so much that teens are unable to get a job or otherwise support a family today?

7. Among the Zoe of South America, the umbepo is a wooden tube placed through a hole in their lower lip. The Zoe consider people who do not have the umbepo to be...

8. Among the Surma women are most attracted to men who are...

9. Among American teens females are often most attracted to males who are...

10. In the Chinese culture mothers who failed to bind their daughter's feet were ...

11. In our society today the average age of marriage for men and women is about...

12. In Chinese culture a woman's beauty was measured by...

13. Chinese men were likely to be sexually excited by reading....

14. In the entire of human history, the ability to read was rare until the last 200 years. Yet today, people can be sexually excited by reading books about sex. The fact that words can elicit a sexual response is most like....

15. In Rachman's study, where he paired women's high heel boots with a picture of a naked lady, he demonstrated that any neutral response can come to elicit a sexual response in males. This is most like....

16. Albert Bandura's study of college males and what parts of a picture (scenery or scenery with a naked lady) they spent most of their time looking at, found that half the males spent most of their time looking at the naked lady, the other half spent most of their time looking at the scenery and only occasionally glanced at the naked lady. This difference was due to....

17. The reason why Surma males are emotionally excited by seeing males hit each other with sticks or seeing a woman with a big lip is described as.... Peer group...

18. The Biological theory of how sexual preference begins is...

19. A Psychological theory of how sexual preference begins is....

20. American's all talk about what we value in education. What teens in high school value is most likely to be determined by what they get excited about in school. So, what do teens in American schools get excited about?

21. We are all reeeeealy stupid. That is why we need the scientific methods.

Psychology, Counseling, and Education are at a "tipping point" on the edge of an active volcano. In the 1970s an average of 25,000 Americans a year committed suicide. Today, that figure stands at 48,000 per year, every year, _before_ the job loss from Covid-19.

Even though we now have six times more psychologists, psychiatrists, and school councilors than we had then, and a 400% increased use of anti-depressive medications in just 20 years, we have failed massively. Unhappiness in life is epidemic. Our schools now have police watching our children, something unheard of in the 1970s. Where did we go wrong?

"The only defense against the world is a thorough knowledge of it." John Locke.

We could easily use the existing educational system for a program of preventive psychology based on the better principles of psychology by the best minds in psychology. Albert Bandura, in an almost unknown experiment, found he could use modeling *films* to prevent panic and counter the fear of dogs in forty children, simply by showing them *films* of a happy boy and a dog. We can use some of the methods in this book to accomplish a similar success with 40 or 400 children or adults at once, something no individual counseling can accomplish.

By combining two of the best scientific methods, Systematic Observation, as used by Copernicus, Galileo, Einstein, Alexander Fleming, Jane Goodall and Margaret Mead, with the Experiments of Albert Bandura and others, it is possible to transform the problems of life for the better. We can deal with cyberbullying, feelings of failure, anxiety, depression, prejudice and more.

Anxiety, Depression, Self-Help, Social Skills, Success: What is it the greatest minds in psychology and those who are the most successful in life know about success and failure? How can we use this knowledge to prevent problems and increase success? Knowledge is a key to success and to surviving failure.

"If only I knew then, what I know now..." is the most common regret of life. It fairly screams the critical importance of knowledge.

Knowledge and understanding can change your brain as effectively as any therapy. Preventing psychological problems can be more effective than treating them after they occur. This book is about how learning from others can protect ourselves and our children from the pain of living and learn the social skills and knowledge that make us successful in our personal lives, raising our children, our families.

This book is an attempt to provide the understanding we need for ourselves and our children to do well in a world that often makes no sense, is often irrational, and difficult to understand. In their own words, we will read about the experiences that inspired the lives and success of others that help give us a hint at a blueprint of life.

See it at https://www.amazon.com/dp/173600252X

ACKNOWLEDGMENTS

Cover background by askandrew
Photos licensed from depositphoto
Illustrations from depositphoto
Additional photos and illustrations as indicated
Permissions and editing by SLG
References are given throughout the book and attributed to the original source.
Apologies if anyone has been missed.

Galileo Nicku
Giordano Bruno pyty
Six cells dividing in Darwin math frenta
Darwin Nicku
Evolution of Human Types nicolasprimola
Four Skulls of Hominids   Liliya.Butenko
Orangutan baby hdamke
Gorilla Baby turtleman
Watson's Spiral Staircase Andreus
E=mc2 nevenova
Einstein, King, Gandhi diego_cervo

PAVLOV marusyachaika
Pavlov's tank maxtor7777
Starving Artist Cartoon andrewgenn
Never Heard of Picasso andrewgenn
Picasso style example pepeemilio2
Artist's hunger for recognition   andrewgenn
Hake fish fotoall
Cow in India mzuuzu
Illusion Footprints on Concrete   motorolka
Illusion lines Furian
Illusion Multiple Boxes Necker Cube Alisher
Line and Motion circle SvetlanaParsh
Zulu Hut Round Dendenal
Schrodinger's Cat
Cats Selfie funny_cats
Dr. viewing EEG yacobchuk1
Necker Cube Variation Iconscout

EEG Record dusan964
EEG WIRE EXAMPLES tumponkrit
EEG WAVE LENGTH Polina_po
Cataract surgery Bork

Tattooed Couple AllaSerebrina
Girl with piercings_sucher
Lesbian Cows Haylight
Mursi tribe, Woman with Liip Plate miroslav_1
2 Mursi women with lip plates   luisapuccini
Child in Thailand with Neck Rings agiampiccolo
Woman in Thailand with Neck Rings agiampiccolo
Theater Masks top of chapter   Morphart
Robert Boyle georgios
Vouban Georgios
heel boot bersenvstudio

Cognition
IQ robot girl chess vitaliy_sokol
Ape head left OlgaTropinina
Sultan sulks head in hand onot
Sultan last bdnz
Sultan chimp thumbs up Cundrawan703
Rat Maze edesignua
Developmental children lemony
2-7 yr girl developmental Victoria Novak
Happy 12-year-old OlgaTropinina

Lorenz Goslings following Mother rhamm
Lorenz duck Victoria_Novak

Frogs Morphart
Puppy chewing toy eriklam
Baboon baby imitates mother WittkePhotos
Harlow rhesus adult andrevoleynik
Rhesus mom with baby Ukususha
Frightened chimp harlow turaevgeniy
Social Smile Baby sborisovHigh

Cute rat Hall Temperament Pakhnyushchyy
Cute puppies temperament Miraswonderland
Cute rat front temperament 2 Pakhnyushchyy
George Washington Pony Tail   DepositNovic
Thomas Jefferson Pony Tail   lenschanger
Color chimp baby on board watman
Young seeing eye dog girls zoeytoja

Seeing Eye Dog Training Belish
Cat and Mouse Friend bloodua
Dog and Cat Friend pyotr021
Male Awareness Weekend   andrewgenn

XY Genetics chapter opening perig76
Egg cell surrounded by sperm   phonlamai
Stork bringing Baby Dazdraperma
China Golden Lotus foot ChinaImages
Chinese Golden Lotus Shoe oqba

Very last chimp hurrumpp DenisPotysiev
SLG Logo Rizw

BIBLIOGRAPHY

Ader, R., and Conklin, P. M. 1963. Handling of pregnant rats: Effects on emotionality of their offspring. *Science* 142:411-12.

Allport, G. W. 1954. *The nature of prejudice.* Boston: Beacon Press.

Allport, G. W., and Pettigrew, T. F. 1957. Cultural influence on the perception of movement: The trapezoidal illusion among Zulus. *Journal of Abnormal and Social Psychology* 55:104-13.

Altus, W. D. 1967. Birth order and its sequelae. *Inter-national Journal of Psychiatry* **3:23-32.**

Anokhin, P. K. 1971. Three giants of Soviet psychology: Conversations and sketches by Michael and Sheka Cole. *Psychology Today* 4, 10:43.

Ardrey, R. 1961. *African genesis.* New York: Atheneum. Ardrey, R. 1966. *The territorial imperative.* New York: Atheneum.

Aronson, E. 1972. *The social animal.* San Francisco: W. H. Freeman.

Asch, S. E. 1956. Studies in independence and con-formity: A minority of one against a unanimous majority. *Psychological Monographs* 9:70.

Ausubel, D. 1958. *Drug addiction.* New York: Random House.

Bandura, A. 1969. *Principles of behavior modification-* New York: Holt, Rinehart, & Winston.

Bandura, A., Ross, D., and Ross, S. A. 1963. Imitation of film-mediated aggressive models. *Journal of Abnormal and Social Psychology* 66:3-11.

Bandura, A., and Walters, R. H. 1959. *Adolescent aggression.* New York: Ronald Press.

Beach, F. A. 1941. Female mating behavior shown by male rats after administration of testosterone propionate. *Endocrinology* 29:409-12.

Beach, F. A. 1942. Analysis of factors involved in **the** arousal, maintenance, and manifestation of **sexual** excitement in male animals. *Psychosomatic Medicine* 4:173-98.

Beach, F. A. 1955. The descent of instinct. *Psycho-logical Review* 62:401-10.

Beach, F. A. 1968. Coital behavior in dogs: Effects olf early isolation on mating in males. ***Behave*** 30:218-38.

Beach, F. A., and Gilmore, R. . 1949. **Responses el** male dogs to urine from females in heat. ***Journal 04 Mammalogy*** 30:391-92.

Beers, C. 1934. A mind *that found itself.* New **Yu&** Longmans Green.

Belmont, L., and Marolla, F. A. 1973. Birth **order,** family size, and intelligence. *Science* **182:1096-**

1101. Collias, N. E. 1944. Aggressive behavior among vertebrate animals. *Physiological Zoology* 17:83-123.

Collias, N. E. 1951. Problems and principles of animal sociology. In *Comparative psychology*, ed. C. P. Stone, pp. 388-422. Englewood Cliffs, N.J.: Prentice- Hall.

Cooley, C. H. 1909. *Social organization.* New York: Scribner.

Cooley, C. H. 1927. *Life and the student: Roadside notes on human nature, society, and letters.* New York: Knopf.

Cooley, C. H. 1964. *Human nature and the social order.* New York: Schocken Books.

Coopersmith, S. 1968. Studies in self-esteem. *Scientific American* 218, 17:96-100.

Cowles, J. T. 1937. Food-tokens as incentives for learning in chimpanzees. *Comparative Psychology Monograph* 14:5.

Darwin, C. 1859. *On the origin of species by means of natural selection.* London: J. Murray.

Darwin, C. *1887. The autobiography of Charles Darwin.* London: Collins.

Darwin, C. 1909. *Voyage of the Beagle.* New York: Collier & Son.

Davis, K. 1947. Final note on a case of extreme isolation. *American Journal of Sociology* 52:432-37.

DeVore, I., and Eimerl, S. 1965. *The primates.* NewYork: Time, Inc.

DeVore, I., and Hall, R. L. 1965. Baboon social behavior. In *Primate behavior,* ed. I. DeVore, pp. 53-110. New York: Holt, Rinehart, & Winston.

Dollard, J., Doob, L., Miller, N. E., Mowrer, 0. H., and Sears, R. R. 1939. *Frustration and aggression.* New Haven: Yale Univ. Press.

Dollard, J., and Miller, N. E. 1950. *Personality* and *psychotherapy: An analysis in terms of learning, thinking,* and *culture.* New York: McGraw-Hill.

Doty, R. W., and Giurgea, C. 1961. Conditioned reflexes established by coupling electrical excitations of two cortical areas. In *Brain mechanisms and learning,* eds.

Fessard, Gerand, Konorski, and Delafresnaye, pp. 133-52. Springfield, Ill.: Charles C. Thomas.

Durant, W., and Durant, A. 1961. *The story of civilization: The age of reason begins.* New York: Simon & Schuster.

Eccles, J. C. 1953. *The neurophysiological basis of mind.* London: Oxford Univ. Press.

Eccles, J. C. 1973. *The understanding of the brain.* New York: McGraw-Hill.

Edwards, J. 1809. *Sinners in the hands of an angry God. The works of President Edwards in eight volumes,* vol. 7. Worcester, Mass: Isaiah Thomas.

Engel, B. T. 1972. Operant conditioning of cardiac function: A status report. *Psychophysiology* 9: 161-77, 207.

Espar, E. A. 1967. Max Meyer in America. *Journal of the History of the Behavioral Sciences* 3, 2: 107-31.

Ferrier, D. 1886. *The functions of the brain.* London: Smith, Elder.

Ferster, C. S., and Skinner, B. F. 1957. *Schedules of reinforcement.* New York: Appleton-Century-Crofts

Festinger, L. 1957. A *theory of cognitive dissonance.* Stanford: Stanford Univ. Press.

Festinger, L., Riecken, H. W., and Schacter, S. 1956. *When prophecy fails.* New York: Harper & Row.

Findley, J. D., and Brady, J. U. 1965. Facilitation of large ratio performances by use of conditioned reinforcement. *Journal of Experimental Analysis of Behavior* 8:125-29.

Flynn, J. P. 1967. The neural basis of aggression in cats. In *Neurophysiology and emotion,* ed. D. C. Glass, pp. 40-60. New York: The Rockefeller Univ. Press.

Ford, C. S., and Beach, F. A. 1951. *Patterns of sexual behavior.* New York: Harper & Row.

Frank, P. 1959. *Alas, Babylon.* New York: Bantam Books.

Frankl, V. E. 1963. *Man's search for meaning,* trans. Ilse Lusch. Boston: Beacon Press.

Franklin, B. 1950. *The autobiography of* Benjamin *Franklin and selections from his other writings.* New York: Modern Library.

Franzblau, A. N. 1958. A *primer of statistics for non-statisticians.* New York: Harcourt, Brace.

Freud, A. 1946. *The ego and the mechanisms of defense.*

New York: International Universities Press. Freud, S. 1920. A *general introduction to psychoanalysis.*

London: Bonji and Liveright, Inc. *Autobiography.* New York: Norton. Freud, S. 1938. *The basic writings of Sigmund Freud.*

The Modern Library. New York: Random House. Freud, S. 1949. *Collected papers,* vol. IV. London: Hogarth. (Also published by Basic Books, N.Y.,1959)

Gallistel, C. R. 1964. Electrical self-stimulation and its theoretical implications. *Psychological Bulletin* 61:23-34.

Gallup, Gordon C. 1971. It's done with mirrors-chimps and self-concept. *Psychology Today* 4, 10:58. Galton, F. 1869. *Hereditary genius: An inquiry into its laws and consequences.* London: MacMillan

Gardner, R. A., and Bardner, B. T. 1967. Teaching signlanguage to a chimpanzee. *Science* 165:664-72. Gazzaniga, M. 5.1967. The split brain in *man.* *ScientificAmerican* 217:24-29.

Gebhard, P. H., Gagnon, J. H., Pomeroy, W. B., and Christenson, C. U. 1965. *Sex offenders: An analysis of types.* New York: Harper & Row.

Gibbon, E. 1896. *The history of the decline and fall of the Roman empire.* London: Methuen & Co. Gibson, E. J., and Walk, R. D. 1960. The "visual cliff." *Scientific American* 202:67-71.

Goodall, J. 1965. Chimpanzees at the Gombe Stream Reserve. In *Primate behavior,* ed. I. DeVore, pp. 423-73. New York: Holt, Rinehart, & Winston.

Goodall, J. 1971. *In the shadow of man.* Boston: Houghton-Mifflin

Gray, P. H. 1966. *The comparative analysis of behavior.* Dubuque, Iowa: Brown.

Gregory, R. L. 1966. *Eye and brain: The psychology of seeing.* New York: McGraw-Hill.

Gregory, R. L., and Wallace, J. G. 1963. *Recovery from early blindness: A case study.* Experimental Psychology Society Monograph 2.

Guhl, A. M. 1961. The development of social organization in the domestic fowl. *Animal Behavior* 6:92-99.

Guthrie, E., and Horton, G. 1946. *Cats in a puzzle box.* New York: Holt, Rinehart, and Winston.

Hall, C. S. 1941. Temperament: A survey of animal studies. *Psychological Bulletin* 38:909-43.

Hall, C. S. 1951. The genetics of behavior. In *Handbook of Experimental Psychology,* ed. S. S. Stevens. New York: Wiley & Sons.

Haney, C., Banks, C., and Zimbardo, P. 1973. Inter-personal dynamics in a simulated prison. *International Journal of Crime and Penology* 38:909-43.

Hansen, C. 1969. *Witchcraft at Salem.* New York: Braziller.

Harlow, H. F. 1949. The formation of learning sets. *Psychological Review* 56:51-65.

Harlow, H. F. 1958. The nature of love. *American Psychologist* 13:673-85.

Harlow, H. F. 1962. The heterosexual affectional system in monkeys. *American Psychologist* 17:1-9.

Harlow, H. F., and Harlow, M. K. 1949. Learning to think. *Scientific American* 181:36-39.

Harlow, H. F., and Harlow, M. K. 1962. Social depriva-tion in monkeys. *Scientific American* 207:137-46.

Harlow, H. F., and Harlow, M. K. 1966. Learning to love. *American Scientist* 54:244-72.

Harlow, H. F., and Suomi, S. J. 1971. From thought to therapy: Lessons from a primate laboratory. *American Scientist* 59:538-49.

Harlow, H. F., and Zimmerman, R. R. 1959. Affectional responses in the infant monkey. *Science* Aug. 21, 1959:421-31.

Hartley, E. E. 1946. *Problems in prejudice.* New York: Kings Crown Press.

Haskins, F. H. 1908. *Adolphe Quetelet as statistician.* New York: Columbia University.

Heath, R. G. 1963. Electrical self-stimulation of the brain in man. *American Journal of Psychiatry* 120, 6:571-77.

Hebb, D. 0. 1949. *The organization of behavior.* New York: Wiley & Sons.

Heidbreder, E. 1933. *Seven psychologies.* New York: Century.

Held, R., and Bauer, J. A., Jr. 1967. Visually guided reaching in infant monkeys after restricted rearing. *Science* 155:718-20.

Held, R., and Hein, A. 1963. Movement-produced stimulation in the development of visually guided behavior. *Journal of Comparative and Physiological Psychology* 56:872-76.

Herodotus. 1956. *The history of Herodotus,* trans. G. Rawlinson. New York: Tudor.

Heron, W., Coone, B. K., and Scott, T. H. 1956. Visual disturbances after prolonged perceptual isolation. *Canadian Journal of Psychology* 10:13-18.

Heussenstaemm, F. K. 1971. Bumper stickers and the cops. *Transaction* Feb.

Hess, E. H. 1959. Imprinting: An effect of early experience. *Science* 130:133-41.

Hess, W. R. 1954. *Diencephalon: Autonomic and extrapyramidal functions.* New York: Grune & Stratton.

Hill, N. 1966. *Think and grow rich.* New York: Hawthorn.

Hilton, I. 1967. Differences in the behavior of mother toward first- and later-born children. *Journal of Personality and Social Psychology* 7:282-90.

Hippocrates. 1952. On the sacred disease. In *The great books of the western world,* vol. 10, ed. R. M. Hutchins. Chicago: Encyclopedia Britannica.

Hitler, A. 1943. *Mein kampf.* Eng. ed. Boston: Houghton-Mifflin. (First edition, 1924.)

Hovland, C. I. 1937. The generalization of conditioned responses: The sensory generalization of conditioned responses with varying frequencies of tone. *Journal of General Psychology* 17:125-48.

Hubel, D. H., and Wiesel, T. N. 1965. Receptive fields and functional architecture in two nonstriate visual areas (18 and 19) of the cat. *Journal of Neurophysiology* 28:229-89.

Hudgins, C. V. 1933. Conditioning and the voluntary control of the pupillary light reflex. *Journal of General Psychology* 8:3-51.

Inhelder, B., and Piaget, J. 1958. *The growth of logical thinking from childhood through adolescence.* New York: Basic Books.

Inhelder, B., and Piaget, J. 1959. *The early growth of logic in the child.* New York: Harper & Row.

Iverson, G. R., Longcor, W. H., Mosteller, F., Gilbert, J. P., and Youtz, C. 1971. Bias and runs in dice- throwing and recording: A few million throws. *Psychometrica* 36:1-17.

James, W. 1892. *Psychology: The briefer course.* New York: Henry Holt & Co. (Later edition, Harper Torchbooks, Harper & Row, 1961.)

Jefferson, L. 1948. *These are my sisters.* Tulsa, Oklahoma: Vickers Publishing Co.

Jones, M. C. 1924. The elimination of children's fear. *Journal of Experimental Psychology* 1:328-90.

Kanwisher, Nancy
https://www.youtube.com/watch?v=5Yj3nGv0kn8

https://www.youtube.com/watch?v=ZueXhzQS1k4

Kellogg, W. N., and Kellogg, L. A. 1933. *The ape and the child.* New York: McGraw-Hill.

Kelly, H. H. 1950. The warm-cold variable in the first impression of persons. *Journal of Personality* 18: 431-39.

Kendler, H. H., and Kendler, T. S. 1962. Vertical and horizontal processes in problem solving. *Psychological Review,* 69:1-16.

Kendler, T. S., and Kendler, H. H. 1962. Inferential behavior in children as a function of age and subgoal constancy. *Journal of Experimental Psychology* 64:460-66.

Kinsey, A. C., Pomeroy, W. B., and Martin, C. E. 1948. *Sexual behavior in the human male.* Philadelphia: W. B. Saunders.

Kinsey, A. C., Pomeroy, W. B., Martin, C. E., and Gebhard, P. H. 1953. *Sexual behavior in the human female*. Philadelphia: W. B. Saunders.

Klukhohn, C. 1949. *Mirror for man: The relation of anthropology to modern life*. New York: Whittlesey House.

Kohler, W. 1925. *The mentality of apes*. New York: Harcourt, Brace.

Kringlen, E. 1966. Schizophrenia in twins: An epidemiological study. *Psychiatry* 29, 2:172-84.

Kuo, A. Y. 1930. Genesis of cat's response to rats. *Journal of Comparative Psychology* 2:1.

Lack, D. L. 1933. *The life of the robin*. London: H. **F.** and G. Whitherby.

Shaping and specificity to discriminative stimulus. *Journal of Comparative and Physiological Psychology* 63:13-49.

Miller, N. E., and Dworkin, B. R. 1973. Visceral learning: Recent difficulties with curarized rats and significant programs for human research. In Contemporary *trends in cardiovascular psychophysiology*, ed. P. Obrist et al. New York: Aldine-Atherton.

Milner, G., and Penfield, W. 1955. The effect of hippocampal lesions on recent memory. *Transactions of the American Neurological Association*, 42-48.

Mind of Man, Film: NET Audio-Visual Center, Office for Academic Affairs, Indiana University, Bloomington, Indiana, 47401.

Money, J. 1961. Hermaphroditism. In *The encyclopedia of sexual behavior*, ed. A. Ellis. New York: Hawthorne Books.

Money, **J.,** Hampson, J. G., and Hampson, J. L. 1956. Sexual incongruities and psychopathology: The evidence of human hermaphroditism. *Bulletin of the Johns Hopkins Hospital* 98, 1:43-57.

Monier-Williams. 1891. *Brahminism and Hinduism*, p. 318. London: MacMillan.

Monkeys, apes, and man. 1971. National Geographic Television Special.

Morgan, C. L. 1894. An *introduction to comparative psychology*. London: Scott.

Moruzzi, G., and Magoun, H. W. 1958. Brainstem reticular formation and actuation of the EEG. *Electroencephalography and Clinical Neurophysiology*, 1:455-73.

Mowrer, 0. H. 1938. Enuresis: A method for its study and treatment. *American Journal of Orthopsychiatry* 8:436-59.

Mowrer, **0.** H. 1939. A stimulus-response analysis of anxiety and its role as a reinforcing agent. *Psychological Review* 46:553-65.

Mowrer, 0. H. 1960a. *Learning theory and behavior*. New York: Wiley & Sons.

Mowrer, 0. H. 1960b. *Learning theory and the symbolic processes*. New York: Wiley & Sons.

Mowrer, 0. H., and Mowrer, W. M. 1965. Enuresis an etiological and therapeutic study. *Journal of Pediatrics* 67:436-59.

Neisser, U. 1967. *Cognitive Psychology*. New York: Appleton-Century-Crofts.

Newell, A., and Simon, H. A. 1972. *Human problem-solving*. Englewood Cliffs, N.J.: Prentice-Hall.

Newton, G., and Levine, S. 1968. *Early experience and behavior: the psychobiology of development* Springfield, Ill.; Charles C. Thomas.

Niemoller, M. 1968. Speech cited in *Choose life*, **ed. B.** Mandelbaum. New York: Random House.

Oesterreich, T. K. 1930. *Possession, demoniacal and other:* Among primitive *races in antiquity,* **the** *Middle Ages, and modern times*. New York: Richard R. Smith.

Olds**, J.** 1958. Self-stimulation of the brain. *Science* 127:315-23.

Olds, **J.,** and Olds, M. 1965. Drives, rewards, and **the** brain. In *New directions in psychology,* ed. **T. %L** Newcomb. New York: Holt, Rinehart, & Winston_

Packard, V. 1968. *The sexual wilderness*. New **York** McKay.

Pascal, B. 1958. *Pensèes*. New York: E. P. **Dutton.**

Pavlov, I. P. 1927. *Conditioned reflexes: An investigation of the physiological activity of the cerebral cortex*, trans. G. Anrep. London: Oxford Univ. **Press_**

Pavlov, I. P. 1928. *Lectures on conditioned reflexes,* trans. H. Grant. New York: International **Publishers.**

Penfield, W. 1959. The interpretive cortex. *Science* 129:1719-25.

Penfield, W., and Jasper, H. 1954. *Epilepsy and the functional anatomy of the human brain.* **Boston:** Little, Brown.

Penfield, W., and Roberts, L. 1959. *Speech and brain mechanisms.* Princeton, N.J.: Princeton Univ. **Press.**

Piaget, J. 1930. *The child's conception of physical causality.* New York: Harcourt, Brace.

Piaget, J. 1948. *The moral judgment of the child.* Glencoe, Ill.: The Free Press.

Piaget, J. 1951. *The child's conception of the world.* New York: Humanities Press.

Piaget, J. 1954. *The construction of reality* in *the child,* trans. M. Cook. New York: Basic Books.

Plato. 1928. *The works of Plato,* ed. I. Edman. (Jowett trans.) New York: Modern Library.

Pomeroy, W. B. 1963. Human sexual behavior. In *Taboo topics,* ed. N. L. Forberow. New York: Atherton.

Powley, T. 1977. The ventromedial hypothalamic syndrome, satiety, and a cephalic phase hypothesis. *Psychological Review* 54, 1:89-126.

Premack, A. J., and Premack, D. 1972. Teaching language to an ape. *Scientific American* Nov.

Pribram, K. 1971. *Languages of the brain.* EnglewoodCliffs, N.J.: Prentice-Hall.

Rachman, S. 1966. Sexual fetishism: An experimental analogue. *Psychological Record* 16:293-96.

Reeves, A., and Plum, F. 1969. Hyperphagia, rage, and dementia accompanying a ventromedial hypothalamic neoplasm. *Archives of Neurology* 52:68-73.

Reynolds, V., and Reynolds, F. 1965. Chimpanzees of the Budongo fOrest. In *Primate behavior,* ed. I. DeVore, pp. 425-73. New York: Holt, Rinehart, & Winston.

Rogers, C. R. 1951. *Client-centered therapy: Its current practice, implications, and theory.* Boston: Houghton-Mifflin.

Rogers, C. R. 1961. *On becoming a person.* Boston: Houghton-Mifflin.

Rosenthal, R. 1966. *Experimenter effects in behavioral research.* New York: Appleton-Century-Crofts.

Rosenzweig, S. 1943. An experimental study of "re-pression" with special reference to need-persistive and ego-defensive reactions to frustrations. *Journal of Experimental Psychology* 32:64-74.

Rowell, T. E. 1967. A quantitative comparison of the behavior of a wild and a caged baboon group. *Animal Behavior* 15, 4:499-509.

Russell, B. 1950. Nobel Prize acceptance speech. Stockholm.

Sackett, G. P. 1965. Effects of rearing conditions upon the behavior of rhesus monkeys. Child Develop¬ment 36:855-68.

Sartre, J. P. 1964. The words, trans. B. Frecthman. New York: Braziller. Scheinfeld, A. 1965. *Your heredity and environment.* Philadelphia: J. P. Lippincott.

Schlipp, P. A. 1970. *Albert Einstein-philosopher-scientist.* Library of Living Philosophers. La Salle, Ill.: Open Court Publishing Co.

Scheinfeld, A. 1965. *Your heredity and environment.* Philadelphia: J. P. Lippincott.

Schneider, D. 1974. The sex-attractant receptor of moths. *Scientific American* 231, 1:28-36.

Schooler, C. 1972. Birth order effects: Not here, not now! *Psychological Bulletin* 78:161-75.

Scott, J. P. 1958. Critical periods in the development of social behavior in puppies. *Psychosomatic Medicine* 20:42-54.

Scott, J. P. 1962. Critical periods in behavioral devel-opment. *Science* 138:949-58.

Scott, J. P. 1963. The process of primary socialization in canine and human infants. *Monogram of Social Research in Child Development* 28, 1:1-47.

Senden, Von. *See* Von Senden.

Sherif, M., Harvey, 0. J., White, B. J., Hood, W. R., and Sherif, C. W. 1961. *Intergroup conflict and cooperation:*

The Robbers Cave experiment. Norman, Okla.: Univ. of Oklahoma Press.

Skinner, B. F. 1948. *Walden two.* New York: Macmillan.

Skinner, B. F. 1951. How to teach animals. *Scientific American* 185, 6:26-9.

Skinner, B. F. 1953. *Science and human behavior.* New York: Macmillan.

Skinner, B. F. 1957. *Cumulative record.* New York: Appleton-Century-Crofts.

Skinner, B. F. 1971. *Beyond freedom and dignity.* New York: Knopf.

Skinner, B. F. 1976. *Particulars of my life.* New York: Knopf.

Smith, M. E. 1926. An investigation of the development of the sentence and the extent of vocabulary in young children. *Univ. Iowa Studies of Child Welfare,* 3, 5.

Solomon, R. L., Kamin, L. S., and Wynne, L. C. 1953. Traumatic avoidance learning: The outcomes of several extinction procedures with dogs. *Journal of Abnormal and Social Psychology* 48:291-302.

Solomon, R. L., and Wynne, L. C. 1953. Traumatic avoidance learning acquisition in normal dogs. *Psychology Monographs* 67, 4:354.

Sorensen, Robert. 1972. *Adolescent sexuality in contemporary America.* New York: World Publishing.

Spelt, D. K. 1948. The conditioning of the human fetus in utero. *Journal of Experimental Psychology* 38:338-46.

Sperry, R. W. 1964. The great cerebral commissure. *Scientific American* 210:42-52.

Sperry, R. W. 1966. Brain bisection and mechanisms of consciousness. In *Brain and conscious experience,* ed. J. C. Eccles. New York: Springer-Verlag.

Sperry, R. W. 1968. Hemisphere disconnection and unity in conscious awareness. *American Psychologist* 23:723-33.

Spitz, R. A. 1945a. Anaclitic depression. In *The psychoanalytic study of the child,* ed. 0. Fenichel et al., vol. 2, pp. 313-42. New York: International Universities Press.

Spitz, R. A. 1945b. Hospitalism. In *The psychoanalytic study of the child,* ed. by 0. Fenichel et al., vol. 1, pp. 54-74. New York: International Universities Press.

Statts, A. W. 1968. *Learning, language, and cognition.* New York: Holt, Rinehart & Winston.

Stewart, J., and Palfaik, T. 1967. Castration, androgens, and dominance status in the rat. *Psychosomic Science* 7, 1:1-2.

Stone, L. J., and Church, J. 1968. *Childhood and adolescence,* 2d ed. New York: Random House.

Stratton, G. M. 1897. Vision without inversion of the retinal image. *Psychological Review* 4:341-60.

Strnhsaker, T. T. 1967. Social structure among vervet monkeys. *Behavior* 29:110-21.

Suomi, S. J., and Harlow, H. F. 1972. Social rehabilitation of isolate reared monkeys. *Developmental Psychology* 6:487-96.

Szasz, T. S. 1961. *The myth of mental illness.* New York: Harper & Row.

Teitelbaum, P. 1961. Disturbances in feeding and drinking behavior after hypothalamic lesions. In *Nebraska symposium on motivation,* ed. M. R. Jones. Lincoln, Neb.: Univ. of Nebraska Press.

Terman, L. M. 1925-59. *Genetic studies of genius: Mental and physical traits of gifted children,* vols. 4 and 5. Stanford: Stanford Univ. Press.

Theios, J. 1962. The partial reinforcement effect sustained through blocks of continuous reinforcement. *Journal of Experimental Psychology* 64:1-6.

Thiel, R. 1957. *And there was light.* New York: Knopf. Thompson, W. R. 1957. Influence of prenatal maternal anxiety on emotionality in young rats. *Science* 125:698-99.

Thorndike, E. L. 1911. *Animal intelligence.* New York: Macmillan.

Thorndike, E. L. 1931. *Human learning.* New York: The Century Co.

Tinklepaugh, 0. L. 1928. An experimental study of representative factors in monkeys. *Journal of Comparative and Physiological Psychology* 8:197-236.

Tolstoi, L. 1887. *My confession.* New York: Crowell.

Toman, W. 1969. *Family constellation: Its effects on personality and social behavior,* 2d ed. New York:Springer.

Twitmyer, E. B. 1905. Knee-jerks without stimulation of the patellar tendon. *Journal of Philosophy, Psychology and Scientific Methods* 2:63.

U.S. Government. 1969. *Crimes of violence: A staff report submitted to the National Commission on the Causes and Prevention of Violence,* vol. 12, pp. 670-77. U.S. GPO.

U.S. Government. 1970a. *Marijuana: A signal of mis-understanding.* First Report of the National Commission on Marijuana and Drug Abuse. U.S. GPO.

Valenstein, E. S., Cox, V. C., and Kakolewski, J. W. 1970. Hypothalamic motivational systems: Fixed or plastic neural circuits? *Science* 163:1084.

Von Senden, M. 1960. *Space and sight: The perception of space and shape in the congenitally blind before and after after operation,* trans. P. Heath. Glencoe, Ill.: The Free Press.

Walters, R. H., Bowen, N. V., and Parke, R. D. 1964. Influence of looking behavior of a social model on subsequent looking behavior of observers of the model. *Perceptual and Motor Skills* 18:469-83.

Warner, L. 1955. What the younger psychologists think about ESP. *Journal of Parapsychology* 19: 228-35.

Warner, L. 1957. The study of social stratification. In *Review of sociology: Analysis of a decade,* ed. J. Gittler, pp. 221-58. New York: Wiley & Sons.

Washburn, S. L. 1960. Tools and human evolution. *Scientific American* 3:3.

Washburn, S. L., and DeVore, I. 1962. Social behavior of baboons and early man. In *Social life of early man,* ed. S. L. Washburn, pp. 91-105. New York: Wenner-Gren Foundation for Anthropological Research.

Wason, P. C., and Johnson-Laird, P. N. 1972. *Psychology of reasoning.* Cambridge: Harvard Univ. Press.

Wason, P. C., and Shapiro, D. 1971. Natural and contrived experience in a reasoning problem. *Quarterly Journal of Experimental Psychology* 73:63-71.

Watson, J. B. 1925. *Behaviorism.* New York: Norton.

Watson, J. B., and Rayner, R. 1920. Conditioned emotional reactions. *Journal of Experimental Psychology* 3:1-14.

Watson, J. D. 1968. *The double helix.* New York: Atheneum.

Watson, R. I. 1968. *The great psychologists.* Philadelphia: J. P. Lippincott.

Weber, M. 1948. *The theory of social and economic organization,* trans. A. N. Henderson and Talcott Parsons. Glencoe, Ill.: The Free Press.

Weber, M. 1958. *The Protestant ethic and the spirit of capitalism,* trans. Talcott Parsons. New York: Scribners.

Weiner, N. 1948. Cybernetics. Cambridge: MIT Press.

Weiner, N. 1963. Nerve, brain, and memory models. Symposium on cybernetics of the nervous system, ed. N. Weiner and J. P. Schade. New York: Elsevier.

Wells, H. G., Huxley, J. S., and Wells, G. P. 1934. The science of life. Garden City, N.Y.: The Literary Guild, Country Life Press.

Whitehead, A. N. 1926. *Science and the modern world.* New York: MacMillan.

Wilkins, M. C. 1928. The effect of changed material on ability to do formal syllogistic reasoning. *Archives of Psychology,* 102.

Williams, T. H., Current, R. N., and Freidel, F. 1969. *A History of the United States to 1865.* New York: Knopf.

Williams, T. H., Current, R. N., and Freidel, F. 1969. *A History of the United States since* 1865. New York: Knopf.

Wolfenstein, M. 1951. The emergence of fun morality. *Journal of Social Issues* 7:15-25.

Wolfenstein, M. 1953. Trends in infant care. *American Journal of Orthopsychiatry* 23:120-30.

Wolpe, J. 1969. *The practice of behavior therapy.* New York: Pergamon Press.

Woodburne, L. S. 1967. *The neural basis of behavior.* Columbus, Ohio: Charles E. Merrill.

Yerkes, R. M. 1929. *The great apes.* New Haven: Yale Univ. Press.

Yerkes, R. M. 1943. *Chimpanzees: A Laboratory colony.* New Haven: Yale Univ. Press.

Zajonic, R. B., and Marcus, G. B. 1975. Birth order and intellectual development. *Psychological Review* 82, 1:74-88.

Zimbardo, P. G. 1972. Pathology of imprisonment. *Society* 9, 6:4-8.

Zuckerman, S. 1932. *The social life of monkeys and apes.* New York: Harcourt, Brace.

Printed in the USA
CPSIA information can be obtained
at www.ICGtesting.com
LVHW070835220224
772419LV00019B/196